Settling the Ebbsfleet Valley

High Speed 1 Excavations at Springhead and Northfleet, Kent

The Late Iron Age, Roman, Saxon, and Medieval Landscape

Volume 4: Saxon and Later Finds and Environmental Reports

by Phil Andrews, Lorraine Mepham, Jörn Schuster and Chris J Stevens

Settling the Ebbsfleet Valley

High Speed 1 Excavations at Springhead and Northfleet, Kent
The Late Iron Age, Roman, Saxon, and Medieval Landscape

Volume 4: Saxon and Later Finds and Environmental Reports

by Phil Andrews, Lorraine Mepham, Jörn Schuster and Chris J Stevens

With contributions from

Leigh Allen, Phil Andrews, Catherine Barnett, Nigel Cameron, Nicholas Cooke, Damian Goodburn, Jessica Grimm, Sheila Hamilton-Dyer, Richard Kelleher, Richard Macphail, Jacqueline I McKinley, Cynthia Poole, Robert Scaife, Ian Scott, David Smith, Wendy Smith, Elizabeth Stafford, Ian Tyers, Alan Vince†, Penelope Walton Rogers, Jacqui Watson, John Whittaker, Robert J Williams, Fay Worley, and Sarah F Wyles

Principal illustrator
Rob Goller

Other illustrations by
Tom Goskar, Nick Griffiths, S E James, Sophie Lamb, Peter Lorimer, Rosalyn Lorimer, Sarah Lucas, Lucy Martin, Rob Read, Rachael Seager Smith, Georgina Slater, and Elaine A Wakefield

Oxford Wessex Archaeology

2011

This book is the fourth of a series of monographs by Oxford Wessex Archaeology (OWA)

978-0-9545970-6-1

British Library Cataloguing in Publication Data
A catalogue record for this book is available from the British Library

Published by Oxford Wessex Archaeology,
a joint venture between Oxford Archaeology and Wessex Archaeology

Oxford Archaeology, Janus House, Osney Mead, Oxford OX2 0ES, Registered Charity No. 285627
Wessex Archaeology, Portway House, Old Sarum Park, Salisbury SP4 6EB, Registered Charity No. 287786

Designed and typeset by Julie Gardiner, Wessex Archaeology
Cover illustration by Peter Lorimer
Printed and bound by Cambrian Printers, Aberystwyth

Contents

Chapter 1 Saxon Pottery, *by Lorraine Mepham with a contribution by Alan Vince[†]*

Chapter 2 Saxon, Medieval, and Post-Medieval Coins, *by Richard Kelleher and Nicholas Cooke*

Chapter 3 Saxon Objects, *by Jörn Schuster, with contributions by Penelope Walton Rogers, Jacqui Watson, and Ian Scott*

Chapter 4 Other Saxon and Medieval Finds

Chapter 5 Human bone from Springhead, *by Jacqueline I McKinley*

Chapter 6 The Saxon Animal Bone from Northfleet and Springhead, *by Jessica M Grimm and Fay Worley with a contribution by Sheila Hamilton-Dyer*

Chapter 7 Post-Roman Sedimentary Sequences and Landscape

Chapter 8 Post-Roman Environmental Evidence for Subsistence and Economy

List of Figures

List of Plates

List of Tables

Preface

by Paul Booth and Phil Andrews

This volume presents specialist reports, and illustrations, on the Saxon and later finds and environmental remains recovered during archaeological investigations in the Ebbsfleet valley, near Gravesend, Kent. It is the fourth part of a four-volume publication on investigations at Springhead and Northfleet, undertaken in connection with engineering works for Section 2 of the Channel Tunnel Rail Link (CTRL), now High Speed 1. The archaeological discoveries made during HS1 Section 2, which range in date from the late Iron Age to the medieval period, are reported in Volume 1. Specialist reports on the Iron Age and Roman artefacts are reported in Volume 2, while those on the Iron Age and Roman human bone, and faunal and environmental remains are reported in Volume 3; additional data is available via the website (http://owarch.co.uk/ hs1/springhead-northfleet/). These reports have been prepared by the Oxford Wessex Archaeology Joint Venture in conjunction with Rail Link Engineering for Union Railways (North) Limited (URN).

High Speed 1 is the new high-speed railway linking London mainline stations to the Channel Tunnel. Section 1 of HS1, running from the tunnel portal at Folkestone, passes through Kent to Pepper Hill near Gravesend, whilst Section 2 continues the line under the Thames at Swanscombe and then runs through Essex and East London to London St Pancras.

The massive engineering and construction project necessitated one of the largest programmes of archaeological works ever undertaken in Britain. Desk-based assessment was followed by extensive evaluation, comprising field walking, trial trenching, test pitting and borehole investigation. This allowed HS1's impact on the finite archaeological resources along the route to be assessed and mitigated. Where archaeological sites could not be bypassed, or preserved *in situ*, excavations were undertaken in advance of construction. The principal archaeological work for Section 1 took place in 1998– 2001, while that for Section 2, commissioned by URN, took place between September 2000 and March 2003.

Construction work relating to Section 2 in the Ebbsfleet valley included HS1 itself, Ebbsfleet International Station and associated access roads, and a connecting line to the existing North Kent Line. Oxford Archaeology undertook detailed excavation and a watching brief on land south of Northfleet, centred on NGR 516413 174196, towards the north end of the valley, while Wessex Archaeology undertook detailed excavation, strip, map and sample excavation, evaluation and a watching brief on various sites around the south end of the valley, at Springhead, centred on NGR 618000 727500.

Following completion of the HS1 programme of work in 2003, there have been further, sometimes extensive investigations within and adjacent to the Ebbsfleet valley, in advance of infrastructure works and housing and commercial developments. Although these have revealed Palaeolithic and other early prehistoric remains, as well as further discoveries of late Iron Age, Roman, and Saxon date, it is not anticipated that any major revisions will be required to what is presented in this publication.

The four volumes of this publication comprise one of two separate archaeological studies reporting on the HS1 Section 2 excavations in the Ebbsfleet valley. The other publication, on *Prehistoric Ebbsfleet*, focuses on Palaeolithic, Mesolithic, Neolithic, Bronze Age and earlier Iron Age activity. The present publication, *Springhead and Northfleet*, concentrates on Roman and later activity, but also takes into account the late prehistoric origins of the Roman occupation of the area. The overlap with the *Prehistoric Ebbsfleet* study, however, is slight as the most important later prehistoric remains – the late Iron Age ritual or ceremonial activity near the Ebbsfleet spring at Springhead – are outside the period covered by the *Prehistoric Ebbsfleet* study.

The *Springhead and Northfleet* publication reports on three major excavations, as well as on minor excavations, evaluations and other investigations, both HS1 and non-HS1. The principal discoveries comprise late prehistoric, Roman, and Saxon features at Springhead, including a sanctuary complex within the Roman town of *Vagniacis*, and two Middle Saxon cemeteries to its east (site code: ARC SPH00); the Roman roadside settlement at

Springhead Nursery (site codes: ARC SHN02 and WA 51724); and late prehistoric, Roman, and Saxon features at Northfleet, where a middle Saxon watermill was discovered immediately adjacent to the Northfleet Roman villa (site code: ARC EBB01). Investigations were also undertaken on the site of a Roman high status walled cemetery south-east of Springhead, first investigated between 1799 and 1802 (site codes ARC WCY02 and WA 52379). This publication also considers the results of excavations at two HS1 Section 1 sites, the Pepper Hill Roman cemetery which is associated with *Vagniacis*, and the rural settlement at West of Northumberland Bottom, to the east of Springhead. Finally, the results of earlier (as well as ongoing) non-HS1 investigations and excavations undertaken by a variety of groups at both Springhead and Northfleet Roman villa, including work on the South Thameside Development Route 4, are considered.

The detailed specialist reports in this volume of the *Springhead and Northfleet* publication cover all the Saxon and later finds recovered during the reported excavations, including human bone and animal bone, and environmental remains and dating evidence relating to contemporary landscape, and subsistence and economy.

These reports include the analysis of over 19 kg of Saxon pottery. Most of it (*c.* 80%) was recovered from Northfleet where it is dated to the 5th–early 6th century, and was recovered from contexts that include demolition layers over the Roman buildings, nine sunken-featured buildings, and the area of the Saxon mill although apparently not directly associated with its period of use. Of the pottery from Springhead, where contexts include two sunken-featured buildings, some of the material was of a similar date to Northfleet, but some appears to be of 6th–7th century date.

Eight Saxon and medieval coins were recovered from Springhead, including two from a grave in the Saxon cemetery and a group of three medieval pennies and a halfpenny close to Watling Street, possibly from a 'pilgrim's purse'. In addition, 31 post-medieval and modern coins and two tokens were recovered, from both Springhead and Northfleet.

The report on Saxon metal small finds provides an overview of grave finds from that part of the two Saxon inhumation cemeteries at Springhead that were excavated in ARC SPH00, comprising 36 graves. The smaller cemetery to the south was fully excavated, while the larger cemetery to its north, which extends to the east, was excavated in 2007-8 (not as part of the HS1 works). The small finds report also provides details on mineral-preserved textiles and other organic remains from the graves. Full analysis of these grave finds will be integrated with those from the further 123 burials to the east, still to be reported. Likewise, the report on the Saxon human remains, deriving from 30 individuals, relates solely to the graves in ARC SPH00.

Other finds reports concern the small quantity of smithing slag recovered from Saxon contexts at Northfleet, although this could be residual Roman material. Medieval and post-medieval ceramic building material was also recovered from Northfleet, and from a tile kiln exposed during a watching brief west of Springhead, and there was also a small quantity of fired clay and daub, much of it from a late Saxon crop dryer at Springhead. There are also reports on a wood plane, and on objects of worked bone, including comb fragments, pin beaters, a spindle whorl, toggles and an antler spearhead, all from Northfleet.

Most of the 4237 fragments of animal bone in the Saxon faunal assemblage came from Northfleet, with only a very small proportion from Springhead. The data indicates animal use focusing on sheep and pig, with horses, dogs and cats also present in the assemblage, but with the hunting of hare, deer, wild boar, and wild fowl making only a limited contribution to the diet. In addition, 51 fish bones were recovered, predominantly of marine species, and the claw of an edible crab. The environmental evidence for Saxon subsistence and economy is presented in reports on waterlogged wood, much of it associated with the Saxon mill, along with charred plant remains, wood charcoal, and marine shell.

Environmental sequences and remains relating the development of the Saxon landscape were recovered mainly from waterlogged deposits at Northfleet, associated with the Saxon mill and millpond. The range of evidence is presented in reports on sediments and soils, soil micromorphology, pollen, diatoms, foraminifera and ostracoda, waterlogged plant remains and insects, with dating evidence presented in reports on radiocarbon dating and dendrochronology.

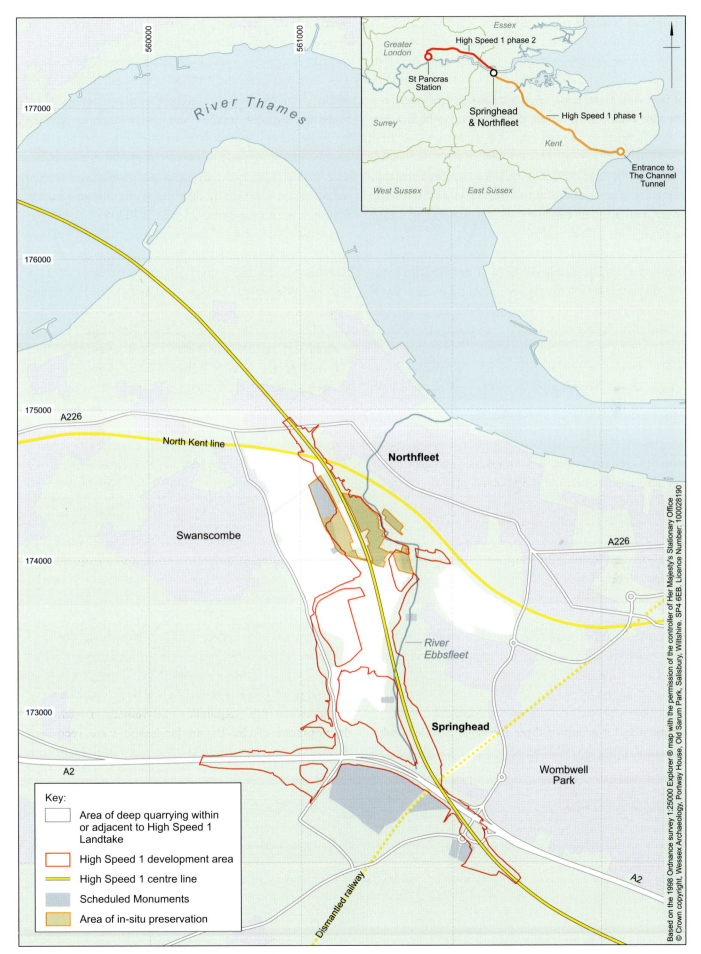

Key:

- ☐ Area of deep quarrying within or adjacent to High Speed 1 Landtake
- ☐ High Speed 1 development area
- — High Speed 1 centre line
- ☐ Scheduled Monuments
- ☐ Area of in-situ preservation

High Speed 1 Sections 1 and 2, and map of the Ebbsfleet Valley and surrounding area showing HS 1 development area at Springhead and Northfleet

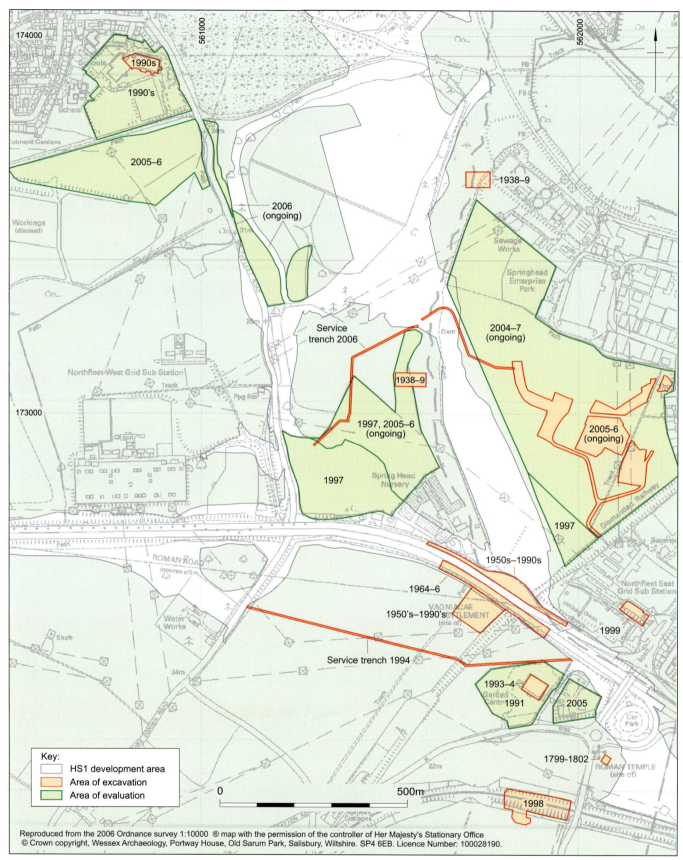

Map of Springhead and surrounding area showing non-HS1 Section 2 archaeological investigations

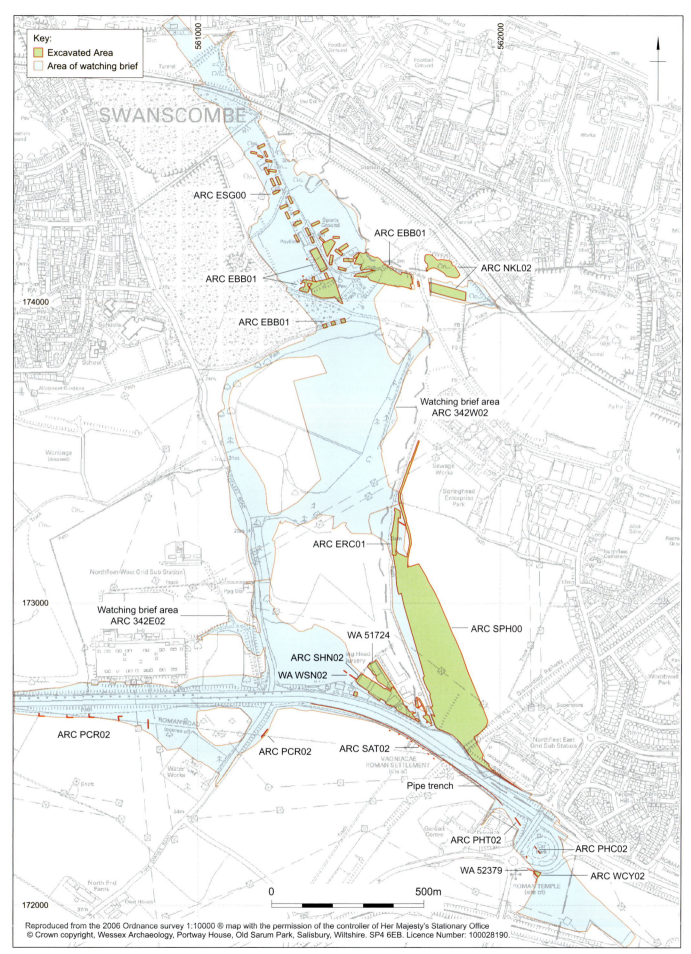

Key:
- Excavated Area
- Area of watching brief

SWANSCOMBE

561000

562000

ARC ESG00

ARC EBB01

ARC EBB01

ARC NKL02

174000

ARC EBB01

Watching brief area
ARC 342W02

173000

Watching brief area
ARC 342E02

ARC ERC01

WA 51724

ARC SPH00

ARC SHN02

WA WSN02

ARC PCR02

ARC PCR02

ARC SAT02

VAGNIACAE
ROMAN SETTLEMENT
(site of)

Pipe trench

172000

ARC PHT02

ARC PHC02

WA 52379

ARC WCY02

ROMAN TEMPLE
(site of)

0   500m

Map of the Ebbsfleet Valley showing HS1 and non-HS1 archaeological investigations (with site codes)

Chapter I

Saxon Pottery

by Lorraine Mepham with a contribution by Alan Vince†

The total Saxon pottery assemblage recovered from Springhead and Northfleet amounts to 1379 sherds (19,250 g), of which the majority (1092 sherds; 15,501 g) came from Northfleet, and a much smaller quantity (287 sherds; 3749 g) from Springhead.

The pottery derived from 99 contexts, for most of which the pottery provides the primary dating evidence. Contexts at Northfleet include nine sunken-featured buildings (SFB), a few other cut features, demolition layers over the Roman buildings, and colluvial layers in the same area. Pottery was recovered in the area of the Saxon mill, but none appears to be directly associated with its period of use. Contexts at Springhead include a sunken-featured building located over the site of the Roman Sanctuary complex, a further SFB and associated contexts excavated during the watching brief to the south, and two isolated features excavated within the cable easement to the north (see Vol 1, Chap 5 for details).

In general the condition of the pottery is fair to good. The assemblage is fragmentary, and there are few reconstructable profiles, but the hard-fired nature of the fabrics has prevented any high degree of surface and/or edge abrasion. Mean sherd weight overall is 14 g, and there is no significant difference in this respect between the assemblages from Northfleet and Springhead.

Methods of Analysis

The whole Saxon assemblage has been analysed following the standard Wessex Archaeology recording system for pottery (Morris 1994), which fulfills nationally recommended minimum standards for post-Roman pottery (MPRG 2001). Fabrics have been defined on the basis of the range, size and frequency of macroscopic inclusions, and coded on the basis of dominant inclusion type (C = calcareous fabrics; P = fabrics containing clay pellets; Q = sandy fabrics; R = rock-tempered fabrics; V = organic-tempered fabrics). This has been supplemented by a limited programme of petrological analysis, carried out by Alan Vince (see below; Table 2).

Rim and other diagnostic sherds have been used as the basis for a vessel type series, whose definition and description follows nationally recommended nomenclature (MPRG 1998).

Fabrics

A total of 28 fabric types has been identified within the five broad fabric groups. Brief descriptions and fabric totals are presented in Table 1. Full fabric descriptions are held in the project archive.

The five-fold division based on dominant inclusion type can be seen to be largely arbitrary, and is used here primarily as a descriptive tool, as the full range of macroscopic inclusions shows overlaps between these groups. It does not, for example, reflect a clear-cut distinction between different source areas, and further exploration of this issue must therefore rely on detailed macroscopic (and microscopic) examination of the fabrics. It was clear from the outset that some of the fabric types contained inclusions which could be regarded as unusual (and thence, possibly, of non-local origin).

Samples of eight fabric types were submitted for thin-section analysis (fabrics Q400, Q403, Q405, Q410, C401, R400, R402, R403), which included examples of both 'unusual' fabrics, and others containing inclusion types which appeared to fall within the expected range for the period and area. The full results are presented below, and show that these eight samples fell into five fabric groups on the basis of the most common or distinctive inclusion types. Of these five groups, three could be suggested to represent regional imports from East Anglia, while the remainder were probably produced in North Kent, but incorporating volcanic rock fragments (perhaps from the re-use of imported rotary quernstones) as tempering material. Table 2 summarises the results.

Table 1 Saxon pottery totals

Potential source	Fabric code	Fabric description	Northfleet		Springhead		Total	
			No.	Wt (g)	No.	Wt (g)	No.	Wt (g)
East Anglia	C401*	Moderately coarse, calcareous (oolitic limestone)	17	209	–	–	17	209
East Anglia	C402	Calcareous (oolitic limestone), quartz	23	332	2	28	25	360
East Anglia	C403	Relatively fine, calcareous inclusions (oolitic limestone)	–	–	1	17	1	17
East Anglia	Q400*	Coarse, prominent quartz	91	1907	1	6	92	1913
East Anglia	Q401	Moderately coarse, quartz (finer variant of Q400?)	396	5376	16	246	412	5622
East Anglia	Q403*	Coarse, sandy, calcareous inclusions (oolitic limestone)	–	–	11	368	11	368
East Anglia	Q408	Sandy, rare calcareous inclusions (oolitic limestone)	10	75	–	–	10	75
East Anglia	R400*	Coarse, rock inclusions (igneous); some quartz	15	141	–	–	15	141
East Anglia	R401	As R400 but no quartz	2	7	–	–	2	7
		Sub-total non-local fabrics	*554*	*8047*	*31*	*665*	*585*	*8712*
North Kent	C400	Moderately fine, calcareous (limestone)	63	1436	6	46	69	1482
North Kent	F400	Sparse flint	6	114	–	–	6	114
North Kent	P400	Slightly soapy, ?clay pellets, rare calcareous inclusions	1	20	–	–	1	20
North Kent	Q402	Moderately fine, sandy, well sorted	134	1482	27	386	161	1868
North Kent	Q404	Sandy, sparse calcareous inclusions (limestone)	96	1437	–	–	96	1437
North Kent	Q405*	Medium-grained sandy (iron-stained quartz)	1	19	3	69	4	88
North Kent	Q406	Fine, sandy, rare organic inclusions	40	384	1	8	41	392
North Kent	Q407	Sandy, rare shell	9	252	–	–	9	252
North Kent	Q409	Fine, sandy, no visible inclusions	11	57	–	–	11	57
North Kent	Q410*	Sandy (iron-stained quartz), rock inclusions	1	11	2	5	3	16
North Kent	Q411	Slightly 'detrital', some quartz, rare rock inclusions (igneous)	4	132	–	–	4	132
North Kent	Q412	Soft, slightly soapy, iron-stained quartz	31	273	–	–	31	273
North Kent	R402*	Sparse rock temper (igneous)	47	392	–	–	47	392
North Kent	R403*	Sandy, rock inclusions (igneous)	11	404	–	–	11	404
North Kent	V400	Coarse, organic temper	43	517	207	2441	250	2958
North Kent	V401	Coarse, organic temper, some quartz	33	388	1	1	34	389
North Kent	V402	Moderately fine, organic temper	–	–	9	128	9	128
North Kent	V403	Coarse, organic temper, calcareous inclusions	2	54	–	–	2	54
North Kent	V404	Coarse, 'detrital', organic & calcareous inclusions, clay pellets & quartz	5	82	–	–	5	82
		Sub-total 'local' fabrics	*538*	*7454*	*256*	*3084*	*794*	*10,538*
		Totals	1092	15,501	287	3749	1379	19,250

* denotes fabric sample submitted for thin-section analysis

Table 2 Summary results of thin-section analysis

Fabric	Fabric group	Suggested source
C401	Oolitic limestone	East Anglia
Q400	Coarse-grained sandstone	East Anglia
Q403	Oolitic limestone	East Anglia
Q405	Sandstone	North Kent
Q410	Volcanic rock	North Kent
R400	Quartz-microcline granite	East Anglia
R402	Volcanic rock	North Kent
R403	Volcanic rock	North Kent

The implications of these results will be further discussed below. On the basis of the thin-section results obtained, comparison with other fabric types enabled the identification of a further five fabrics as potentially non-local in origin (fabrics C402, C403, Q401, Q408, R401), while the remainder are likely to represent products of the local area (ie, within 20 km of the site), some also containing volcanic rock inclusions.

Table 1 presents the full quantification of 'local' and 'non-local' fabrics. The latter group make up a surprisingly large proportion of the total assemblage (45.3% by weight), but the results from the two sites vary significantly – non-local fabrics make up 51.9% by weight of the Northfleet assemblage, but only 17.7% of the smaller Springhead assemblage.

Vessel Forms

The problems of formulating any form type series for early Saxon vessels are well rehearsed, for example by Hamerow (1993, 37), and centre on the unstandardised nature of the handmade forms, combined with the (generally) fragmentary condition of assemblages, in which rims and other featured sherds can rarely be assigned to complete vessel profiles. The typology offered by Myres (1977) is based primarily on whole vessels and is therefore biased in favour of cemetery vessels, and against domestic assemblages in which whole vessels are far less likely to survive; moreover, Myres' chronology has been shown to require some revision. The hierarchical scheme proposed for the Mucking assemblage is better designed for such domestic assemblages (Hamerow 1993, 37–40); within this scheme, most if not all of the definable vessel form types from Springhead and Northfleet would fall within

the range of 'bowls', with either 'simple' or 'complex' profiles (but see below). It is debatable, in any case, how valid such classificatory systems are, given the probable multi-functional nature of many vessels.

Thirteen vessel form types have been defined here, based largely on rim/upper body forms; there are few complete or near complete profiles. The number of rims which could be assigned to vessel form was relatively small – out of 123 rims only 54 could be assigned to specific form, and even here, classification into separate categories is not always clear cut. A broad approach has been taken here which combines overall body profile (where known) with rim orientation. Despite the Mucking scheme, the distinction between 'jar' and 'bowl' on the basis of open/closed body profile, presence/absence of rim constriction, or width:height ratio (see also MPRG 1998, forms 4.1, 5.1) cannot be consistently maintained here, and is not attempted apart from obvious examples (forms 2, 4, 6). Size is also variable (and not all rims have measurable diameters), and may or may not have functional implications, but obviously small vessels have been classified separately as 'cups'. Forms have also been identified from carinated body sherds (form 5), handles (forms 11, 12), and pedestal base sherds (forms 13). The two vertical looped handles, which are the only examples of form 12, are from vessels of uncertain form, although a possible parallel is provided by a 5th century vessel from Empingham, Rutland, illustrated by Myres (1977, fig 74, 3336). The vessel form types are listed below, and Table 3 gives the correlation of fabric to vessel form type.

Form 1: small to medium, convex vessel, profile neutral to closed; short upright or everted rim (Fig 1, 1–4).

Form 2: medium to large, rounded jar, profile closed; short upright or everted rim (Fig 1, 5).

Form 3: medium convex or rounded vessel, profile neutral to closed; plain, inturned rim (Fig 1, 6–7).

Form 4: small to medium, convex or hemispherical bowl, profile open; plain, upright rim (Fig 1, 8).

Form 5: small to medium, carinated vessel; profile neutral to closed; short everted rim; frequently decorated (Fig 1, 9–13).

Form 6: small to medium, convex bowl, profile neutral to open; short, everted rim (Fig 1, 14–15).

Form 7: small to medium vessel, almost upright profile; upright rim (not illus).

Form 8: small, shouldered cup; rounded base (Fig 1, 16).

Table 3 Correlation of vessel form type to fabric type (Northfleet in regular font, Springhead totals in ())

Vessel form	Non-local fabrics			Local fabrics											Total
	C401	Q401	Q408	C400	Q402	Q404	Q405	Q406	Q407	R402	R403	V400	V401	V404	
Form 1: small/medium convex vessel	1	6	–	3	6	1	4	–	1	1	–	1(1)	2	–	26(1)
Form 2: medium/large rounded jar	–	1(1)	–	1	1	–	–	–	–	–	–	–	1	–	4(1)
Form 3: convex vessel, inturned rim	–	–	–	–	1	–	1	1	1	–	1	–	–	–	5
Form 4: convex/hemispherical bowl	–	1	–	–	3	–	1	–	–	–	–	(1)	1	1	6(1)
Form 5: carinated vessel	–	5	–	–	2	–	1	–	–	1	–	–	–	–	9
Form 6: convex bowl, everted rim	–	–	–	1	–	1	–	–	1	–	–	(1)	–	–	3(1)
Form 7: straight-sided vessel	–	–	–	–	–	–	–	–	–	–	–	(2)	–	–	1(2)
Form 8: small, shouldered cup	–	1	–	–	–	–	–	–	–	–	–	–	–	–	1
Form 9: small, rounded cup	–	–	–	–	–	–	1	–	–	–	–	–	–	–	1
Form 10: small, carinated cup	–	1	–	–	–	–	–	–	–	–	–	–	–	–	1
Form 11: handled bowl	–	–	–	–	(1)	–	–	–	–	–	–	–	–	–	(1)
Form 12: handled vessel, form unknown	–	–	–	–	–	1	1	–	–	–	–	–	–	–	2
Form 13: vessel with splayed or pedestal base	–	–	1	–	1	–	–	–	–	–	–	–	–	–	2
Total	1	15(1)	1	5	14(1)	3	9	1	3	2	1	1(5)	4	1	61(7)

Form 9: small, rounded cup; neck constriction; everted rim (Fig 2, 17).

Form 10: small, carinated cup; neck constriction; everted rim (Fig 2, 18).

Form 11: bowl; upright lug handles, either perforated (Fig 2, 19; post-firing perforation) or unperforated.

Form 12: handled vessel, form unknown (Fig 2, 20).

Form 13: vessel; footring or pedestal base.

Table 3 shows that most of the more commonly occurring types (forms 1, 2, 4, 5) are found in both 'local' and 'non-local' fabrics. Of these, only the carinated types (form 5) are chronologically distinctive, belonging largely to the 5th century, according to Myres (1977, 2–3). Of the two splayed/pedestal bases, another 'early' form, one is in a local and one in a non-local fabric. Two of the cups (forms 8 and 10) are in non-local fabrics, and one (form 9) in a local fabric. In other words, there is no clear evidence for a distinction in vessel form between local and non-local products.

The vessel with the upright, perforated lug (Fig 2, 19), presumably one of two opposed lugs, warrants some further comment. This is an unusual form, not least because the lug carries a post-firing perforation (although it is always possible that an original, smaller, pre-firing perforation was subsequently enlarged after firing). Myres (1977, 9) comments that vessels with these paired upright lugs are normally wide-mouthed cauldrons, but he offers no firm dating. Published examples, however, seem generally to date from the 6th or 7th century, for example from West Stow and Mucking (West 1985, fig 64, 1; Hamerow 1993, figs 134, 9 and 168, 7). Blackmore notes their general absence from early Saxon rural sites in the London area, perhaps because most of the latter sites date to the 5th or 6th century (Blackmore 2008, 185).

Decoration and Surface Treatment

A small proportion of sherds carry decoration (46 examples, counting joining sherds as one, from a maximum of 35 vessels). Most of this comprises relatively simple schemes involving combed, incised or tooled lines, mostly arranged horizontally on vessel shoulders (32 examples: Fig 1, 10, 12, 13; Fig 2, 17–18). Seven sherds have applied solid lugs, on six of which the lugs are placed on the shoulder or carination (Fig 1, 10; Fig 1, 14; Fig 2, 21). Myres (1977, 10) claims a functional rather than decorative purpose for these

Table 4 Decoration by fabric (no of examples)

Fabric	Tooled	Incised	Jug(s)	Lug(s)+ tooled	Stamped	Complex	Total
C401	1	–	–	–	1	–	2
C403	–	–	1	–	–	–	1
Q401	13	4	1	1	–	–	19
Q402	4	2	–	–	–	–	6
Q404	–	2	–	–	–	–	2
Q405	6	4	2	–	1	1	14
Q412	1	–	–	–	–	–	1
V401	4	–	1	–	–	–	5
Total	29	12	5	1	1	1	50

vessels, where the lugs (usually three in number) support a suspension cord. The seventh example, however, provides the single most complex decorative scheme from the site – elongated bosses divided by vertical incised lines, with horizontal tooling above and quartered circle stamps below (Fig 1, 11). Apart from this only one other sherd is stamped, with a rosette stamp on the rim (Fig 2, 24). One vessel has a faceted carination (Fig 1, 12), and a small, carinated cup has multiple impressions around the carination (Fig 1, 18).

Decoration occurs on only eight fabrics (see Table 4), of which the most frequently represented are fabrics

Table 5 Surface treatment by fabric (no of sherds)

Fabric	Burnish	Wiping	Scoring/ combing	Rustica- tion	Coarse slipping	Total
C400	12	–	–	–	–	12
C401	8	–	–	–	–	8
Q400	10	–	–	8	21	39
Q401	35	–	–	4	17	56
Q402	57	–	2	–	–	59
Q404	16	–	2	–	–	18
Q405	87	4	3	5	6	105
Q406	5	–	–	–	–	5
Q407	1	–	–	–	–	1
Q408	9	–	–	–	–	9
Q409	3	–	–	–	–	3
Q411	1	–	–	1	–	2
Q412	1	–	–	–	–	1
R400	1	–	–	–	3	4
R402	–	4	–	–	–	4
R403	10	–	–	–	–	10
V400	19	1	–	–	–	20
V401	8	–	–	–	–	8
V402	5	–	–	–	–	5
Total	288	9	7	18	47	369

Q401 and Q405. Where vessel form type is known, seven examples are on carinated vessels (form 5), and one is on a convex vessel (form 1). In terms of 'local' versus 'non-local' fabrics, 17 out of the 46 examples of decoration occurred on non-local fabrics (C401 and Q401).

Surface treatments can be divided into two broad categories: those that involve the smoothing, wiping or burnishing of the vessel surface, and those that involve the deliberate roughening of the surface (always the exterior). The latter can be achieved by scoring or combing (Fig 2, 21), by 'rustication' using fingernail impression or finger-pinching (Fig 2, 22, 23), or by the application of a coarse slip, a technique known as *Schlickung*. Table 5 gives the breakdown of surface treatment by fabric type. Burnishing is the most common, used on a number of different fabrics, but most commonly on fabrics Q401, Q402, and Q405. Eleven of the 30 rusticated sherds come from a single vessel in fabric Q403, and 36 of the 47 coarse-slipped sherds, in fabrics Q400, Q401 and R400 derived from two contexts within SFB 10271 (contexts 10272, 10274), and probably represent a small number of vessels (a minimum of four).

The more common surface treatments (burnishing, rustication and coarse-slipping) were all used on both local and non-local fabrics – wiping and scoring/ combing are confined to local fabrics. Rustication and coarse-slipping, however, occur most commonly on non-local fabrics (Q400, Q401, Q403, R400), although local fabric Q405 is also well represented here.

Only a small proportion of the sherds with surface treatment can be assigned to vessel form type, but burnishing occurs on vessels of forms 1, 3, 4, 5, 7, and 11. What little evidence there is for position suggests that treatments involving surface roughening are found on the lower parts of vessels (eg, Fig 2, 21–3), a pattern also observed at Mucking, where the argument was advanced that surface roughening was designed to facilitate the handling of large or slippery vessels (Hamerow 1993, 35).

Pottery Chronology and Affinities

Setting the Springhead and Northfleet assemblages within their local and regional context, and from this attempting to draw conclusions as to chronology and affinities, is not straightforward, and raises some interesting questions as to patterns of pottery production and distribution operating at this period.

Certain *caveats* should be considered before any discussion of chronology. First, the number of published early Saxon assemblages of any size in north Kent, or indeed the surrounding area, is minimal. The majority of parallels here must inevitably be drawn from the large and well published assemblages from Canterbury (Macpherson-Grant and Mainman 1995) and Mucking, Essex (Hamerow 1993) although, as will become apparent, the assemblage from Springhead and Northfleet may have closer affinities with the London area. Second, the dating of assemblages from this period is often based solely on typological evidence, although corroboration of these dates can come from associated artefacts (mainly jewellery) and the occasional radiocarbon date. Both are available (although scarce) for Springhead and Northfleet.

Various aspects of the pottery should be considered in any discussion of chronology, including fabric, form, decoration and surface treatment. The majority of the vessel forms, with convex and rounded profiles, do not lend themselves to close dating, beyond a general impression that the 'hollow-necked' vessels (those with a pronounced rim curvature) dated by Myres (1977, 2–5) to the 5th and early 6th centuries are absent, and that the rim forms seen here, short and upright or weakly everted, are more characteristic of the 6th/7th century, as is the lugged rim. The carinated vessels, on the other hand, can be highlighted as indications of an early date range; Myres (*ibid*, 2–3) places these amongst the earliest in the Saxon sequence, in the 5th century. Within this category, faceted carinated bowls are conventionally dated to the first half of the century, although this dating may now be revised to allow a more extended date range into the early 6th century, in the light of more recent evidence from both the Continent and from England (Hamerow 1993, 42–4). Pedestal bases, too, of which there are two examples, are of 5th to early 6th century date. Other more distinctive forms, such as the handled vessels (forms 11 and 12), are not closely datable.

Decoration is not common within the assemblage, and the predominant techniques and motifs used (linear tooled and incised schemes) are apparently long-lived, as seen in Canterbury (Macpherson-Grant and Mainman 1995, 864). Stamping, however, as seen on two vessels, is not regarded as an early technique, and at Mucking,

for example, was observed to increase in popularity in the 6th and 7th centuries (Hamerow 1993, 52).

Burnishing is common throughout the assemblage, but is not chronologically distinctive. What is significant, however, is the occurrence of surface roughening in the form of fingernail, finger-pinched and scored rustication, and coarse-slipping (*Schlickung*). At Mucking, both rustication and coarse-slipping appear to be predominantly 5th to early 6th century phenomena (Hamerow 1993, 37), although evidence from Canterbury suggests a slightly later date for the *floruit* of coarse-slipping (Macpherson-Grant and Mainman 1995, 868).

While parallels for the range of forms, decorative techniques and surface treatments are known, for example within the published early Saxon sequences from Canterbury and Mucking, as well as other, smaller and less well dated assemblages from north Kent and south Essex (eg, Raymond 2003; Tyler 1995; 1998), the emphasis on a range of non-local fabrics is less easily matched. What published information there is for the Dartford/Gravesend area, and indeed elsewhere in north Kent, suggests that the fabric types in use during the early Saxon period were either organic-tempered or sandy (Pollard 1988, 161; Tester 1956; Philp 1973, 155, 161; Raymond 2003, 38) or, in Canterbury, chalk-tempered (Macpherson-Grant and Mainman 1995, 822), although information on fabrics is generally lacking from early published reports. In Canterbury, where the Saxon ceramic sequence runs from the 5th century, evidence suggests that the organic-tempered fabrics did not constitute a significant part of the assemblage until the later 6th century (*ibid*, 852), and this pattern is echoed on the other side of the Thames at Mucking (Hamerow 1993, 31). On none of these sites is there any suggestion of the use of non-local fabrics before the mid-Saxon period.

Non-local fabrics are, however, recorded for a small but increasing number of early Saxon sites in the London area, such as Harmondsworth (Laidlaw and Mepham 1999), Twickenham and Hammersmith (Blackmore 2008) and recently from Southend, Essex (WA 2007b), although the general pattern still echoes that seen in Kent and Essex, of sandy fabrics gradually replaced by organic-tempered fabrics during the 6th century (Blackmore 1993).

There seems to be sufficient evidence here to suggest a date range, at least for the Northfleet assemblage, focusing on the 5th/6th century, although there may be some later elements. Clearly diagnostic 'early' forms (eg,

Table 6 Springhead: pottery by context (no./wt (g))

Site	Feature	C400	C402	C403	Q400	Q401	Q402	Q403	Q405	Q406	Q410	V400	V401	V402	Total
342 Watching Brief East															
	gully 102	–	–	–	–	–	–	–	–	–	–	3/6	–	–	3/6
	pit 105	–	–	1/17	–	1/8	2/5	–	–	–	2/5	62/682	–	1/6	69/723
	pit 113	–	–	–	–	5/142 form 2	5/11	–	–	–	–	17/96 form 6	–	1/2	28/251
	SFB 127	6/46	–	–	–	–	–	–	1/12	1/8	–	58/480	–	2/45	68/591
Ebbsfleet river crossing															
	layer 496	–	–	–	–	1/5	–	–	–	–	–	–	–	–	1/5
Roman Roadside settlement															
	ditch 11441	–	–	–	–	–	–	–	–	–	–	1/22	–	–	1/22
	pit 16740	–	–	–	–	–	–	–	–	–	–	1/5	–	–	1/5
Sanctuary site															
	ditch 2871	–	–	–	–	–	–	–	1/36	–	–	–	–	–	1/36
	ditch 3187	–	–	–	–	–	1/54 rustic.	–	–	–	–	–	–	–	1/54
	layer 5247	–	–	–	–	–	18/225 rustic.	–	–	–	–	8/70	–	5/75	31/370
	pit 2856	–	–	–	–	–	–	–	–	–	–	1/29 form 7	–	–	1/29
	pit 2868	–	–	–	–	9/91	–	11/368 rustic.	–	–	–	–	–	–	20/459
	pit 2874	–	2/28	–	1/6	–	–	–	–	–	–	–	–	–	3/34
	pit 3181	–	–	–	–	–	–	–	–	–	–	1/13	–	–	1/13
	pit 6540	–	–	–	–	–	–	–	–	–	–	1/63	–	–	1/63
	SFB 5809	–	–	–	–	–	1/91 form 11	–	–	–	–	45/875 form 1, 4	1/1	–	47/967
	surface 5707	–	–	–	–	–	–	–	1/21 dec.	–	–	–	–	–	1/21
	well 3674	–	–	–	–	–	–	–	–	–	–	9/100 form 7	–	–	9/100
Total		6/46	2/28	1/17	1/6	16/246	27/386	11/368	3/69	1/8	2/5	207/2441	1/1	9/128	287/3749

carinated vessels, particularly those with faceted carinations) and surface treatments (fingernail rustication and coarse-slipping) can be isolated, although the majority of the vessel forms are not particularly chronologically distinctive, and the most common decorative techniques have a long currency. The predominance of non-local fabrics and a corresponding scarcity of organic-tempered fabrics (6.24% of the total by weight from Northfleet) can be paralleled amongst other sites in the London area which are currently dated as 5th or early 6th century. Supporting evidence for the early dating comes in the form of radiocarbon dates for SFB 16639 of cal AD 420–570 (NZA 27437) and for SFB 30107 of cal AD 430–600 (NZA 27442).

In contrast, although 'early' elements are also identifiable at Springhead, including the use of non-local fabrics and surface rustication (although mainly confined to a single feature – see below), the majority of the pottery may well be later, with a focus in the 6th/7th century. This is, however, based purely on the predominance here of organic-tempered fabrics (69.4% of the total by weight) rather than on any chronologically distinctive forms or decoration, and it may be observed that organic-tempered fabrics do continue in use later than the 7th century, for example at *Hamwic* (Timby 1988, 111–2). A 6th/7th century focus is, however, supported by two radiocarbon dates from pit 105 in the watching brief area (ARC 342E02), of cal AD 500–630 (NZA 27432) and cal AD 530–640 (NZA 27431).

Pottery Distribution

Springhead

Pottery derived from 15 features and three layers at Springhead, mostly within the Springhead Sanctuary site (ARC SPH00), but with a small group of features from the watching brief area (ARC 342E02) to the south (see Vol 1, Fig 5.4). Some pottery came from the upper parts of Roman features or layers on ARC SPH00, with two sherds from the top fills of Roman features on the Roadside settlement site (ARC SHN02) and one sherd from a layer at Ebbsfleet River Crossing (ARC ERC01) (see Table 6).

Potentially the earliest group here comprises 20 sherds from pit 2868, an isolated feature found in the easement at the northern end of ARC SPH00 (see Vol 1, Fig 5.2). These sherds were associated with a late 5th/early 6th century Visigothic brooch (see Schuster

below, Chap 3). Eleven of the 20 sherds, almost certainly all from a single vessel, are in a non-local fabric (Q403) containing oolitic limestone and sandstone; the vessel has surface rustication in the form of multiple fingernail impressions (Fig 2, 22). Both fabric and surface treatment would support the late 5th to early 6th century date range suggested by the brooch. The other nine sherds are in fabric Q401.

A further sherd with fingernail rustication (Fig 2, 23), in fabric Q402, came from the top of the Iron Age enclosure ditch 3187, and could be regarded as of similar late 5th/early 6th century date.

The remainder of the Springhead assemblage seems likely to be of later date, within a 6th–7th century date range, as suggested by the preponderance of organic-tempered fabrics and the absence of clearly diagnostic 5th/early 6th century features such as carinated forms and surface rustication.

Just over half of the total assemblage (159 sherds) derived from three features excavated to the south during the watching brief (ARC 342E02; Vol 1, Fig 5.4) – pit 105 (69 sherds), pit 113 (28 sherds) and SFB 127 (68 sherds). The majority of these sherds (141) are in organic-tempered fabrics, and the only diagnostic sherds are from a form 2 vessel in fabric Q401 (Fig 1, 5) and a form 6 vessel in fabric V400 (both from pit 113). Pit 105 yielded radiocarbon dates of cal AD 500–630 and cal AD 530–640.

A second SFB (5809), cut into the Sanctuary area (ARC SPH00; see Vol 1, Fig 5.3) produced 47 sherds, again mostly in organic-tempered fabrics, including sherds from form 1 and form 4 vessels. In addition, there is a perforated lug handle (form 11) in fabric Q402 (Fig 2, 19). This was the only cut feature of Saxon date encountered in the Sanctuary area, but other sherds were recovered from the surface of Roman layers in the immediate vicinity, including a body sherd with complex bossed and stamped decoration (Fig 1, 11). The pottery from this area and that from the area to the south is certainly of similar character, and could, arguably, represent part of the assemblage from a single settlement area of which only two ends were excavated.

Northfleet

At Northfleet (ARC EBB01) pottery was recovered from a number of layers and cut features, but the majority of the assemblage (931 sherds from a total of 1092) came from nine SFBs (see Vol 1, Figs 5.7–8).

Table 7 Northfleet (SFBs only): pottery by context (no./wt (g))

Fabric		16635	16636	16637	16638	16699	20186	30057	30107	30119	Total
Non-local fabrics	C401	5/94	–	2/5	9/76	–	–	–	1/3	1/20	18/198
	C402	–	–	4/20	1/3	17/292	–	1/17	–	–	23/332
	C403	–	–	–	–	–	–	–	1/18	–	1/18
	Q400	7/109	9/201	6/75	42/1172	9/179	–	2/5	4/88	4/22	83/1851
	Q401	8/75	1/9	17/138	34/603	48/656	–	28/331	27/230	43/560	206/2602
	Q408	–	–	–	10/75	–	–	–	–	–	10/75
	R400	–	–	–	15/141	–	–	–	–	–	15/141
	R401	–	–	–	–	–	–	–	–	2/7	2/7
Local fabrics	C400	1/28	–	–	9/389	14/94	–	1/9	2/29	29/757	56/1306
	Q402	33/334	1/16	1/6	13/143	6/46	3/87	16/127	5/65	10/96	88/920
	Q404	9/102	–	8/63	10/218	11/130	–	4/74	2/7	37/538	81/1132
	Q405	41/756	14/462	3/66	82/923	6/77	–	6/56	7/85	–	159/2425
	Q406	2/42	–	–	7/74	–	19/178	7/53	1/2	–	36/349
	Q407	7/172	–	–	–	–	–	–	–	–	7/172
	Q409	8/50	–	–	–	–	–	2/5	–	–	10/55
	Q411	–	1/16	–	–	–	–	2/68	–	–	3/84
	Q412	–	–	–	–	–	–	–	–	15/126	15/126
	R402	–	–	–	–	32/61	–	1/3	12/280	–	45/344
	R403	8/357	–	–	–	2/22	–	–	–	–	10/379
	V400	16/167	–	–	4/113	2/11	–	2/30	–	1/8	25/329
	V401	9/141	–	–	–	5/41	–	2/10	3/15	12/157	31/364
	V403	–	–	–	2/54	–	–	–	–	–	2/54
	V404	4/77	–	1/5	–	–	–	–	–	–	5/82
Totals		158/2504	26/704	42/378	238/3984	152/1609	74/788	22/265	65/822	154/2291	931/13,345

Table 8 Northfleet: vessel form types by SFB

Feature	Form 1	Form 2	Form 3	Form 4	Form 5	Form 6	Form 7	Form 8	Form 9	Form 13	Total
16635	3	1	2	2	2	1	–	–	1	–	12
16636	1	–	–	–	–	–	–	–	–	–	1
16637	–	–	–	–	1	–	–	–	–	–	1
16638	5	–	1	1	3	–	1	–	–	1	12
16699	5	–	–	–	–	1	–	1	–	–	7
20186	–	2	2	–	–	–	–	–	–	–	4
30057	1	–	–	–	–	–	–	–	–	–	1
30107	2	–	–	2	1	–	–	–	–	1	6
30119	4	1	–	–	1	2	–	–	–	–	8
Total	21	4	5	5	8	4	1	1	1	2	52

These were located in two groups – four from Northfleet villa (SFBs 16635, 16636, 16637 and 16638) and three from Area 6 (SFBs 30057, 30107, 30119) – with two outliers, SFB 16699 to the west of the main group at Northfleet villa, and SFB 20186 at Ebbsfleet Sportsground.

These individual feature groups, deriving from the backfill of the SFBs, are assumed to relate largely (if not totally) to the abandonment/disuse of these structures rather than to the period of their occupation and use ('secondary' rather than 'primary' refuse), and cannot be considered as necessarily representative of the ceramics used within the SFB in which they were deposited. They are more likely to derive from nearby midden deposits subsequently incorporated in backfills. Nevertheless, the distribution of pottery amongst these structures could give at least a crude indication of the original pattern of deposition, and could reveal chronological and/or functional trends across the site. Moreover, there are some contexts which have been interpreted as possible occupation deposits (eg, 30060 in SFB 30057), and which might therefore be expected to provide more direct evidence for the use of the structures.

Table 7 gives a breakdown of the quantities of pottery recovered from each SFB, and Table 8 gives the numbers of diagnostic vessel form types by SFB. Numbers of sherds per SFB range from 22 (30057) to 238 (16638). All SFBs contained diagnostic vessel form types, and all forms are represented within the SFBs except for the carinated cup (form 10) and the handled types (forms 11 and 12). Numbers of identifiable vessels (from rim sherds or, in the case of form 13, base sherds) range from one to 21; 52 of the 60 identifiable vessels from the site came from the SFBs.

Beyond basic quantities of pottery, no significant patterning could be observed in the distribution of pottery across the site and between individual SFBs, or between groups of SFBs. All SFBs produced pottery with some 'early' features, eg, carinated or pedestal vessel forms, non-local fabrics, and the use of *Schlickung* or rusticated surface treatments. A degree of contemporaneity is supported by radiocarbon dates from a hearth in SFB 16699 of cal AD 420–570 (NZA 27437) and from a posthole in SFB 30107 of cal AD 430–600 (NZA 27442).

Of the four instances where secondary (or 'upper') and/or primary (or 'lower') fills were recorded within SFBs (20186, 30057, 30107, 30119), pottery was concentrated in the primary/lower fills in three cases (20186, 30107, 30119); in the fourth (30057), quantities were approximately equal between 'occupation deposit' 30060 and 'final infill' 30061. Pottery with 'early' features was recorded from secondary/upper fills as well as primary/lower fills. In all three cases where both primary/lower and secondary/upper fills produced pottery (30057, 30107, 30119), mean sherd weight from the secondary/upper fills was less than for the primary/lower fills (12.1 g lower/7.1 g upper fill; 14.6 g/9.6 g; 15 g/14.7 g respectively), suggesting a higher degree of post-depositional movement.

To summarise, the whole assemblage from the SFBs is unlikely to represent a wide timespan in terms of use, and both occupation and abandonment of all SFBs are likely to have been more or less contemporaneous across the site, although deposition and redeposition of the material culture resulting from use may have occurred over a considerable period after abandonment of the SFBs.

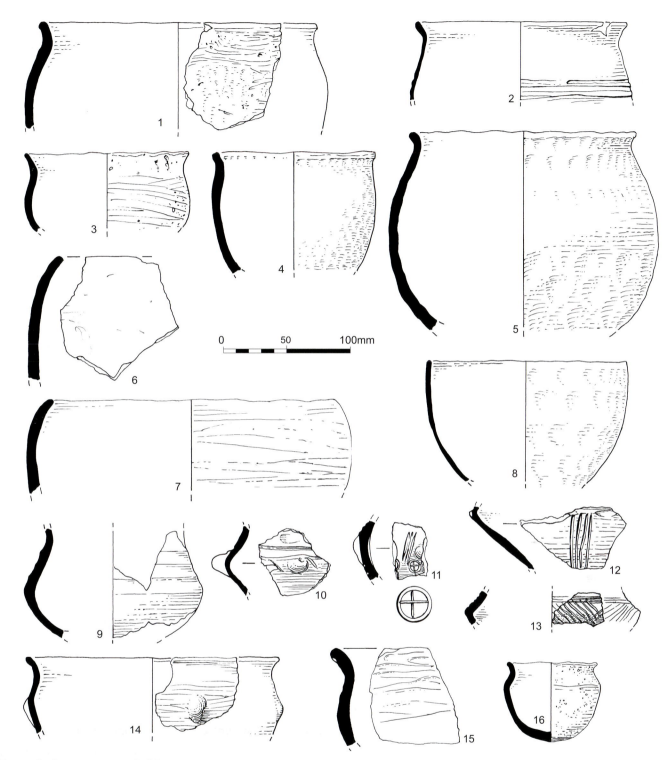

Figure 1 Saxon pottery 1–16

Eighteen other features (ditches, pits, tree throws, construction cuts and a posthole) produced pottery, but none more than 20 sherds, and most fewer than ten. The dating of these features thus remains slightly ambiguous since such small quantities of pottery could be regarded as residual. Overall, however, the range of fabrics and forms (eg, Fig 1, 9) is matched in the SFBs, and there is nothing to suggest that any of the features is anything other than broadly contemporaneous with the SFBs.

Conclusions

Although relatively small, the assemblage from Springhead and Northfleet has proved a valuable addition to the known range of early Saxon material from the region, for which findspots are relatively scarce. In particular, the identification of a range of unusual fabric types, including non-local fabrics, is significant, and serves to link this assemblage more closely with sites

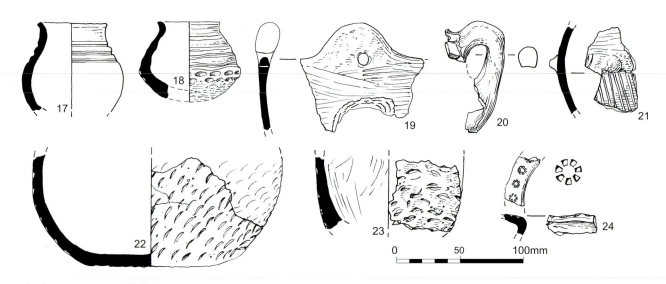

Figure 2 Saxon pottery 17–24

in the London area than with other sites in north Kent. In this respect, the use of petrological analysis has proved crucial in highlighting potential source areas, and this assemblage can thus be added to the growing number of early Saxon sites in south-east England which have produced wares which can be sourced to the east Midlands or East Anglia (Williams and Vince 1997). The mechanisms by which these wares were distributed is still a matter for debate, although Vince (see below) suggests that the wares found at Springhead and Northfleet may have been exported through Ipswich and thence down the coast to the Thames estuary. The use of volcanic rock as a tempering agent has, however, been shown by the petrological analysis to be probably a local (but as yet unparalleled) phenomenon, perhaps through the re-use of imported quernstones.

Radiocarbon dating has provided a useful chronological framework for the pottery assemblage, and supports the typological dating based on fabric, form, decoration and surface treatment, suggesting that the majority of the assemblage, perhaps all of the material from Northfleet and some of the material from Springhead (eg, pit 2868), is of 5th–early 6th century date, although the remainder of the Springhead assemblage appears to be later, perhaps 6th to 7th century. There is insufficient evidence, however, to suggest any sort of chronological sequence within the Northfleet assemblage and thus any potential sequence within the group of SFBs and associated features.

List of illustrated vessels
(Fig 1)

1.   Large convex vessel with everted rim (form 1); fabric V401. PRN 93, rim 6, context 30082, SFB 30119.

2.   Convex, thin-walled vessel with everted rim (form 1); horizontal tooling on shoulder; burnished all over; fabric Q401. PRN 423, rim 61, context 10272, SFB 16638.

3.   Small convex vessel with everted rim (form 1); fabric C400. PRN 263, context 15001, SFB 16699.

4.   Slightly convex vessel with everted rim (form 1); burnished all over; fabric Q401. PRN 252, rim 35, context 10155, SFB 16636.

5.   Large rounded vessel with everted rim (form 2); fabric Q401. PRN 987, ARC 342E02, context 112, pit 113.

6.   Convex bowl with inturned rim (form 3); fabric R403. PRN 224, Rim 33, context 10537, SFB 16635.

7.   Convex bowl with inturned rim (form 3); burnished inside and over rim; burnished inside; fabric Q401. PRN 435, rim 57, context 10272, SFB 16638.

8.   Thin-walled, hemispherical bowl (form 4); burnished inside; fabric Q401. PRN 421, rim 59, context 10272, SFB 16638.

9.   Carinated vessel (form 5); horizontal tooling on shoulder; fabric Q401. PRN 126, context 15785, pit 15676.

10. Small, carinated vessel (form 5); applied solid lugs on carination, separated by diagonal incisions, horizontal tooling on shoulder; fabric Q401. PRN 77, context 30083, SFB 30119.

11. Carinated vessel (form 5); applied elongated bosses around carination, separated by vertical incisions; horizontal tooling below, stamped (quartered circles) above; burnished inside; fabric Q405. PRN 940, ARC SPH00, surface 5707.

12. Sharply carinated vessel (form 5); faceted around carination; band(s) of vertical scoring below; burnished inside; fabric Q401. PRN 138, context 10321, SFB 16637.

13. Sharply carinated vessel (form 5); two-directional diagonal incision across carination; horizontal incision

above; burnished outside; fabric Q401. PRN 434, context 10272, SFB 16638.

14. Convex bowl with everted rim (form 6); applied solid lugs on shoulder; fabric V401. PRN 91, rim 12, context 30082, SFB 30119.

15. Convex bowl with everted, thickened rim (form 6); burnished over rim; fabric C400. PRN 103, rim 3, context 30082, SFB 30119.

16. Small shouldered cup with rounded base (form 8); fabric Q400. PRN 161, SF 11655, context 10897, SFB 16699.

(Fig 2)

17. Small rounded cup with constricted neck and everted rim (form 9); horizontal tooling on shoulder; fabric Q401. PRN 220, rim 32, context 10537, SFB 16635.

18. Small carinated cup with neck constriction and everted rim (form 10); impressions (fingertip?) on carination; horizontal tooling on shoulder; fabric Q401. PRN 300, unstratified.

19. Handled bowl, perforated lug (post-firing perforation) extending upwards from rim (form 11); fabric Q402. PRN 937, ARC SPH00, context 5904.

20. Vertically looped rod handle (form 12); mortise attachments at both ends for insertion through vessel wall; burnished; fabric Q401. PRN 430, context 10272, SFB 16638.

21. Decorated body sherd from rounded vessel; applied solid lug(s) on girth; scored below; externally burnished above; fabric Q401. PRN 215, context 10537, SFB 16635.

22. Lower part of convex or rounded vessel with rounded basal angle; fingernail rustication all over; fabric Q403. PRN 961, ARC SPH00, context 2869, pit 2868.

23. Body sherd from lower part of small vessel; fingernail rustication all over; fabric Q402. PRN 960, ARC SPH00, context 3188, ditch 3187.

24. Stamped rim sherd (rosettes); form unknown; fabric C401. PRN 228, SF 11538, context 10272, SFB 16638.

Petrological Analysis of Selected Early Saxon Pottery from Springhead and Northfleet, Kent

by Alan Vince†

Samples of eight early Saxon pottery vessels from excavations at Springhead and Northfleet, Kent, were submitted for thin-section analysis following a visual study which suggested that they contained unusual inclusions (Table 9). This analysis indicated that all but one of the samples did indeed contain rock fragments not local to North Kent. The vessels could be grouped

Table 9 Fabric samples submitted for thin-section analysis

TSNO	Context	Sub-fabric
Sanctuary ARC SPH00		
V4541	2869	Q403
Ebbsfleet Valley: ARC EBB01		
V4540	30076	Q400
V4539	10045	Q405
V4538	10179	R403
V4537	391012/3971012	R402
V4536	10274	R400
V4535	10536	C401
V4534	10415	Q410

into five fabric groups on the basis of the most common or distinctive inclusion types: oolitic limestone; quartz-microcline granite; coarse-grained sandstone; volcanic rock; and sandstone. It is suggested that three of these fabrics are regional imports from East Anglia whilst the remainder were produced in North Kent, but with the addition of angular volcanic rock fragments to the fabric.

Oolitic Limestone (V4535 and V4541)

The two sections containing oolitic limestone are sufficiently similar to be given a single fabric description. Even so, there is a considerable difference in the range of inclusions found in the two sections. The following inclusion types were noted:

Oolitic limestone. Mainly moderate ooliths, usually with no trace of cement. The ooliths range from c 0.3 mm to 1 mm across. The outer layer usually consists of almost colourless micrite whilst the inner layers consist of brown-stained micrite surrounding a core composed often of an angular shell fragment or amorphous micrite pellet. In a few cases rock fragments composed of several ooliths occur, ranging up to 1.5 mm across. These show no signs of rounding. The cement consists of light brown micrite.

Fossiliferous Limestone (only in V4535). Moderate angular fragments up to 0.5 mm across consisting of a ferroan calcite groundmass containing small angular fragments of shell and amorphous brown micrite. One fragment contains a brown spherical grain c 0.3 mm across.

Quartz. Moderate angular overgrown grains were present in V4541 and sparse well-rounded grains up to 0.5 mm across were present in V4535.

Coarse-grained sandstone (only in V4541). Sparse fragments of coarse-grained sandstone composed of overgrown quartz grains with a grey kaolinitic cement filling some pores.

Flint (only in V4535). Rare angular fragments of unstained flint.

Organics (only in V4535). Sparse carbonised matter in elongate voids.

Microcline feldspar. Rare angular fragment up to 0.3 mm across.

Plagioclase feldspar. Rare angular fragments up to 0.3 mm across.

Opaques. Sparse rounded grains up to 0.5 mm across.

Chert. Sparse brown grains.

Gastropod (only in V4541). Rare fragment of non-ferroan calcite gastropod shell 1.5 mm across with non-ferroan calcite micrite filling.

Bivalve shell. Sparse fragments of thin-walled shell (*c* 0.05 mm thick and up to 0.3 mm long).

Siltstone (only in V4541). Rare rounded fragment of brown siltstone finer in texture than the groundmass.

Mudstone (only in V4541). Rare rounded fragment of brown mudstone finer in texture than the groundmass.

The groundmass consists of dark brown optically anisotropic baked clay minerals, moderate angular quartz and feldspar laths up to 0.2 mm long and sparse rounded opaque grains up to 0.1 mm across.

Interpretation

No oolitic limestones outcrop in the geology of south-east England although oolitic limestone fragments do sometimes occur in calcareous Thames gravels. Similarly, no source for the overgrown quartz grains and coarse-grained sandstone fragments found in V4541 outcrops within the Wealden district and the material is identical in thin section to coarse-grained Carboniferous sandstones, such as the Millstone Grit and the Pennant sandstone of the Forest of Dean and the Bristol coalfield. Oolitic limestones and Millstone Grit sandstones occur together in fluvio-glacial deposits in East Anglia (predominantly in Suffolk, in the Chalky-Jurassic drift) and examples have been noted in thin-sections of early Saxon pottery vessels from Thetford, interpreted there as being of local production. The presence of flint excludes the possibility of a Leicestershire source but a source in a boulder clay to the southeast of the Mountsorrel outcrop, in Cambridgeshire, south Norfolk or Suffolk is quite possible.

Quartz/Microcline Granite (V4536)

The following inclusion types were noted:

Acid igneous rock. Angular fragments of a rock composed of microcline feldspar, quartz, perthite and zoned orthoclase feldspar with the inner zone being heavily altered to sericite and biotite. The fragments range up to 2 mm across.

Coarse-grained sandstone. A rock composed of overgrown quartz grains.

Limestone. Sparse rock fragments up to 0.5 mm with a ferroan calcite groundmass containing grains of rounded brown micrite and shell fragments, including punctate brachiopods.

Oolitic limestone. Sparse fragments up to 0.5 mm across. Similar to those in V4535 and V4531.

The groundmass consists of optically anisotropic baked clay minerals, moderate angular quartz and feldspar, muscovite laths up to 0.2 mm long and sparse angular opaque grains up to 0.1 mm across.

Interpretation

The groundmass of this sample is very similar to that of the two oolitic limestone-tempered samples and probably the interpretation of all three should be considered together. The angular igneous rock fragments could be erratics of Scottish or Scandinavian origin or could be from the Mountsorrel granodiorite outcrop in north-east Leicestershire. Given the presence of oolitic limestone, which does not outcrop along the east coast of England and is not a feature of Northern Drift deposits of Scottish/Scandinavian origin in Yorkshire, Lincolnshire or Norfolk, a Leicestershire origin for the igneous rock seems certain. Chalky-Jurassic boulder clays outcrop in south Cambridgeshire, South Norfolk and Suffolk.

Coarse-grained Sandstone (V4540)

The following inclusion types were noted in thin section:

Coarse-grained Sandstone. Abundant fragments of similar character to those in the oolitic limestone-tempered and granite-tempered fabrics.

Opaques. Rounded grains up to 1 mm across with sparse angular quartz inclusions.

Biotite. A single large sheaf of biotite 1 mm long.

Organics. Sparse elongate voids containing carbonised material and surrounded by darkened haloes.

Plagioclase feldspar. Sparse angular fragments up to 0.5 mm long.

The groundmass consists of optically anisotropic baked clay minerals, moderate angular quartz and feldspar, muscovite laths up to 0.2 mm long and sparse angular opaque grains up to 0.1 mm across.

Interpretation

The groundmass in this section is identical to those found in the oolitic limestone and granitic fabrics. All the inclusions are of types found in those two fabrics, differing in the much greater frequency of coarse-grained sandstone fragments.

Volcanic Rock (V4534, V4537–8)

The four sections containing volcanic rock fragments are all sufficiently different to be given individual fabric descriptions. The volcanic rock fragments are similar in each case.

Volcanic rock fragments. Sparse to rare fragments *c* 0.2–1 mm across. The larger fragments show some sign of rounding but the smaller ones are angular. The rock has a cryptocrystalline groundmass similar to that of chert but with laths of feldspar and some unidentified minerals with a zoned structure, up to 0.2 mm long and abundant euhedral opaque grains <0.05 mm across. There are sparse pores up to 0.1 mm across, some of which are filled with ferroan calcite.

The glassy groundmass is recrystallised, indicating a possible Palaeozoic date. Such volcanic outcrops occur in Leicestershire, Devon, the Welsh border and the Scottish border. Tertiary volcanic activity in the Massif Central and the Eifel mountains produced rocks which are similar in appearance in thin section but there are no obvious geological processes which could have led to the deposition of rounded fragments from these sources in North Kent. An ash fall would consist solely of sharply angular shards or spheroidal glass, neither of which is present and given the distance from either of these sources the size of the fragments precludes these sources. The pores are not numerous enough for the material to have drifted, the explanation for pumice found along the strand line around the Mediterranean coast (pumice has an average porosity of 90% (http://en.wikipedia.org/wiki/Pumice). Thus a Canary Islands or Mediterranean source can be excluded.

The closest sources of volcanic rock to Northfleet are the pre-glacial gravels of the proto-Thames, which ran well to the north of the modern river and the pebble beds of the Wealden Series (Gallois 1965, 22) which have been identified as being of Old Red Sandstone age. The author's experience of these Devonian rocks, in the sand used to temper Exeter Bedford Garage ware, suggests that they would be more altered than those in these samples (Vince in Allan 1984) but this is also true of the volcanic rocks found in the Kesgrave gravels (Sumbler 1996, fig 31). The other possibility is that the volcanic rock fragments are weathered or deliberately added fragments of central French or Rhenish lava

artefacts, of Roman date (importation of lava querns did not resume until the 7th century). Non-volcanic inclusions in each sample suggest a local source.

Sample V4534 (Q410)

Fossiliferous limestone. Moderate angular fragments with a ferroan calcite groundmass and angular non-ferroan calcite fossil sand. One fragment includes a sponge spicule.

Rounded quartz. Sparse well-rounded grains up to 0.5 mm across, many with dark brown veins and some with a dark brown coating.

Overgrown quartz. Moderate grains with euhedral faces and often the ghost of the original rounded surface within, between *c* 0.2 mm and 0.5 mm across.

Sandstone. Sparse fragments composed of overgrown quartz grains up to 0.5 mm across.

Flint. Sparse fragments. One well-rounded, spherical grain *c* 0.4 mm across and one brown-stained with a dark brown coating.

The groundmass consists of optically anisotropic baked clay minerals, abundant angular quartz, sparse muscovite, ferroan calcite, and rounded opaques.

Interpretation

Without the volcanic grains, the inclusions in this sample suggest a source in the Weald, or an alluvial deposit from a river draining the Weald. The flint fragments indicate a small contribution from Tertiary deposits, indicating that the source lies close to the mouth of the river.

Sample V4537 (R402)

Volcanic rocks. All the fragments have exactly the same mineralogy and could be derived from a single larger fragment. The fragments range from *c* 0.2–1.5 mm across and are all angular.

Sandstone. Moderate angular fragments of a sandstone up to 2 mm across consisting of rounded quartz grains, rounded opaque grains and rounded brown grains, all *c* 0.2–0.5 mm across in a groundmass of isotropic light brown phosphate. Some of the quartz grains have brown veins.

Quartz. Sparse well-rounded grains, some with brown veins, up to 0.5 mm across.

Flint. Sparse angular colourless fragments up to 0.5 mm across.

Opaques. Moderate rounded grains up to 0.5 mm across.

The groundmass consists of dark brown and black optically anisotropic baked clay minerals, abundant angular quartz, sparse feldspar, and angular flint, all up to 0.2 mm long, and muscovite laths up to 0.1 mm long.

Interpretation

In this section the volcanic rocks have the same size range and distribution as the sandstone fragments, and both inclusion types probably therefore share the same history. Most likely they were added to the pottery fabric as crushed rock, although a complex geological process cannot be completely dismissed. The sandstone is of lower Cretaceous origin and phosphatic nodule beds occur in several of the members of the Lower Greensand (BGS 1965). Excluding the rounded quartz, which probably originated in the sandstone fragments, the remaining inclusions and the groundmass are consistent with an estuarine origin on the north Kent coast or a Tertiary silty clay.

Sample V4538 (R403)

Volcanic rocks. Moderate subangular fragments ranging *c* 0.3–1.5 mm across. All of very similar lithology.

Silicious limestone. Moderate angular fragments of a mixed colloidal silica and fine-grained calcite rock *c* 0.3–*c* 1.5 mm across. Some fragments contain chalcedony-filled spheres. This is probably a Malmstone from the Upper Greensand.

Limestone. Moderate fragments of a ferroan-calcite cemented limestone *c* 0.1–*c* 0.5 mm across. The rock contains fragments of non-ferroan calcite polyzoa and shell together with thin lenses of gypsum.

Quartz. Sparse well-rounded grains up to 0.5 mm across.

Opaques. Sparse rounded grains up to 0.3 mm across.

The groundmass consists of dark brown and black optically anisotropic baked clay minerals, abundant angular quartz up to 0.2 mm across, and flint.

Interpretation

The limestone fragments and the volcanic rocks have a similar size range distribution and rounding and probably entered the pot through the same route. The identification of the silicious limestone as an Upper Greensand Malmstone leads one to look for suitable candidates of similar age for the ferroan calcite-cemented limestone, but no Wealden limestone is noted as containing gypsum in the BGS regional guide (1965) and the fossil fragments are too small and fragmentary for close identification.

The flint-bearing silty groundmass is similar to that of V4537 and also must have a Tertiary or Quaternary source.

Sandstone (V4539)

The following inclusion types were noted:

Quartz. Abundant overgrown grains *c* 0.3–0.5 mm across. The original rounded grain boundary is often visible, due to the presence of brown veins and inclusion trails in the original grain.

Organics. Sparse elongate voids, some containing carbonised materials.

Flint. Rare brown-stained angular grains up to 0.5 mm across.

Sandstone. Sparse fragments composed of overgrown quartz grains.

Altered glauconite. Sparse red grains *c* 0.2 mm across.

The groundmass consists of optically anisotropic baked clay minerals, abundant angular quartz, sparse angular flint, and sparse muscovite laths up to 0.1 mm long.

Interpretation

The sandstone and quartz inclusions are derived from one of the Lower Cretaceous sandstones. The purity of the sand suggests the Folkestone Beds. The remaining inclusions are probably naturally present in a Tertiary silty clay or Quaternary estuarine silt.

Discussion

These samples fall into two groups. The first consists of four vessels which have inclusions which in combination only occur in boulder clay in East Anglia. The groundmass in all four samples is similar in texture and mineralogy and is reminiscent of Mercian Mudstones, which because of their deposition in a desert environment contain a high proportion of feldspar in the silt fraction which in a more humid environment would be altered to micaceous minerals. The presence of Mountsorrel granodiorite indicates that this is a Chalky-Jurassic boulder clay whilst the presence of flint indicates that the till is somewhere to the east of the chalk outcrop. This limits the potential source to south-east Cambridgeshire, Suffolk or north Essex. Given its later dominance in coastal trade, it is possible that the vessels were exported through Ipswich.

The second group of vessels is the volcanic rock group. Omitting these rock fragments, the three samples all consist of angular rock fragments in a silty groundmass containing angular flint. This indicates either the use of a Tertiary Clay, probably the London Clay, or Quaternary estuarine silt. The rock fragments in each sample differ in type and frequency but all can be matched in the Lower Cretaceous geology of the south-east. Most likely all were present in Quaternary sand and the presence of relatively soft inclusions, such as

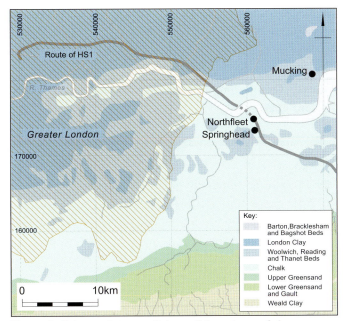

Figure 3 Schematic map of the solid geology of the Springhead area

phosphate nodules and limestones, suggests that this sand originated in one of the rivers which cut through the North Downs, such as the Darent or the Medway, rather than the Thames itself, whose gravels do contain the harder, non-calcareous Lower Cretaceous rock fragments. The Ebbsfleet only rises at Springhead and cannot therefore be the source of this sand. The lack of chalk inclusions is remarkable, given that the sand is calcareous and that the presence of rounded flint and angular flint grains in the matrix clearly indicates that the clay was obtained from a deposit to the north of the North Downs. Figure 3 shows a schematic map of the solid geology of the Springhead area. The groundmass of the Volcanic rock and sandstone groups matches the Woolwich Beds and London Clay and small outcrops occur to the south of the sites as well as extensively elsewhere in this part of the lower Thames.

The variations in the character of the sand fraction in the Volcanic rock and sandstone groups could indicate different sources for each sample but is more likely to reflect the variable nature of the sand. The presence of volcanic rock in three of the samples makes it likely that these three samples at least come from a single source. It is conceivable that this volcanic rock is of natural origin, derived from the Wealden pebble beds, and the presence of lower Cretaceous rock fragments in the sand would be consistent with this. However, this would require testing through the sampling and analysis of sands from the area. A more likely possibility is that the rock fragments are derived from lava quernstones, although the similarity in size, roundness and sorting of the volcanic rock fragments to the other coarser inclusions in these three samples suggests that all the coarser inclusions have a similar origin. Either a selection of rocks was crushed for used as temper, or a sand incorporating weathered quern fragments was used.

The suggestion that the samples essentially come from two sources, East Anglia and North Kent, could be tested by chemical analysis of the clays to see if they fall into two groups.

Chapter 2

Saxon, Medieval and Post-Medieval Coins

by Richard Kelleher and Nicholas Cooke

Saxon and Medieval Coins

by Richard Kelleher

All of the Saxon and medieval coins came from the Springhead Sanctuary site (ARC SPH00). The coins have been ordered below according to their presumed date of striking. For the later English hammered coinage the standard work followed for identification is North (1989; 2004). Details of each entry include, where relevant, a brief description of the coin, the weight (g), the degree of preservation/wear and the die axis (in degrees). Legends are only transcribed where they differ in detail from the given standard catalogue entry (underlining indicates ligatured lettering). A date of loss/deposition is thereafter suggested.

Grave Finds

Two sceattas were found in grave 2129 which contained an adult male accompanied by a spear (see Vol 1, Fig 5.21).

SF 273. Series BIB silver sceatta (BMC 27b). Obv. Blundered legend, diademed bust right within serpent circle. Rev. Blundered legend, bird on cross with annulet at end of each arm. 1.18 g. Little worn. Die axis 180°. Context 2131 (Pl. 1, 1).

SF 274. Series BIB silver sceatta (BMC 27b). Obv. Blundered legend, diademed bust right within serpent circle. Rev. Blundered legend, bird on cross with annulet at end of each arm. 1.22 g. Little worn. Die axis 90°. Context 2131 (Pl. 1, 2).

The coins (Pl 1) show little evidence of wear and as such it can be proposed that they were interred with the body soon after striking. On this basis they suggest a date for the grave which could be as early as *c* AD 685–90. Single finds of series B sceattas suggest an origin north of the Thames, with Metcalf (1993, 104) tentatively proposing the possibility of London as the mint-place.

The occurrence of sceattas is well-known from a number of Saxon graves and series B coins, such as those here, are attested from cemetery sites across southern and eastern England. There are finds of two sceattas from graves at Sarre and Buckland, for example, both in east Kent, and outside the county grave-finds of just two sceattas are the norm. However, several cemeteries in Kent have produced larger numbers, including the recently investigated example at Bridge where four of the 11 graves contained coins of series A and B, with each of these interments being female. These four graves contained 12, 14, 17 and 21 coins respectively (Williams in prep.). The mean weight, excluding the fused examples, for the B I coins from Bridge is 1.23 g, making the two Springhead coins slightly underweight in comparison.

Other Finds

Two single coins were found, one from a possible late Saxon crop dryer and the other in the subsoil.

1. Charles the Bald, King of the West Franks, 843–77. Silver denier, class 1d (Morrison and Grunthal 624). Obv. +CAROLVSREX around cross. Rev. +PALATNNAMONEAT around the KRLS monogram*. 1.39 g. Some wear. SF 1266. Context 3190. Crop dryer 3227 (Pl. 1, 3).

Coins of Charles the Bald, though uncommon, do occur as finds in England as large numbers were minted in order to pay the ransoms to the Northmen from AD 845 (Grierson and Blackburn 1986, 230). This coin displays the PALATINA mint name, which was for the 'Palace', but no specific mint can be identified and it is possible that these coins were struck by moneyers moving with the court. Dating coins of

Plate I Saxon coins from Springhead

c 1248–51 based on the form of the beard, the inclusion of lines for the neck on the obverse and the positioning of the lettering in this quarter of the coin. The practice of cutting pennies into halves and quarters is well attested from the late Saxon period as rarely were any fractional denominations struck. The reverse cross on these coins aided the cutting into smaller denominations. The long-cross pennies of Henry III were introduced in 1248 to replace the short-cross pence which had been struck under Henry and his three predecessors, and would have been removed from circulation by Edward I's recoinage of 1279 (Wren 1993). Therefore, it is overwhelmingly likely that this coin was lost within a couple of years of striking.

The 'pilgrim's purse'

A group of three pennies and a halfpenny was found, by use of a metal detector, within an area of a few square metres, and is likely to have formed a purse or small hoard group. The find spot lay close to the head of the Ebbsfleet and near Roman Watling Street which survived into the medieval period as a route between London and Canterbury. The coins are as follows:

3. Edward I, 1272–1307. Penny, class 4b, Berwick (North 1079). 0.70 g. Clipped, chipped and worn. SF 1456. Subsoil.
4. Edward I, 1272–1307. Halfpenny, class 4c, London (North 1046/1; Withers class 3). 0.62 g. Slightly chipped. SF 1482. Subsoil.
5. Edward I/II, 1272–1307/1307–1327. Penny, class 10cf^3(b^2), London (North 1042/2). 1.13 g. Bent. SF 1452. Subsoil.
6. Richard II, 1377–1379. Penny, class 1a, York (North 1329). 0.89 g. Bent, scratched and worn. SF 1451. Subsoil.

This group, perhaps a 'pilgrim's purse', is likely to have been lost or deposited sometime in the 15th century given the latest coin dating from the reign of Richard II and the conditions of wear and clipping displayed by the group overall. Pence of Edward I and II are found in hoards deposited into the 14th and 15th centuries, with some examples present in the Ryther hoard which was deposited as late as *c* 1487. In this hoard the pre-1412 pennies account for 18% of the total coins, with 5% from the sterling coinages of Edward I and II (Barclay 1995, 132–50). Each adjustment to the weight standards of the currency, which occurred in 1351, 1412, 1464/5 and 1526, was effective in reducing the number of coins

this type is problematic as they continued to be struck in this style in Aquitaine when other areas had adopted the *Gratia Dei Rex* type. This coin is likely to have been lost in the last quarter of the 9th century.

2. Henry III, 1216–1272. Voided long-cross cut farthing (North 986–90). Class 3 or 4 struck *c* 1248–51. Mint: unknown. Moneyer: Nicole. 0.23 g. Slightly bent but otherwise in good condition. SF 273. Subsoil.

As only one-quarter of the original remains, identifying the mint and moneyer becomes problematic. The extant letters OLE come from the second part of the moneyers name NICOLE, and moneyers with this name are known to have struck coins at Canterbury, London, Winchester and Shrewsbury. It is impossible to assign to a specific class other than to say it dates from

which carried over from the previous, heavier issue. Those that do survive into the later periods display clipping in accordance with the new weight standard and as such the condition of this group suggests that it was deposited prior to the 1464/5 reduction.

Post-medieval and Modern Coins and Tokens

by Nicholas Cooke

Ten post-medieval and modern coins and one token were recovered from the Springhead Roadside settlement site (ARC SHN02), the majority from unstratified layers. The single token recovered is of interest – it is a ¼d token struck by Richard Wicking, a grocer in Maidstone, and probably dates to AD 1650–70. The coins are all small issues of the 18th–20th centuries, some undoubtedly relating to the existence of pleasure gardens, watercress beds and, latterly, a nursery on the site.

A further 16 post-medieval and modern coins and one token were recovered from the Springhead Sanctuary site (ARC SPH00), predominantly from topsoil, subsoil and colluvial layers. None are particularly interesting or unusual.

A single post-medieval coin weight came from the hand dug test pits (ARC SAT02) on the south side of the A2. Struck after 1772, probably during the reign of George II, this weight would have been used by traders to check the weight of guineas minted prior to 1772, and weighs some 8.3 g (5.6 grains).

Four post-medieval coins were recovered from the excavations at Northfleet villa (ARC EBB01). The earliest was a fragmentary 'Rose farthing' issued by Charles I, found intrusive in a late Roman layer. Other identifiable coins included a half penny of George II, minted in 1738, and a farthing of George IV, struck in 1826. Both were recovered from post-medieval contexts. A fourth, illegible, post-medieval coin was an unstratified find.

Chapter 3

Saxon Objects

by Jörn Schuster
with contributions by Penelope Walton Rogers (PWR, mineral-preserved textiles),
Jacqui Watson (JW, mineral-preserved organic material), and Ian Scott (glass beads)

This report describes all illustrated Saxon metal small finds from the HS 1 Section 2 excavations at Springhead and Northfleet, but an attempt has been made also to mention those finds only described in the finds database, which are referred to by their original small find number (SF ...), in order to find them on the database available online at http://owarch.co.uk/hs1/springhead-northfleet/. Apart from basic descriptions and all measurements for both catalogued and non-catalogued finds, this database also contains digital photos of most non-ferrous metal objects. Grave finds are only referred to by their small find number, and these are also used on the grave plans. Most metal objects were x-radiographed, and conservation was carried out on selected objects by Wiltshire Conservation Service, Salisbury (now Chippenham).

Catalogue of Saxon Grave Finds from Springhead

This catalogue provides an overview of the grave finds from the Saxon cemetery discovered at the eastern edge of the Sanctuary site (ARC SPH00; see Vol 1, Fig 5.2). Subsequent excavation of the area immediately adjacent to the east, carried out in 2007–8, which was not part of the HS 1 investigations in the Ebbsfleet Valley, revealed further Saxon graves. Additional to the 36 graves discovered on the ARC SPH00 site, of which 27 graves contained grave finds, a further c 123 inhumation burials were excavated in the new area to the east. Therefore, it was decided that post-excavation work on the grave finds from the ARC SPH00 site should be largely confined to conservation and analysis of mineral-preserved textiles and other organic remains, the results of which have been included in this catalogue. The analysis of these objects will be integrated with that of the recently excavated, larger part of the cemetery (Stoodley in prep.), as it is now clear that the northern half of the ARC SPH00 cemetery (300258; Vol 1, Fig 5.19) continues seamlessly to the east; in contrast, no continuation has been discovered relating to the southern half of the cemetery (300257; Vol 1, Fig 5.9) within the north-eastern corner of late Iron Age enclosure 300030.

The grave goods are here grouped irrespective of their location in either the northern or southern part of the cemetery but are instead presented in numerical order by grave number.

Grave 2101 (Vol 1, Fig 5.10)

SF 1678. Socketed spearhead (probably part of spear with ferrule recorded as SF 1677). Iron. Context 2102.

SF 1677. Ferrule. Fragments of a ferrule with a flat, probably closed base, mineralised wood attached on the inside (probably part of spear with spearhead SF 1678). Iron. Mineral-preserved organic remains (JW): wood preserved in socket, not well enough preserved to identify, but nothing on spearhead blade SF 1678. Context 2102.

SF 1679. Knife. Back and edge both curve to join in the median line of the blade. The whittle tang sits below this line, leaving only a short shoulder between it and the cutting edge. Four small fragments of copper alloy: probably of same object, two conjoining pieces have small perforation towards one edge. Wood and copper-alloy rivet fragments attached. Iron. Mineral-preserved organic remains (JW): iron knife with the remains of a horn handle, and where it extends over tang and shoulder of blade has been highlighted by the cleaning. Traces of leather sheath on the blade tip. On the broken cross-section the leather is continuous over the back and joined at the blade edge, where a section remains of the layers of leather with stitches of plyed thread. Context 2102.

Grave 2105 (Vol 1, Fig 5.11)

SF 187. Knife. Very corroded, tip missing. Iron. Context 2107.

SF 190. Ferrule. Tubular collar/cap with one closed end. Mineral remains preserved around inner perimeter.

Central square ?shaft visible in x-radiograph. Iron. Mineral-preserved organic remains (JW): possibly an ox-goad, with mineral-preserved wood in the socket, *Alnus* sp. (alder). The annual ring boundary appears to follow the inner circumference of the socket, so the shaft was probably made from young grown wood. Context 2107.

Grave 2112 (Vol 1, Fig 5.12)

SF 194. Knife. Tip and end of whittle tang missing. Tang set slightly above median line of blade. Iron. Context 2111.

SF 1680. Spearhead. Socketed spearhead with leaf-shaped blade of flat lozengiform section. Iron. Context 2111.

Grave 2121 (Vol 1, Fig 5.20)

SF 1681. Seax (a) and knife (b): a) broad seax with straight cutting edge and slightly arched back both curving gently to tip in the median line of the blade. Base of wide tang leaves only short shoulder either side. Groove below back visible in x-radiograph along most of the length of the blade. Iron. Mineral-preserved organic remains (JW): no trace of handle. Single piece leather sheath, grain pattern suggests it was pigskin. No evidence as to how it was joined at the blade edge; b) incomplete knife blade, possibly originally with rounded tip (L 70 mm). Context 2123. Saxon.

SF 1682. Spearhead. Socketed spearhead with gently curving leaf-shaped blade of lozengiform section; max width of blade 27.8 mm, max width/diam of socket 17.7 mm. Iron. Context 2123.

Grave 2129 (Vol 1, Fig 5.21)

SF 273 and SF 274. Silver sceattas (see coins above). Context 2131.

SF 278. Spearhead. Socketed spearhead with gently curving leaf-shaped blade of lozengiform section. Iron. Mineral-preserved textile remains (PWR): remains of some organic material enveloped the spearhead and in places this had the general appearance of a coarse textile, approximately 8 x 8 threads per cm. No further technical details possible. Mineral-preserved organic remains (JW): wood in socket: possibly *Fraxinus* sp. (ash). Context 2131. Saxon.

Grave 2134 (Vol 1, Fig 5.22)

SF 279. Spearhead. Socketed spearhead with leaf-shaped blade of lozengiform section and almost parallel edges in its central part. Iron. Mineral-preserved organic remains (JW): wood present in socket: *Alnus* sp. (alder). Context 2132.

SF 282. Sheet fragments (not illus). Mineral-preserved organic remains (JW): this appears to be a copper alloy mount/repair attached to the rim of a wooden vessel with iron pins, possibly *Betula* sp. (birch). As they are attached to a radial surface it is more likely to be a mount rather than a repair, but the sheet is too flattened to get a reliable profile or diameter for the original vessel. Context 2132.

SF 283. Seax. Broad seax with back and tip gently curving to the tip in the median line of the blade. Long tang with remains of iron pommel plate. Sheath/scabbard mouth retains fragments of mouth-band. Iron. Mineral-preserved organic remains (JW): the handle appears to be made from a single piece of horn and the sheath or scabbard from a single piece of leather. The sheath still retains areas with a grain pattern that resemble pigskin, and although badly damaged it is still possible to see that the leather covers the back of the blade and was originally joined at the blade edge – but there is no evidence for stitching, thong or wire closures. Context 2132.

Grave 2522 (Vol 1, Fig 5.23)

SF 395. Spearhead. Socketed spearhead with leaf-shaped blade of lozengiform section and almost parallel edges in its central part. Iron. Context 2524.

Grave 2616 (Vol 1, Fig 5.24)

SF 432. Ring. Incomplete. Penannular, oval cross-section, loop tapers slightly towards ends. One end loops round as though to hook onto other (now broken) end. Silver. Group No. 428, Context 2619

SF 468. Ring. Incomplete, half loop only. Circular cross-section, tapering slightly towards one end. Silver. Group No. 465, Context 2619.

SF 469. Wire. Incomplete. Probably from a ring with terminals coiled around each other (*cf* SF 528, grave 2827). Circular cross-section, coiled into two spiral turns at one end, bent into small hook at other. Silver. Group No. 465, Context 2619.

SF 470. Ring. Collar from glass melon bead SF 467. Two fragments join to make complete tiny ring of oval cross-section, transverse grooves on one side. Third fragment (not illustrated) possibly from another similar object, oval cross section, grooved on one side, broken both ends. Silver. Group No. 465, Context 2619.

Beads from Grave 2616:

SF 429. Biconical bead. Opaque brick red. D 10 mm; Ht 7 mm. Context 2619. [ID 9].

SF 430. Small biconical bead. Opaque brick red. D 7 mm; Ht 4 mm. Context 2619. [ID 10].

SF 431. Bead made from shell? Slightly irregular flattened diamond section. Opaque umber. L 15 mm; W 7 mm. Context 2619. [ID 11].

SF 467. Melon bead. Turquoise frit. D 17 x 18 mm; Ht 13 mm. Roman bead. Context 2619. [ID 12].

SF 656. Bun-shaped annular bead. Translucent very pale blue-green. D 9 mm; Th 3 mm. Context 2617. [ID 7]. Good Roman form.

Grave 2620 (Vol 1, Fig 5.25)

SF 414. Seax. Narrow seax with back curving gently towards tip in median line of blade, curve of cutting edge towards tip starts nearer the end. End half of tang with remains of grip separate but complete. Incomplete triangular chape now separate from blade. Iron. Mineral-preserved organic remains (JW): handle made from a single piece of horn. There are fragments of leather along the blade and over the back, even extending over part of the handle. Context 2623.

SF 415. Spearhead. Socketed spearhead with leaf-shaped blade of lozengiform section and very gentle transition between blade and socket. Iron. Mineral-preserved organic remains (JW): wood in socket: *Corylus* sp. (hazel), from mature timber. Context 2622.

SF 433. Fitting. Four fragments, three are flat, quite thin, the two smallest pieces have incised crosses. Larger flat piece has a square base with three straight sides and thin strip with hole at the end extending from the other. Fourth fragment is bent shaft or ?chain link of circular cross-section. Copper alloy. Context 2625.

SF 443. Strike-a-light. Triangular with curled ends and straight back. Iron. Mineral-preserved organic remains (JW): iron mount has leather remains on both sides, and on one side are wood remains which on closer inspection turned out to be a small iron point with wooden handle, possibly *Alnus* sp. (alder), and appears to be attached to the strike-a-light with a plyed cord. Both the cord and part of this object seem to be inserted inside the leather container with the strike-a-light. Context 2624.

SF 454. Knife. Blade with parallel sides curving to the tip in the median line of the blade. Triangular whittle tang set near the cutting edge, possibly without choil, and only a short, stepped shoulder on the side of the back. Iron. Mineral-preserved organic remains (JW): the iron knife has the remains of a horn handle with traces of the leather sheath partially enclosing it. Context 2630.

SF 462. Belt. Oval buckle (2 fragments), square belt plate with three triangular openings near one edge, bases of triangles facing towards three ?copper alloy rivets/dot inlays near edge. One square belt plate with three ?copper alloy rivets/dot inlays, but no openings. Six fragments of rectangular belt fittings with similar ?rivets/inlays. three other fragments, one perhaps part of buckle (not illus). Iron. Context 2631.

Grave 2626 (Vol 1, Fig 5.26)

SF 453. Knife. Very corroded (not illus), found together with fragmented small cramp or bracket. Iron. Context 2628.

SF 438. Spiral wound tubular bead. Opaque yellow-green. D 7 mm; Ht 7 mm. Context 2628. [ID 13].

Grave 2629 (Vol 1, Figs 5.27–28)

SF 417. Workbox. Fragmentary. Cylindrical, sheet metal (Th 0.63 mm) rolled, secured by four rivets that also fixed hinge plate to main body and hinge for ?lid (separate fragment, axial rod still in place). Lid and base both circular, slightly domed. Decoration on all three fragments made from repeated rows and concentric rings of dots stamped from the internal side. Hinge plate attached to decorated 'arm'/handle with lozenge-shaped base with diamond shaped openings and punched ring-and-dot decoration, tapering to cylindrical shaft with repeated transverse grooves, ring terminal at end contains part of iron ?loop. Copper alloy. Context 2633. Very similar decoration of repoussé dots arranged in bands of one or two on workbox from Didcot grave 12 (Boyle 1995, 223–4; 253 fig 97,14; very close parallel Barton-on-Humber grave II; Drinkall and Foreman 1998, 207 fig 121, 2).

SF 426. Brooch. Penannular brooch with blue glass melon bead attached. Terminals flattened and coiled back at right angles to ring, they are decorated with two longitudinal grooves, ring is oval sectioned. Either side of terminals are nine transverse grooves and another set opposite terminals. Wear marks on opposing sides of brooch indicate where pin may have been, now missing. Silver. Group No. 427, Context 2633.

SF 444. Bracelet. Penannular, rectangular section, tapers towards perforated terminals which flatten to rectangular-section at right-angled axis to body of bracelet. Terminals overlap where they meet. Broken, two pieces join. Probably originally riveted. Copper alloy. Context 2633.

SF 445. Knife. Blade slightly S-shaped with raised tip. Short triangular tang set near cutting edge, shoulder only on side of back. Iron. Context 2633.

SF 446. Chain. Probably with long rod-like square-sectioned links with looped ends. Probably for suspension of workbox SF 417 to ?organic belt (no trace of belt discovered in grave). L at least 415 mm. Iron. Context 2633.

SF 448. Pin. Circular flat head on same axis as shaft, on its reverse is part of a perforated possible lug (slightly broken), riveted to head. Faint trace of two transverse raised lines immediately below head. Circular cross-section, tapers slightly. ?Pin possibly attached to chain SF 450–1. SF 449 probably its counterpart but without head. Silver. Group 447, Context 2633.

SF 449. Pin (not illus). Incomplete, shaft only, circular cross-section, tapers slightly. Shaft is split/damaged. Possibly part of disc at ?head end. Probably the counterpart to SF 448. Silver. Group 447, Context 2633.

SF 450. Fitting. Two fragments possibly join. Small cylinders, join visible, small rivet survives. On larger piece wire twisted loop attached at one end and thin silver wires gathered inside tube. Silver. Group No. 447, Context 2633.

SF 451. Chain. Now in four fragments. Longest fragment (L 22.7 mm W 1.8 mm) plaited, still free-moving. Silver. Group No. 447, Context 2633.

Beads from Grave 2629:

SF 425. Spiral wound tubular bead. Opaque brick red. D 7 mm; Ht 5 mm. Context 2633. [ID 8].

SF 426. Melon bead on penannular brooch. Turquoise frit. D 16 mm; Ht 13 mm. Roman bead. Context 2633.

Grave 2634 (Vol 1, Fig 5.29)

SF 463. Knife. Narrow blade with straight back and cutting edge which curves up to tip at line of back. Triangular tang continues with gentle curve into line of back, short choil to cutting edge. Iron. Mineral-preserved organic remains (JW): the knife has traces of the horn handle which extends over the shoulder of the blade, and remains of the leather sheath. Context 2636.

SF 9462. Belt. Long oval buckle with square belt plate. Two rectangular fittings, each with three rivets either side. Iron. Context 2636.

Grave 2637 (Vol 1, Fig 5.30)

SF 456. Knife. Blade with straight cutting edge and gently arched back, both curving to now missing tip in median line of blade. Whittle tang set slightly below median line of blade. Iron. Context 2639.

Grave 2640 (Vol 1, Fig 5.31)

SF 441. Knife (a) and socket (b): a) Narrow blade with slightly convex back and straight cutting edge, tip missing. Long triangular tang. Iron. Mineral-preserved organic remains (JW): on the iron knife there are traces of the leather sheath, but little remains of the tang and no identifiable organic material relating to the original handle; b) Base of split socket, top end of object missing. Iron. Mineral-preserved organic remains (JW): small iron socket with mineral-preserved wood, possibly *Fagus* sp. (beech), in cross-section this appears to be from young growth such as a sapling or branch wood. This is possibly the socket from an arrowhead. Context 2641.

Grave 2643 (Vol 1, Fig 5.32)

SF 413. Sword (a) and spearhead (b): a) Spatha. Mineralised remains analysis (JW): the sword is heavily corroded in several fragments, and preserved in the corrosion layers are traces of the organic materials that originally formed the hilt and scabbard. The hilt is made up of sections of horn, but only the grip and lower guard remain and the components can be distinguished by a change in grain direction. The lower guard is 13 mm thick. There are grooves about 3 mm wide on the inside of the horn sheath that forms the grip section, these can be seen as a raised area along the tang and in the cross-section of the broken end of the tang. No packing material, such as wood or horn wedges, seems to have been used to fill this void and provide a more secure fit for the horn sections of the hilt, as has been noted on a seax hilt from Mucking (Watson in Hirst and Clarke 2009, 567). The composite organic scabbard comprises a 'fleece' lining with the hairs next to the blade. On top of this are two thin wooden stiffeners, which have a radial surface. Wood: *Fraxinus* sp. (ash). The iron blade is *c.* 54 mm wide, and the scabbard 66 mm. There are the remains of an outer leather covering on top of the wood, and near the hilt are marks in the soil and corrosion which possibly correspond to the position of three bands of leather strapping often found in this position on sword scabbards (Cameron 2000). All the organic components present on this sword have been noted on other Saxon swords (Cameron 2000; Watson and Edwards 1990); b) Small socketed spearhead found with sword. Tip missing. Iron. Mineral-preserved organic remains (JW): wood preserved in socket, *Corylus* sp. (hazel) from mature timber. Context 2645.

Grave 2776 (Vol 1, Fig 5.33)

SF 508. Knife. Blade with ?straight edge and slightly arched back, tip missing. Whittle tang continues line of cutting edge and joins back with a gently curved shoulder. Length (97 mm) measured for three fragments of ?knife that join together. Iron. Context 2778.

Grave 2783 (Vol 1, Fig 5.34)

SF 494 (not illus). Unidentifiable lump, mostly iron corrosion products and soil. Context 2785.

SF 511 (not illus). Spearhead. Fragment of socketed spearhead. Iron. Context 2785.

SF 513. Knife. Blade with straight edge and back curving down to tip. Tang in median line of blade; straight shoulder, convex choil. Iron. Context 2785.

Grave 2827 (Vol 1, Fig 5.35)

SF 522. Shears. U-shaped shears, blades corroded onto each other, handle broken. A knife is placed above (or below) the shears (only discovered during mineral-preserved organics analysis); tip of the blade and end of tang are missing; tang and probably tip in median line of blade. Iron. Mineral-preserved textile remains (PWR): running across one face of the shears (on the opposite face from the knife) are loose folds of organic material, which incorporate two relatively well preserved patches of textile, 6 x 6 mm and 4 x 4 mm. The textile is a tabby weave, 26/Z x 18/Z per cm; fibre not identified. Context 2828.

SF 525. Ring. Fragments, possible fitting or ?annular brooch. Flat cross section, circular. Ring and dot decoration visible on one side of two pieces. Copper alloy. Group No. 523, Context 2828.

SF 528. Ring. Complete. Circular cross-section. Two opposing groups of transverse grooves on internal edge. Terminals are coiled around each other with six turns on each side. Silver. Group No. 523, Context 2828.

SF 531 (Pl 2). Brooch. Incomplete. Keystone garnet disc brooch. Plate of bronze/gunmetal, gilded on front, reverse partly covered with white metal containing lead, tin and zinc. Approximately one third of brooch is missing, deliberately broken off. Originally decoration would have consisted of three keystone ?garnet inlays (two empty settings remain), alternating with three round inlays of which only two empty settings remain. At centre was large inlay (this also missing) with beaded silver wire border which was soldered on to plate with leaded solder (fragments retained separately). Gilded surface with punched dot decoration, arranged in more or less parallel lines radiating from centre, covers remainder of surface. Textile fragments adhere to back, possibly where hinge/lug for pin was located. Part of small square catchplate, cast together with plate, survives on reverse. Copper alloy, with gilding and white metal coating. Mineral-preserved textile remains (PWR): on back, in two flat layers over pin support, but not engaged with pin, 15 x 12 mm of textile woven in tabby, 24/Z x 18/Z per cm. The fibre is probably flax, or possibly hemp, identified from the narrow diameter range, 10–15 microns, smooth profile and fine central lumen. Context 2828.

Plate 2 Silver-gilt keystone garnet disc brooch SF 531, grave 2827. Diam. 51 mm. Photo: E. Wakefield

Beads from Grave 2827:

SF 524. Hexagonal-section tubular bead. Opaque green. L 8 mm; D 5 mm. Context 2828. [ID 35]. Roman form of bead (see Brugmann 2004, figs 67 and 70).

SF 526. Spiral wound tubular or barrel-shaped bead. Opaque green. D 8 mm; Ht 6 mm. Context 2828. [ID 34].

SF 527. Annular bead. Semi-opaque with marvered white spiral trail. Blue-green/white trail. D 15 mm; Th 6 mm. Context 2828. [ID 36]. For parallels see Guido (1999, 335–337 and pl. 11a).

SF 529. Spiral wound tubular or barrel-shaped bead. Opaque brick red. D 7 mm; Ht 5 mm. Context 2828. [ID 37].

Grave 2829 (Vol 1, Fig 5.36)

Beads from Grave 2829:

SF 9550. Thin biconical or annular bead, flawed. Opaque yellow. D 11 mm; Ht 6 mm. Context 2830. [ID 38].

SF 9551. Biconical bead with flat central band. Translucent dark blue-green. D 9 mm; Ht 8 mm. Context 2830. [ID 39]. Roman bead.

SF 9552. Biconical bead. Blue green. D 8 mm; Ht 6 mm. Context 2830. [ID 40]. Roman?

SF 9553. Spiral wound tubular or barrel-shaped bead. Opaque pale sandy green. D 7 mm; Ht 5 mm. Context 2830. [ID 41].

SF 9554. Spiral wound tubular bead. Opaque brick red. D 6 mm; Ht 5 mm. Context 2830. [ID 42]. Saxon.

Grave 2888 (Vol 1, Fig 5.38)

SF 534. Probably knife. If pieces belong to the same object, cutting edge may have been slightly raised near tip, back ?straight. Iron. Context 2890.

Grave 3703 (Vol 1, Fig 5.13)

SF 1648. Spearhead. Socketed spearhead with long slender blade of lozengiform section. Socket nearly as long as blade. Iron. Mineralised remains in socket not analysed. Context 3704.

Grave 3829 (Vol 1, Fig 5.14)

SF 1649. Knife. Complete. Back and edge of blade both curve to tip in median line of blade. Triangular whittle tang continues line of cutting edge and leaves only a short shoulder on side of back. Iron. Context 3828.

Grave 3903 (Vol 1, Fig 5.39)

SF 6004 (not illus). Uncertain fragments. a) probably knife in three fragments; b) and c) unidentifiable. Iron. Context 3908.

Grave 3991 (Vol 1, Fig 5.15)

SF 192. Knife. Tip and end of tang missing, back of blade slightly arched in middle, cutting edge ?straight. Iron. Context 3992.

SF 1667 (Pl 3). Brooch. Incomplete. Garnet inlaid disc brooch, silver base, gilding applied to face. Central setting with garnet in beaded border, originally set on boss of white material, of which only traces remain, set within circular silver band and beaded ring. Four elongated petal-shaped settings holding garnets arranged in cruciform around central setting. Four intermediate areas filled with chip-carved interlacing animal-style II design arranged around intermediate settings with raised, beaded borders. All intermediate settings lack ?white material filling; two settings still contain round garnets set on cross-hatched gold foil; one only has gold foil with solder raising it to similar height as complete settings. Outer edge decoration of zigzag lines, second ring decoration of four grooved rectangular panels alternating with four rectangular garnet inlays. Textile and ?bone attached to back. Plain lug for spring and catchplate

Plate 3 Silver-gilt garnet-set disc brooch SF 1667, grave 3991. Diam. 48 mm. Photo: E. Wakefield

(visible in x-radiograph), cast with base plate. Silver with gilding. Mineral-preserved textile remains (PWR): on back, visible in area over pin support, 20 x 15 mm, but covered by consolidated earth, textile woven in 2/2 diamond twill, 20/Z x 16–18/S per cm; fibre not identified, but the ZS spin suggests wool. The Z-spun system runs across the line of the brooch. Context 3992.

SF 1668. Pin. Disc-headed pin with flat oval shaped head in same plane as shaft, remains of suspension loop at top. Shaft circular sectioned. Very abraded. Copper alloy. Context 3992.

Beads from Grave 3991:

SF 1671. Biconical bead. Translucent dark turquoise. D 9 mm; Ht 8 mm. Context 3992. [ID 66]. Roman bead.

SF 1672. Spiral wound tubular bead. Asymmetrical. Opaque green. D 9 mm; Ht 6 mm. Context 3992. [ID 67].

Grave 3993 (Vol 1, Fig 5.16)

SF 207. Buckle. Oval-shaped angled buckle frame, grooved line decoration, some beading visible. Pin has trapezoid plate at base end below which sits perforated lug for attachment to plate. Body of pin arched, D-shaped section, flares outwards at tip which is decorated with animal-like head (dots for eyes, snout-like nose at end). Iron axis holds pin, frame and decorative plate together. Lyre-shaped plate with profiled edges, tapers slightly to one end, three perforated lugs on reverse, upper side decorated with pattern of drop and lozenge shapes, five roundels around edge. Copper alloy. Context 3994.

So far without close parallels, the individual details of ornamentation of this buckle relate it to Byzantine belt buckles with lyre-shaped plates. Such belt buckles are found from Trabzon on the Turkish Black Sea coast to Burgos in Northern Spain throughout the Mediterranean basin and are dated to the middle to second half of the 7th century (Werner 1955, 37; 47 Karte 2, Typ Trabzunt). The decoration on some of these plates shows the fight of a crocodile with a double-headed snake, a scene alluding to one of the fables from the Physiologus (*ibid*, 36 with note 6; Taf. 4,3.5–7). The best comparison with regards to the outline of the plate and the arrangement of ornamental subdivisions is provided by an unprovenanced belt plate, probably from the area of the Roman province of Hispania Baetica in southern Spain (Ripoll López 1998, 153 fig 25,91 and lám. 32,91). The plate shows a bearded face in the drop-shaped element at the end, accompanied by a fish-bladder-shaped element either side; at the base near the hinges for the attachment of the belt-frame are two outward-facing heads of birds of prey. Ripoll López

(1998, 136) could not find a close parallel for this buckle but loosely related it to her type D of lyre-shaped buckles. The five small roundels found on the Springhead plate are familiar from plates of' 'Typ Gerena' by Ebel-Zepezauer (2000, 67). The arrangement of the drop and lozenge shapes on SF 207 can be understood as reinterpretations or degradations of the snake-and-crocodile or bearded face scenes, possibly influenced by the floral patterns employed in the decoration of another type of Byzantine belt buckle with a more heart-shaped plate, named 'Typ Syrakus' and dated to the first half of the 7th century by Werner (1955, 37 Abb. 2; 46 Karte 1; Taf. 5,8–12.14–16). At least two examples of this type (*cf* Marzinzik 2003, type 22.b-i) are known from England: one from Kent (Werner 1955, 37 Abb. 2,3) and another one from The Broyle, Chichester (Welch 1983, 642 fig 126b; this was still mentioned as unprovenanced by Werner (1955, 47 Liste 2 No. 31)). A link between 'Typ Syrakus' and the Springhead plate might be provided by a belt plate from Niederbreisig, Germany, which has an open-work decoration alluding to the palmettes familiar from 'Typ Syrakus', and oval motifs which Wamers suggests may be eyes reminiscent of Germanic animal ornament, while its oval buckle frame and shield-shaped pin are familiar elements of Merovingian buckles (Wamers 1986, 72 No. 53). Like the late 5th/early 6th-century bow brooch of type Estagel found in pit 2868 *c* 500 m to the north-northwest of grave 3993 (see below, Cat. No. 2), belt buckle SF 207 points to contacts with the Romanised Mediterranean, and possibly more specifically Visigothic, sphere. A buckle plate of a different but related type (Ripoll Lopéz type G2), recently found near Maidstone (PAS no LON-8577D6; *Medieval Archaeology* 52, 2008, 325 fig 14), adds support to the suggested contacts with Visigothic Spain.

SF 1674. Spearhead. Socketed spearhead with leaf-shaped blade of lozengiform section, tip missing. Iron. Mineral-preserved organic remains (JW): wood in socket: *Alnus* sp. (alder) from mature timber. Context 3994.

Grave 3997 (Vol 1, Fig 5.17)
SF 193. Point. Possible lace end? Sheet rolled into cylinder that tapers to point. Part of punched hole (D 1.5 mm) visible at widest point. Copper alloy. Context 3998.

Beads from the Saxon Graves
by Ian Scott

Many of the beads from the graves at Springhead (ARC SPH00) are either spiral wound tubular or tubular/barrel-shaped beads and opaque. Brugmann (2004, 41, for parallels see figs 93–96 and 99) has dated this type of bead to the 7th–8th centuries. Biconical beads in opaque glass are Saxon, but by contrast the translucent biconical beads – SF 1671 (Grave 3991) and SF 9551 (Grave 2829) – are of Roman origin, as is the tubular bead of hexagonal cross-section (SF 524, Grave 2827). The melon beads, in turquoise frit, are another Roman form.

Mineral-preserved Textiles from Springhead Saxon Cemetery
by Penelope Walton Rogers (Anglo-Saxon Laboratory)

Traces of textile have been recorded in association with metal artefacts in three graves, 2129, 2827 and 3991. The most important are from grave 3991, on the back of brooch SF 1667, where there is a fine 2/2 diamond (or chevron) twill which, to judge from its Z x S spin, is made from wool (Walton Rogers 2007, 72). This is a good quality fabric, of a type used for outer garments for both men and women (*ibid*). It can be assumed from the grave layout that the brooch was originally in the region of the neck or upper chest and the close relationship between the textile and the brooch hinge suggests that the brooch clasped the textile.

Comparable brooches can be seen fastening cloaks and mantles in illustrations in the Stuttgart Psalter, dated *c* AD 800 (Walton Rogers 2007, 177), but there is little textile evidence to show how they were worn in Kent. Only one other 7th century brooch of similar size and weight has retained remains of the garment that it fastened, and that is a plated disc brooch, 47 mm diameter, from Saltwood grave 6421. In that instance the brooch clasped the worked edge of a lightweight linen, of a quality more appropriate to a chemise or veil than a mantle (Walton Rogers 2006). The garment accessories and their arrangement in the grave place both Saltwood 6421 and Springhead 3991 in Kentish Dress Style VI. Style VI is defined by a short pin on the upper chest, a small number of beads, sometimes an ornate brooch, and no buckle at the waist, and it has been provisionally dated to *c* AD 625–700 (Walton Rogers 2007, 193; in prep). The exact appearance of the clothing represented by Dress Style VI is as yet unclear, but the Springhead burial has at least added some useful new data.

A fine linen tabby weave, 24–26/Z x 18/Z per cm, was found on two separate artefacts in grave 2827. It lay in two flat layers on the back of the keystone garnet disc brooch SF 531 in the region of the left hip; and in loose folds on one face of the shears (and knife) SF 522 in the

Plate 4 Detail of mineral-preserved knife sheath SF 522, Grave 2827. Calfskin with fine diagonal nick-marks, each about 1 mm long. Photo: I. Panter, York Archaeological Trust Conservation Department

area of the waist. The brooch does not pin the textile and it was probably simply placed against the linen clothing, along with the knife and shears. Textiles of this nature are particularly common in late graves: in a recent survey, ZZ tabby represented 50% of all textiles in burials confidently dated to the late 6th or 7th century (Walton Rogers 2007, 104–7).

Part of the sheath has been preserved on the knife SF 522 from grave 2827. It has been made from an animal skin and although the method of skin preparation cannot be determined from fully mineralised material (Cameron 2000, 54), it has the appearance of tanned leather, with no hairs visible in the follicles. The leather, approximately 2 mm thick, curves over the spine of the blade, which implies that the sheath seam ran along the cutting edge. The grain pattern is particularly clear and has been identified by Ian Panter, York Archaeological Trust Conservation Department, as calfskin, based on the even distribution and small size of the empty hair follicles. On the best-preserved area of the leather, there is a row of fine diagonal nick-marks, each about 1 mm long, and there are further similar marks elsewhere (Pl 4): it is not clear whether these represent decoration or damage during use.

This item fits the evidence for knife sheaths of the 5th to 7th centuries collected by Cameron (2000, 53–6). They were close-fitting sheaths, generally with the seam along the cutting edge and they were mostly made from calf, occasionally sheep or goat. They sometimes had simple linear decoration, although this was usually impressed, rather than incised.

The poorly preserved coarse fabric on both faces of spearhead SF 278 in grave 2129 almost certainly represents a cloth wrapper. Similar fabrics have been recorded in a number of other cemeteries, some held in place by a cord tied around the spear socket (Walton Rogers 2007, 228), and the small pins alongside spearheads in other burials in Kent probably also represent a fastening for a wrapper (Evison 1987, 82–3).

Mineral-preserved Organic Remains from Springhead Saxon Cemetery
by Jacqui Watson

Most of the organic material has been preserved by iron corrosion, and even those materials in close proximity to copper alloy objects have been preserved by iron salts produced by small nails or rivets. In many cases it has been possible to identify the original organic material and some wood species with the aid of a binocular microscope. In other cases samples have been examined using a scanning electron microscope (SEM). A few objects required investigative conservation, but this only amounted to the repair of loose flakes with HMG (nitro-cellulose adhesive) and the removal of accretions to facilitate the identification of traces of organic materials.

Spears
Six spearheads with wood remains in their sockets were submitted for analysis (alder (2), hazel (2), ash (1), and not identifiable (1)). Three have clearly been fashioned from mature timber, with the annual rings visible as horizontal bands across the width of the socket. The use of mature wood rather than a sapling probably allows greater control and accuracy when throwing the spear in much the same way that medieval arrow shafts were made from carefully selected mature timber rather than using saplings or branches of an appropriate size (Urbon 1991).

Seaxes
Although similar materials are preserved on seaxes as on swords, it is more common for seax hilts to be made from a single piece of horn rather than several pieces, and to have a leather sheath encasing the blade, and often the hilt, rather than a composite wood and leather scabbard. The sheaths are usually made from a single piece of thick leather, such as cattle hide or like SFs 283 and 1681 of pigskin, and joined at the blade edge with copper alloy rivets, studs or wire. The three analysed seaxes (SFs 283, 414 and 1681) from Springhead, at least in part, follow the same construction (Cameron 2000).

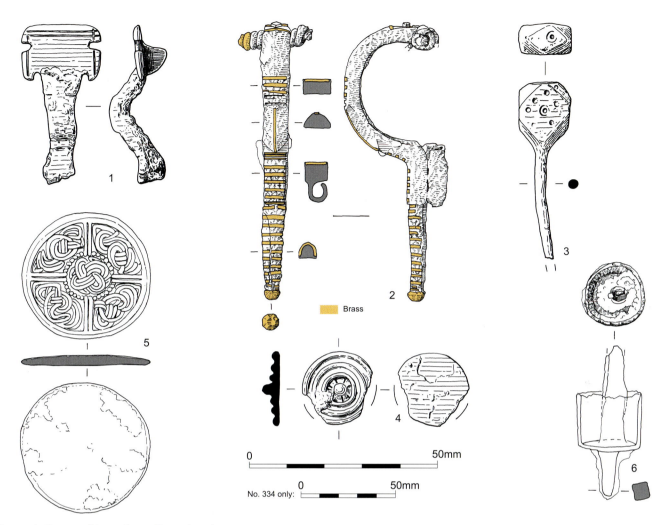

Figure 4 Saxon objects from Springhead

Knives

Four knives from different graves have been analysed, all with the remains of leather sheaths, and where the tang remains all have evidence for a horn handle. There is some evidence for the construction of the leather sheaths, which can be seen to be made from a single piece of leather that was joined along the blade edge and in at least one case it also covers the handle. In most cases the condition of the mineral-preserved leather is little more than a compact powder.

Catalogue of Other Saxon Metal Objects from Springhead

1. Brooch. Incomplete. Rectangular-shaped flat head plate with incised line decoration around edges and small rectangular notches below upper edges and next to bow. Two perforated lugs on reverse for spring. Pin missing. Knee-shaped, oval-sectioned bow, transverse ribbed

decoration, Foot tapers slightly, with catchplate attached; foot end missing. (Leaded) copper alloy. SF 1726, Context 6379, Intervention 1001 (Spring), SG 300015 (Deposits). Early Roman.

Cat. No. 1 (Fig 4, 1) is an Anglo-Saxon small-long brooch, a type most common in the Anglian areas in the east of England but also the Midlands and the north; it is less frequent in Saxon areas, although it is not unusual to find one or two graves in a cemetery with a pair of such brooches at the shoulders (Walton Rogers 2007, 119). As Cat. No. 1 was found in the Ebbsfleet a date is entirely reliant on comparison to parallels. The last comprehensive study of the type was conducted by Leeds (1945, 4–44), and subsequently criticised by Vierck for not adequately exploring the influence of cruciform brooches on the development of the type (Vierck 1972; 1977, 42–3; references after Stoodley 1999, 18 footnote 12). Vierck's suggestion that small-long brooches were basically only simpler versions of

Plate 5 Visigothic brooch Cat. No. 2, iron body inlaid with brass cramps and brass knobs. L 75 mm.
Photo: E. Wakefield

cruciform brooches has recently been challenged by Walton Rogers (2007, 119) who claims that they are often well made, but while they can sometimes be found as fasteners in positions on the shoulder like cruciform brooches, their variation of orientation and position is greater than that of cruciforms and thus indicating a more versatile brooch type. Very similar examples with notched headplates like Cat. No. 1 have been found in Sussex, eg, at Alfriston, grave K (Welch 1983, 559 fig 43d) and Chichester (*ibid*, 642 fig 126a). On account of their more distant relationship to North German '*Fibeln mit gelappter Kopfplatte*', Welch (*ibid*, 169) suggests a date in the later 5th or early 6th century for these.

2.   Brooch. Bow and foot inlaid with transverse brass cramps on foot, bow with facetted fields, which have longitudinal inlays on their ridges, intersected by rectangular sections with transverse cramps. Brass knobs at foot end and left side of axis bar, right one missing. Iron with brass. SF 564, Context 2869, Intervention 2868 (Pit), Springhead Sanctuary. Early Saxon.

The brooch (Fig 4, 2; Pl 5) belongs to Schulze-Dörlamm's type Estagel, a Visigothic type dated to the end of the 5th and the beginning of the 6th centuries AD (Schulze-Dörlamm 1986; Kazanski 1998, fig 4). A distribution map of Visigothic bow brooches by A. Koch (1998, 83 Abb. 17) shows type Estagel, predominantly found in southern France and central Spain, to have some outliers in Normandy, Picardy and the Île-de-France. Cat. No. 2 has very close parallels in two iron brooches from grave 529 at Frénouville, Dép. Calvados,

France (Pilet 1980, pl 141). These have a similar, but silver, decoration of cramps and knobs either side of the spring and at the end of the foot. Whether the Springhead brooch indicates the presence of Visigothic persons in south-east Britain, which is the interpretation suggested for their presence in Northern France (A. Koch 1998, 82 ff. Abb. 15–16; U. Koch *et al* 1996, 841; 847), or whether they are simply indicative of the wider political and economic circumstances providing a framework for the exchange of such objects, cannot be decided at present. There are several other objects, mainly from south-eastern England, including coins and dress accessories, with Visigothic or more broadly western Mediterranean rather than East Germanic origin (see eg, Eagles and Ager 2004), for instance a three-lobed small long brooch from *Grubenhaus* 81 at Mucking (Hamerow 1993, 61, 244; fig 132, 1) with affinities to a Visigothic type of 'Blechfibeln'. Visigothic coins found in eastern England have been discussed by Rigold (1975) and Archibald (1991, 36), and among the latest of these is a tremissis, dated to the end of the 6th century, found at the Dover-Buckland cemetery (Evison 1987, 181).

Cat. No. 2 was the only metal find from an as yet isolated pit (2868) almost half way along the Ebbsfleet between Springhead and Northfleet (see Vol 1, Fig 5.5). As has been discussed elsewhere in this volume (see Mepham, Chap 1), the other finds from the pit are sherds of ceramic vessels with parallels among the early Saxon pottery from Mucking, just across the Thames in Essex. About 150 m further north from this pit another pit (2874) contained a Saxon bucket handle (SF 542), a copper alloy sheet fragment, an unidentified iron object, a shale spindle whorl and a 1st-century Roman dolphin brooch (see Schuster Vol 2, Chap 3, Cat. No. 89) as well as one Roman and two Saxon pottery sherds. Recent excavations in an area further to the east have revealed a Saxon sunken-featured building (SFB). In synopsis, these finds may be indicative of an early Saxon settlement area in the vicinity.

3.   Pin. Incomplete. Faceted cuboid head. Ring and dot decoration on top and both sides, cordon/collar just below head at top of shaft. Circular cross-sectioned shaft bent and broken at tip. Severely corroded. SF 108.

This pin (Fig 4, 3) belongs to Hinton and Parsons' Type Bb2ii, dated to the mid-Saxon period at Hamwic (Hinton and Parsons 1996, 22 fig 9, 32/457 and

169/1905), and similar pins from Lundenwic and other mid-Saxon sites support a dating in the 8th–9th century (eg, Ross 1989, 119 fig 41,196; I. Riddler, pers. comm.).

4. Disc or pendant. Incomplete disc, reverse plain. Front with three concentric ridges around edge, centre with cross whose arms are created by two parallel ridges each, with large boss in the centre. If it was a brooch, corrosion pattern on back may be reminiscent of spring or catchplate fittings. ?Leaded copper alloy or lead/tin alloy. SF 52002, Context 411, Intervention 411 (post-Roman river channel, Ebbsfleet Crossing).

Plate 6 Bracteate die Cat. No. 5, copper alloy. Diam. 34 mm. Photo: E. Wakefield

While it is uncertain whether this small disc (Fig 4, 4) was originally part of a pendant or a fitting, the elements of its design find parallels in a variety of mainly mid- to late Saxon objects. Small scutiform pendants of silver sheet metal are common 7th-century grave goods, mostly in the eastern half of England (Walton Rogers 2007, 128). They frequently have a central raised boss with cruciform decorations of lines of punched dots forming the four arms of a cross (eg, Dover-Buckland, graves 32, 35, 38, 67 (Evison 1987), or Finglesham, graves 84, 138, 174, 187 (Chadwick Hawkes and Grainger 2006)). However, the treatment of the decoration on the small disc from Springhead finds closer comparisons on later Saxon and Ottonian brooches both in England and on the Continent. A much larger pewter disc brooch from a 10th–11th century AD context at Thetford has the central boss, a cross with – slightly flaring – arms consisting of two ribs and an outer rim of three circular bands created by four concentric ribs. Both the cross arms and the bands are additionally subdivided by small square cells (Goodall 1984, 70, fig 109, 1). Ottonian circular cast disc brooches show similar designs (eg, from Mainz, (Wamers 1994, 86 Abb. 54, 170–1, cross rather like his 173–4 but lacking the central knob)) but can clearly be identified as brooches by their catchplates and pin hinges cast as part of the disc. Cat. No. 4 was found in a post-Roman river channel fill on the eastern side of the Ebbsfleet, which was partly covered by Saxon or later peat layers, and as it was the only object from the context no closer dating is possible.

5. Bracteate die (Pl 6). Circular disc, flat rectangular section. Engraved decoration on one side: within dotted circular border a central knotwork pattern of two intertwined loops consisting of three lines, the central one dotted with what looks like bifurcated ?feet in the corners of the cruciform arrangement; four panels arranged around this, separated by two parallel lines arranged to create a cross with the knotwork field in its centre, all contain Style-II animal decoration. Reverse appears to be plain. Orange patches adhere to front and back of object suggesting presence of iron/iron corrosion nearby. Very abraded. 12.2 g. Copper alloy. SF 50905, Context 34wb, Intervention 34wb.

Cat. No. 5 (Fig 4, 5; Pl 6) is a die for the production of repoussé sheet metal (Preßblech). The process would involve placing a sheet on the die, followed by a piece of leather or lead which is then struck by a hammer and thus transfers the ornament onto the thin sheet which through the process is also stiffened. The Style-II ornament in a cruciform arrangement, denoting the increasing influence of Christianity, suggests a date in the later 7th century. Bracteate brooches with similar ornaments are common in the Rhine-Neckar region in Germany (cf Roth and Wamers 1984, 283–4, no. 199.2) where they have been interpreted in a similar way. Wamers (1986, 49) discusses the possibility that even the apotropaic 'worm' ornament, similar to that found on Cat. No. 5, could already have been reinterpreted in a Christian way, much as other more evidently Christian motifs like eagles or deer found on such brooches. Other circular bracteate dies are known eg, from Hyldagergard, Denmark (Roth 1986, 52 Abb. 22a), Petersberg near Bonn, Germany (ibid, Abb. 22b) or Barton-on-Humber (ibid, Abb. 22e; Drinkall and Foreman 1998, 204 fig 118, 3; pl 18), the latter found in a grave containing a set of balances and weights. And while use as a weight cannot be excluded for the Barton die – Scull points out its weight of 12.98 g which is close to 10 siliquae at a standard of 1.30 g (ibid, 204 table 10) – its use as a die has been stressed in connection with the grave's interpretation as that of a goldsmith (Drinkall in

Drinkall and Foreman 1998, 291). Nevertheless, it is interesting to note that the weight of Cat. No. 5 of 12.2 g would correspond well with that of a tremisses struck to the Byzantine standard of 8 siliquae at avoirdupois of 1.52 g (*ibid*, 160). Unfortunately, as the Springhead die was found in subsoil approximately 100 m down slope west of the Saxon cemetery, there are no context associations which would aid the interpretation of its use or dating.

6. Ferrule. Ferrule with one side either closed or the rim folded inwards, remains of iron shaft in its centre, extending beyond the closed end. Mineralised wood remains on shaft identified as hazel (*Corylus avellana*; ident: C Barnett). Iron. SF 196, Context 2125, Intervention 2125 (Layer). Saxon (from area of Saxon ring ditches).

It is unfortunate that Cat. No. 6 (Fig 4, 6) was not found in a secure context as this might have helped to determine its original function. Similar ferrules are known from a late Roman ladle at Worms Nordfriedhof, grave 58 (Grünewald 1990, 216–7 No. F15). More commonly, such ferrules have been referred to as *Stabdorne*, the fittings to protect the lower end of a stick which may have been a sign of office of a village elder, an interpretation which has been refuted by Kleemann (1991, 272–3; 451) and Schmid (1994, 254–7) on account of their occurring too frequently in Continental Saxon and Frisian cemeteries in northern Germany. Other possible uses include ferrules of spears or lances, like those found in graves 117 and 133 at Finglesham (Chadwick Hawkes and Grainger 2006, 272 fig 2.110, 1.2; 277 fig 2.115,1.2), or crutches (*cf* Schön 2001, 110–1).

Catalogue of Saxon Metalwork from Northfleet

Only two metal objects recovered during the Northfleet excavations are intrinsically datable to the Saxon period, although a further 203 individually recorded items come from contexts phased as Saxon, but these are mostly colluvial or alluvial layers containing redeposited material of which the majority is likely to derive from the demolition debris of the Roman buildings in the area. Where relevant, these objects have been discussed in the section on Roman metalwork (see Schuster, Vol 2, Chap 4). However, a number of fills from SFBs contained

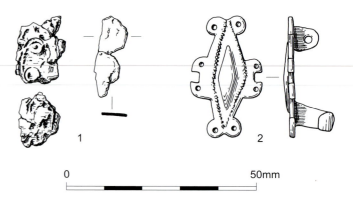

0   50mm

Figure 5   Saxon brooches from Northfleet

large numbers of lead discs possibly used as weights which will be discussed below.

Personal Adornment or Dress

1. Fragments of applied saucer brooch. Repoussé cover plate with remains of one double-tendril ornament facing outwards, rim set off by band filled with small raised dots. Three other fragments are part of the base plate and solder used to attach cover plate to base. Very corroded. Copper alloy. SF 11075, Context 10272, Intervention 10271 (foundation cut), SG 16638 (wall). Saxon.

Due to the extremely corroded condition of Cat. No. 1 (Fig 5, 1), the following identification is very tentative. Applied saucer brooches with tendril ornaments similar to this piece are found on Böhme's (1974, 25 Abb. 8) types Westerwanna or especially Bad Lippspringe; a very close parallel comes from Oosterbeintum, Netherlands, where the irregularities in the ornament include equally shallow tendrils (Böhme 1974, Taf. 58, 15). English examples were for instance found at Mitcham, grave 1 and 5, (Wheeler 1935, 117 fig 9,2; 120 fig 10,1). The type of ornament also occurs on saucer brooches with applied chip-carved plates of Böhme type Altenbühl-stedt. Continental examples of these types date to the end of the 4th and the 5th centuries, and in England they may even run into the 6th (Böhme 1974, 28; Walton Rogers 2007, 113–4). The brooch fragments were found in the backfill of Saxon SFB 16638 (see Vol 1, Chap 5, Fig 5.7), located only *c* 15 m south-east of the villa buildings. Because of the fragmentary condition of the brooch and the possibility of residuality it should be mentioned that brooches with applied cover plates featuring tendril ornaments already occur during the Roman period, but the arrangements of the tendrils tend to be slightly different to those of the types mentioned above (Bayley and Butcher 2004, 130 fig 98, 373; 173).

2. Plate brooch. Incomplete. Hinged, perforated lug on reverse of head, pin missing. Symmetrical lozenge shape, two circular lugs/lobes at top and bottom with ring and dot decoration, 2 almost rectangular shaped lugs either side also with ring and dot decoration. Raised central lozenge with beaded decoration surround. Large rectangular catchplate. Casting sprue/marks on reverse. Copper alloy. SF 30938, Context 30060, Intervention 30058 (foundation cut), SG 30057 (floor). Saxon.

This unusual brooch (Fig 5, 2) was found in the fill of Saxon SFB 30057 (see Vol 1, Chap 5, Fig 5.8). No immediate comparisons for this brooch are known to the author, but the workmanship of the brooch suggests that it may perhaps be a crude imitation of 2nd-century Roman lozengiform brooches like Feugère type 26d1. A later 4th-century fitting from grave 1107a at Krefeld-Gellep, Germany, bears some resemblance to Cat. No. 2 but lacks the lugs on the long sides (Böhme 1974, Taf. 80, 2). Another possible influence for the design of Cat. No. 2 may come from square plate brooches of a type more commonly found in northern France and the Rhine valley; a pair of such brooches with ring-and-dot punches in the roundels comes from Mucking, grave 552 (Hirst and Clark 2009, 56 fig 29, 552.1–2; 484–5), and a pair set with garnets was found in grave 71, Mill Hill, Deal (Parfitt and Brugmann 1997, 176 fig 39, 71c), which belongs to Kentish Phase II dated *c* 500– 530/40. As Cat. No. 2 was found in a Saxon context, the later Roman/early Saxon influences may provide more plausible explanations for the origin of its design.

Weighing and Measuring

Twenty-five lead weights were recorded from various Northfleet sites (Table 10; Fig 6). The majority (18) of the weights are disc-shaped, but of the five Roman weights only two are of that form while there are also two hemispherical weights and one biconical weight. The latter (SF 11762) has iron corrosion products at one end, most likely deriving from a suspension loop for its use on a steelyard; it is the only one of the Roman weights where its use as a weight is beyond reasonable doubt. However, neither this nor the two hemispherical and one of the disc-shaped weights are close to known

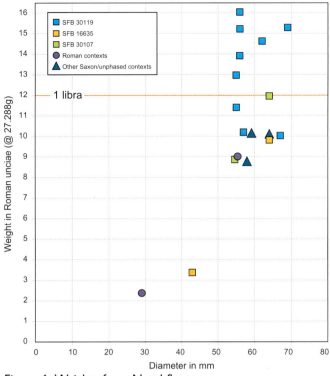

Figure 6 Weights from Northfleet

multiples of the uncial scale (*cf* Chantraine 1961, col. 620), much in contrast to the weights from Saxon contexts, while the only weight from an early Roman ditch in the Western Roman Complex site is just *c* 1.5 g or 0.65% lighter than 9 *unciae*.

As can be seen from Figure 6, most disc-shaped weights have diameters between 55 mm and 70 mm, with the majority of the nine weights from Saxon SFB 30119 ranging between 55 mm and 57 mm, while their weights in the range between 244 g and 438 g are more variable. Plotted against an uncial scale based on a Roman ounce at 27.288 g, seven of the nine discs from SFB 30119 appear to vary by less than 2% from known multiples of the *uncia*. A cluster of five weights from various Saxon contexts exists around 273 g (268–78 g), the equivalent of ten Roman *unciae* or one *dextans* at 272.88 g. Apart from one disc from SFB 30119, the central holes of the other eight discs show signs of uneven wear, suggesting they were perhaps suspended from a thread.

Considering the wear marks on most of the holes of the perforated lead discs, a use as loom weights could be a possible interpretation of these objects, an explanation which has also been discussed for some of the 28 lead discs from Mucking just across the Thames from Northfleet (Hamerow 1993, 70–1). Disregarding a lighter group of six discs with weights between *c* 25 g and 50 g

Table 10 Weights from Northfleet

SF	Width/diam.	Wt (g)	Comment	Shape	Trench	Context	Cut	Sub-group	Phase & feature description
10979	29	65	–	Disc	NVGS	10036	–	–	Late Roman; alluvial sediment, N edge of gravel spur
10980	37	171	–	Biconical	NVGS	10033	–	–	Saxon; colluvium
10984	17	21	–	Truncated–spherical	NVGS	10039	–	–	Unphased; alluvial sediment
11076	58	317	–	Cone–section	NVGS	10274	10273	16638	Saxon; backfill SFB quadrant 10273 & post-hole 10350
11581	43	92	–	Disc	NVGS	10536	10180	16635	Saxon; fill N/W quadrant SFB
11582	64	268	Close to a *dextans* = 10 *unciae* = 272.88 g	Disc	NVGS	10536	10180	16635	
11672	58	239	Close to a *dodrans* = 9 *unciae* = 245.59 g	Disc	NVGS	15001	10809	15003	Saxon; SW quadrant of SFB
11762	20	33	–	Biconical	Wetlands	12344	–	19651	Late Roman; interface between alluvial & flint surface in channel
12710	48	285	–	Hemispherical	Wetlands	12618	–	19651	Late Roman; finds ref. number given for interface
12729	27	68	–	Hemispherical	Wetlands	12618	–	19651	
11786	19	23	–	Truncated–spherical	Wetlands	12588	–	–	Saxon; organic top soil sealing structure 12591
20965	55	244	Close to a *dodrans* = 9 *unciae* = 245.59 g	Disc	ESPORTS	20041	20042	20439	Early Roman; fill of ditch
30901	59	276	Almost exactly a *dextans* = 10 *unciae* = 272.88 g	Disc	3971 TT	3971012/30085	3971016/30084	30107	Saxon; silt accumulation in top of SFB
30920	64	326	Almost exactly a *libra* = 327.46 g	Disc	Area6Ex	30090	30087	30107	Saxon; primary fill of post pipe 30087
30921	55	244	Almost exactly a *dodrans* = 9 *unciae* = 245.59 g	Disc	Area6Ex	30086	30084	30107	Saxon; lower fill of SFB
30927	56	438	Almost exactly a *mina* = 436.61 g	Disc	Area6Ex	30082	30081	30119	Saxon; primary silting fill of SFB
30928	62	399	–	Disc	Area6Ex	30082	30081	30119	
30929	56	380	Almost exactly 1 *libra* and 2 *unciae* = 382.032 g	Disc	Area6Ex	30082	30081	30119	
30930	57	278	Close to a *dextans* = 10 *unciae* = 272.88 g	Disc	Area6Ex	30082	30081	30119	
30931	55	311	–	Disc	Area6Ex	30082	30081	30119	
30932	69	417	–	Disc	Area6Ex	30082	30081	30119	
30933	56	415	–	Disc	Area6Ex	30082	30081	30119	
30934	55	354	Almost exactly 1 *libra* + 1 *uncia* = 354.74 g	Disc	Area6Ex	30082	30081	30119	
30944	67	274	Almost exactly a *dextans* = 10 *unciae* = 272.88 g	Disc	Area6Ex	30082	30081	30119	
401,821	64	275	Almost exactly a *dextans* = 10 *unciae* = 272.88 g	Disc	–	0	–	–	

which are convincingly interpreted as spindle whorls (for weights of clay spindle whorls *cf* Walton Rogers 2007, 26), the heavier lead discs range between *c* 150 g and 280 g and are thus on the whole lighter than the assemblage from Northfleet (Hamerow 1993, 71 fig 47). The same also holds true for the disc diameters. At Mucking there are three groups clustering around *c* 25 mm, 32 mm and 40 mm respectively. Compared to the assemblage from Northfleet they are thus on average only half the size. Interestingly though, groups of discs from individual *Grubenhäuser* at Mucking have essentially identical diameters within each group, while their weights can vary by as much as *c* 130 g. The same is evident in the group from SFB 30119 at Northfleet, but while here the intervals of weights more or less increase by an *uncia* from weight to weight, the intervals at Mucking are much more gradual (N.B. no attempt has been made here to check these increases against smaller subdivisions of the *uncia*).

An interpretation of these discs as loom weights is certainly feasible; they fall well within the two maxima in the range of clay loom weights from Mucking (*ibid*, 67 fig 46), and similar interpretations have also been put forward for lead discs from other Saxon sites, eg, from Hanwell, Middlesex (Wheeler 1935, 136 fig 19) or Linford, Essex (Barton 1962, 76 fig 17). With regards to the uncial increments of the Northfleet discs it is, however, not inconceivable that they may have been lead weights or ingots; the latter has for instance been suggested for a group of discs from the Allemanic settlement on the Runde Berg near Urach, Germany (Koch 1984, 185, Taf. 30, 17–19).

Chapter 4

Other Saxon and Medieval Finds

Slag

by Phil Andrews

All of the slag that might be of Saxon date came from the Northfleet villa site (ARC EBB01). This amounted to just 0.77 kg of iron smithing slag, including one smithing hearth bottom fragment, most coming from context 30060 (0.42 kg, including the smithing hearth bottom fragment), with lesser amounts from 10274 (0.19 kg) and 10272 (0.16 kg). Both of the latter were fills of SFB 16638 and the former the fill of SFB 30057 (see Vol 1, Fig 5.6). The slag may all be residual Roman material, but could equally be Saxon, with small quantities of smithing debris quite often occurring in features, particularly sunken-featured buildings, of early–mid-Saxon date.

Medieval–Post-Medieval Ceramic Building Material

by Cynthia Poole

A small quantity of medieval and post-medieval brick and tile was identified during the assessment of ceramic building material from Northfleet (ARC EBB01) (Pringle 2005). None was identified from the Springhead Sanctuary (ARC SPH00) and Roadside settlement (ARC SHN02) sites, but a small quantity was recovered during a watching brief (ARC 342E02) when a tile kiln was exposed.

The post-Roman material from Northfleet accounted for less than 1% by weight of the site assemblage (3.06 kg). The forms present are set out in Table 11. The material comprised fragments of peg tile and brick, from unstratified, colluvial, alluvial and dumped deposits, as well as from a post-medieval field drain. Although not closely datable, the roof tiles appear to be not earlier than the 16th century and the bricks to date from the 17th–18th century or later. The material is archaeologically insignificant.

The material from Springhead came from an otherwise undated tile kiln (350), which produced peg tiles (see Vol 1, Fig 5.43). A total of 30 fragments weighing 6425 g were recovered from two layers (354, 367) around and infilling the kiln. The tiles from 354 had patches of mortar adhering to some, suggesting they may have formed part of the kiln structure, whilst the other group included wasters and overfired tiles, suggesting this was waste debris dumped after firing.

The majority of the tiles were peg tiles, but one was certainly a hip tile and another may have been a distorted peg tile, a ridge or a hip tile. No complete tiles were recovered, but several peg tiles provided complete widths of 149 mm, 150 mm, 152 mm, 155 mm and 160 mm and were 10–15 mm thick; the maximum surviving length was >190 mm. Nearly all the fragments collected from layer 367 retained one or two peg or nail holes. These included circular/oval, square and sub-square holes, some set at an angle of 45° to the edge so as to appear diamond-shaped, but others at different angles so as to appear merely skewed. The shapes, sizes and positions in relation to the tile edge of the peg holes are listed in *Table 12*. It was suggested of the peg tiles at Parsonage Farm (Betts and Smith 2006) that the shape of peg holes might be personal to the tiler, so each could identify their output. However, the mix of square and circular holes on the same tile appears to negate this and may reflect the shape of the tool used: if the punch had a cross-section that changed from squared to circular it may reflect the depth to which the punch was pressed into the tile. The angle of the square holes appears to be fortuitous rather than carefully positioned to achieve deliberately a square- or diamond-shaped hole.

The tiles are fairly well made and evenly finished, though it would appear that little effort was made to

Table 11 Count and weight of post-Roman tile types from Northfleet villa (ARC EBB01)

Form	No of frags	Wt (g)
Peg tile	4	224
Post-medieval brick	4	2814
Unidentified tile	1	20
Total	9	3058

place the peg holes regularly and symmetrically. There was less variation in distance to the top of the tile, but there was much greater variation in relation to the sides and each other. In date they are likely to be later medieval or even early post-medieval, probably falling within the range of late 14th–early 16th century.

The clay fabric used for the tiles showed considerable variation, but this probably reflects local variations in the clay source and the degree of preparation of the clay. The basic clay matrix was a fine sandy silty micaceous clay containing quartz sand and lesser quantities of a dark rock, probably iron. In the finest version virtually all grains are <0.1 mm in size with very rare larger rounded quartz sand up to 0.5 mm. The coarser version contains a high density of medium sand of the same rock types in the size range 0.1–0.5 mm, but rarely larger than this. The sand is evenly distributed and the fabric well mixed.

There were, in addition, examples of both the finer and coarser matrix in a poorly mixed, strongly laminated fabric (some of these tiles were very brittle and sheared and fragmented along the laminations) containing coarse buff rounded clay pellets and angular unwedged clay up to 8 mm and smaller red pellets of iron rich clay, and occasional red, possibly burnt, sandstone grit. The fabric fired to red and reddish-brown, as well as grey and purplish in the more overfired tiles.

Fired Clay and Daub from Springhead

by Cynthia Poole

A small quantity of fired clay and daub (204 fragments; 40,883 g) was found in contexts assigned a Saxon date. Of this nearly 95% by weight was found in one late Saxon feature (3475) at Springhead Sanctuary (ARC SPH00) interpreted as a crop dryer (see Vol 1, Fig 5.2). Some of the fired clay, certainly pieces of wall daub with roller stamped impression, in the early Saxon contexts are residual Roman.

Early Saxon

A small concentration in an early Saxon SFB (5809; see Vol 1, Fig 5.3) included vitrified furnace wall with a 35 mm wide perforation for a tuyère amongst a scatter of undiagnostic fragments of fired clay and may indicate the building was used for some form of industrial activity.

Late Saxon

The late Saxon material is concentrated in two features (3217, 3475) that have been interpreted as crop dryers (see Vol 1, Chap 5). Pit 3217 produced the smaller quantity (3%) of fired clay (89 fragments, 1337 g), much of which was amorphous. Most of the remainder had one or occasionally two surfaces, forming flat slabs 13– >30 mm thick. A few faint wattle impressions with a diameter of *c* 13 mm were visible, but insufficient diagnostic material survived to judge whether this was oven wall or floor (or even residual Roman wall daub). A few thin sub-oval or sub-rectangular plates with lentoidal section up to 14 mm thick measured over 70 mm long. Similar objects are sometimes associated with ovens or kilns and may have been used as spacers. All the fired clay was found in the final fill of the feature and therefore represents material dumped in the pit after it had gone out of use. The shape of the feature is consistent with a large oven or kiln and the fired clay may represent demolished superstructure and furniture thrown back into the disused structure.

Pit 3475 produced the largest group of material (73 fragments, 38,642 g) which formed a concentrated layer across the lower part of the pit and overlying primary layers of charcoal. All the pieces had a fairly flat, even surface on one side and interwoven wattle impressions on the other. Some pieces had a thinner coating of daub of 8–20 mm over the wattles compared to 40–60 mm over others. Only one piece, measuring 75 mm thick, retained evidence of the surface on both sides of the wattles. Other pieces were >80 mm thick and it is estimated that the full thickness for much of the structure would be *c* 100–110 mm.

Though initially recorded as oven wall, it is now thought more likely to be the remains of the drying floor of the probable crop dryer. The flat character of the

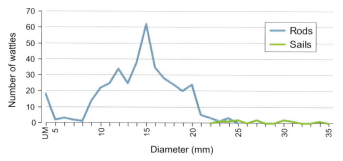

Figure 7 Wattle diameters from late Saxon crop dryer 3475

fragments are more consistent with floor material. The surviving fired clay surface was estimated to cover a minimum area of 1 m². The horizontal rod impressions were closely set and interlaced around vertical roundwood sails, set between 0.15 and 0.25 m apart. The wattles were very regular and rods and sails were distinct in terms of size (Fig 7). It is possible a hurdle was used as the basis for the floor. A variety of edge fragments were present, including a moulded edge with rounded cross-section, a straight edge with recessed ledge and flat straight edges, some with wattles projecting through the edge of the fired clay. The moulded edge probably represents the edge over the flue, whilst the other edges may have finished against the edge of the pit or a surrounding kerb. The shallow recessed ledge on one piece may indicate planks were used to prevent the drying grain from spilling off the floor.

Wooden Objects from Northfleet

Apart from the wood plane and the wooden bowl which are discussed below, brief mention should also be made of a perforated disc, made of oak, which contained a series of holes of different sizes arranged in concentric rings, some containing pegs, set around a large central hole (Fig 8, 3). It may have been the collar at the entrance to the fish trap 19441 (Hardy and Andrews, Vol 1, Chap 5). This device would allow the fish or eel to enter the basket through the central hole, but not to escape again; a function common to basketry fish traps worldwide, and as such not intrinsically datable.

Wood Plane
by Robert J Williams

The stock of a wooden plane (SF 12737; Fig 8, 1; Pl 7) was recovered from the interface of two clay and rubble deposits (contexts 12617 and 12619) that overlay the Roman quayside structures (see Vol 1, Fig 3.24). The plane has been extensively charred, although parts of the original surface have survived. It has been fashioned from a close-grained block of roundwood, although no obvious sapwood or knots are evident. The exact wood species has not been identified; it may be boxwood (D Goodburn, pers comm) although the visible grain may indicate that it is, more likely, another fruitwood.

The plane is 139 mm long, 38 mm wide, and tapers from 21 mm to 26 mm deep from front to back. The toe

Plate 7 Wood plane from Northfleet

is square, whereas the heel is tapered across its width and then rounded with triangular notches in both sides, creating a 'pinched' appearance, with traces of flanges on the sole. The throat is regular and has been carefully carved to give a maximum cut width of 18 mm. It is central to the stock leaving substantial cheeks, each approximately 10 mm wide. The front of the throat is nearly vertical but the bed of the throat (often referred to as 'pitch') is at an angle of 52° to the surviving sole. Both the wedge and the iron are missing, but the remains of two circular, 6 mm diameter holes in each cheek survive, indicating that the wedge and iron were held in place by a simple cross bar, which is also missing. The rounded heel of the plane has been set out by a compass and both the indentation of the point and a scribed arc (where it has not been cut away) are still clearly visible. The rounded heel also retains traces of vertical facets where it was pared to shape with a knife or chisel. The surviving squared sides and top of the plane are otherwise relatively flat, indicating that it was carefully made and finished, with little evidence of any tool marks. However, on the right-hand side and, particularly, on the top just behind the wedge position are the remains of fine incised cut marks. The sole of the plane exhibits a very clear longitudinal groove, 18 mm wide at its maximum width at the front and tapering slightly towards the heel but running at an angle across the sole and off-centre to the mouth. This groove is clearly the result of considerable wear from use.

The function of this plane can be ascertained from the wear on the sole. A groove with a minimum diameter of 18 mm is clearly visible and especially pronounced at up to 3 mm deep at the toe. In modern times such a plane would be known as a spar or oar plane (Sellens 1978, 72) and used to smooth large poles but, in this context, it is highly probable that the plane was used to fashion and finish spear or arrow shafts. It is interesting that the angle of the iron at 52° is very similar to post-medieval planes used for working hardwoods or cutting grooves. Lower angles are traditionally used for cutting end grain or soft woods (Whelan 1993, 385). No similar Roman examples for smoothing/rounding shafts are known, although a more decorative example with a hollow in the sole and dated to about AD 300 was found in the Vimose bog in Denmark (Long 2006, 16). The exact method of use of a plane of the size of the Nortfleet example must remain speculative, but there is some suggestion that small planes of this general form may have been pulled as opposed to pushed. While the rounded heel might fit comfortably in the palm of the hand, equally the notched and 'pinched' heel provides a good grip for the thumb and forefinger if the tool is pulled, giving even more control. The deeper groove at the toe end also seems to support this suggestion.

The plane was found at the interface between two layers (12617 and 12619) which comprised building rubble and clay dumped in the late 4th century to raise the level of the Roman quayside. These layers were subsequently pulled into the channel in the mid-Saxon period during construction of the mill pond. Consequently it remains possible that the plane is Saxon, but it could equally be of Roman date.

Establishing the ancestry of this significant discovery is extremely important, as so few wooden tools, and particularly planes, survive before about AD 1600 in Britain or indeed in Europe. Most extant Roman planes are of the jack plane type, usually over 300 mm long, constructed with an iron or sometimes bronze sole with varying degrees of infill of wood and ivory and used for smoothing timber (Goodman 1964, 43–53; Ulrich 2007, 41–5). Where there is good survival of the stock they are usually characterised by a slotted rear, and sometimes a front grip. This characteristic is particularly well developed in the Goodmanham plane of 4th century date found in East Yorkshire in 2000 (Long et al 2002, 9–20), although a similar Saxon example, dated to about AD 600, was also found in Kent at Sarre in 1863 (Dunning and Goodman 1959, 196–201).

Although the Sarre plane is made of horn and bronze its dimensions are very similar to the Northfleet plane at 153 mm long and only 32 mm wide. Planes made entirely of wood with no metal fittings of post-Roman and pre-medieval date are extremely rare, although several have been found in Holland in the terps at Hallum, Beetgum, and Oosterbeintum and illustrated by Goodman (1964, 54, pl 55), and one from Straubing in Germany is described by Long (2006, 17, fig 4). Another plane made of horn with a bronze sole was also found at Finkum in Friesland (Goodman 1964, 54), and in this example the rear handle is in the form of a scroll abutting a circular pillar at the heel and dates to the middle of the 1st millennium AD. All these planes of this date are about 150 mm long and of very similar proportions to the Northfleet plane. The Dutch examples referred to above, and dating to about AD 700, are also all characterised by a rear handle with a scroll-like appearance and/or with a circular pillar at the heel. It is interesting, and probably typologically relevant, to note that the circular and notched heel of the Northfleet plane suggests that it derives from a very similar tradition, where the fully slotted handle has regressed into a simpler solid but more decorative form. While it remains impossible to establish the absolute date of the Northfleet plane, all of the evidence suggests that it is of early Saxon date, having evolved from a common Roman ancestry, along similar lines to those found in the Low Countries. Equally the possibility remains that it is of Roman date and of a type of small rounding plane that has never been found before, as so few planes made entirely of wood have survived.

Wooden Bowl
by Damian Goodburn

During the excavation of fill deposits (19118) around the mill chutes, the remains of a broken wooden bowl (SF 12771) were found. The well-sealed location of the find dates its deposition to AD 692–3, a period from which turned vessels are extremely rare (Earwood 1993, 92). The findspot might lead one to suggest it had been used for bailing out parts of the area into a bucket during the setting up of the mill. Another slight possibility might be that it was some form of ritual foundation deposit, but no clear contents were noticed.

It was possible to largely reconstruct the vessel (Fig 8, 2). It is c 170 mm in diameter and has a damaged height of 85 mm. The form of the vessel is fairly deep and slightly incurving towards the top, with traces of a shallow horizontal line below the rim. The outside and inside are slightly abraded but clearly show fine concentric striations from lathe turning. We cannot be certain what form of lathe was used from the form or

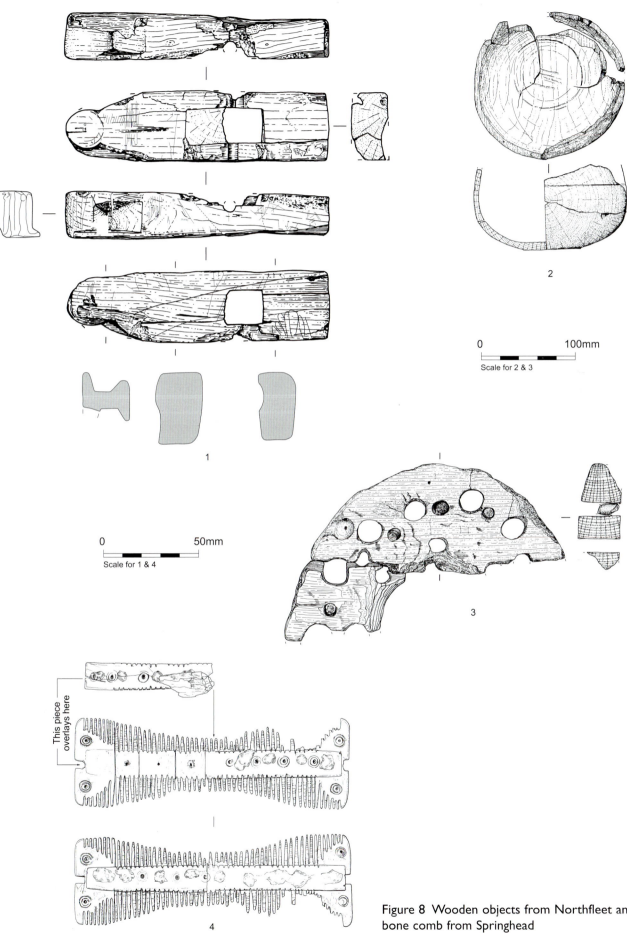

0   100mm
Scale for 2 & 3

0   50mm
Scale for 1 & 4

This piece overlays here

Figure 8 Wooden objects from Northfleet and
bone comb from Springhead

size of the vessel. The turning was carefully carried out, resulting in even, fairly smooth walls *c* 8 mm thick and a base around 12 mm thick where there was a very vestigial foot ring. Cut marks from a knife or small fine bladed adze are visible inside the base where the central waste core has been detached.

Although there are no close parallels to this find, which may have once been a relatively common class of domestic object, some of the forms of wooden bowls found on early medieval Irish sites are slightly reminiscent of it (Earwood 1993, 95). Two other features of the bowl are clearly extremely rare compared to the much more numerous earlier and later examples. First, it was made using most of a whole small log with the pith included, whereas the vast majority of vessels were made using roughed out half-logs as the starting blanks or, less commonly, they were 'spindle turned' (Morris 2000, 212–3; Wood 2005, 31). With a half-log bowl the grain runs across the face. The pith was generally avoided because distortion and splitting tend to radiate out from it. The species of tree used has been identified as hornbeam, a dense, tough, deciduous wood very rarely used for bowl turning, as the grain can be awkward and sinuous. It commonly grows in the steep hanger woods of the Chalk North Downs today and could have grown a short walk away from the Ebbsfleet itself. In recent times the species has generally been managed as coppice or pollarded and used for mill parts and machinery or high quality firewood. Both systems tend to produce relatively small logs which are knot free over short lengths suitable for turning; perhaps the relatively small size of the parent logs available encouraged the turner to use a whole log which he must have known would have been weak and split-prone.

Worked Bone Objects from Northfleet and Springhead
by Leigh Allen

Nine worked bone objects were recovered from Saxon contexts at Northfleet, Ebbsfleet Sports Ground, most of these from the fills of sunken-featured buildings (SFB). The primary fill of SFB 30119 produced two of the three 'cigar'shaped' pin beaters and the fragmentary remains of one of the double-sided composite combs (a similar comb came from an unstratified context). The backfill of SFB 16638 produced the third 'cigar-shaped' pin beater, the spindlewhorl and the spearhead. Fills of

SFBs 16635 and 16636 produced the two toggles. These personal and domestic items hint at the daily life of the inhabitants; comb fragments and toggles for personal adornment, pin beaters and spindlewhorls for spinning and weaving and the spearhead for hunting.

Additionally, one complete composite bone comb was found in a Saxon SFB at Springhead (ARC SPH00).

Combs

At Ebbsfleet Sports Ground, two fragments from combs (SF 11531 and No SF) were recovered from contexts 10288 (unstratified) and 30086 (lower fill of SFB 30107). Both fragments are from the tooth plates from double-sided bone combs, they have fine and coarse teeth and a perforation (or a perforation with an iron rivet) to secure the connecting plates to the tooth plate.

At Springhead, a complete double-sided composite comb (SF 754; Fig 8, 4) was recovered from context 5845 in SFB 5809 (Vol 1, Fig 5, 2–3). It has an elongated outline and narrow rectangular end plates decorated with a rectangular central notch and a ring-and-dot motif. The connecting plates are attached to the main body of the comb by nine iron rivets alternating with ring-and-dot motifs. The comb has coarse teeth on both sides and notches are visible where the base of the teeth meet the connecting plate, indicating that the teeth were cut (or re-cut) after the connecting plate was attached. The teeth are worn into a curve on both sides.

Pin Beaters

Three examples of 'cigar-shaped' pin beaters (SF 11077, 30943 and 30947) were recovered from contexts 10274 (backfill of SFB 16638) and 30082 (primary silting fill of SFB 30119). They all have ovate sections and taper to a point at either end from an intermediate swelling. These items are associated with weaving and are commonly found in Saxon contexts.

Spindlewhorl

A fragment from a small burnt spindlewhorl (SF 11078) came from context 10274 (backfill of SFB 16638). It is discoidal in shape and has an incised groove running around the perforation on both faces.

0   50mm

Plate 8 Antler spearhead from Northfleet SF11525

Toggles

Two possible toggles were recovered from the site (SF 11067 and no SF). The first toggle is from context 10155 (backfill of SFB 16636). It is a small polished cylinder of bone with a worn groove running half way round it at roughly the centre point. The second from context 10537 (fill of SFB 16635) is a sheep/goat metacarpal with a circular perforation through the centre (but otherwise unworked). Similar items have been variously interpreted as either fastenings, bobbins for winding wool and even musical instruments that are attached to a string and swung round (MacGregor 1985, 102–3). These toggle type objects are known from the Iron Age through to the medieval period and are commonly found on late Saxon sites.

Spearhead

A beautifully fashioned antler spearhead (SF 11525; Pl 8. The author is grateful to Ian Riddler for his identification of this object) was recovered from context 10272 (the backfill of SFB 16638). The spearhead is highly polished with a rectangular-sectioned body tapering to a diamond-sectioned point. There is a central rib running down the centre of the point on the top and bottom faces. The object has been hollowed axially and has a perforated lug on either side, suggesting that it was originally fastened to a shaft. These implements could have been used in hunting or as fish spears. Similar examples recovered from South Manor, Sandtun and Wharram are middle to late Saxon in date (Riddler pers comm).

Chapter 5

Human Bone from Springhead

by Jacqueline I McKinley

The Saxon material (29 contexts) all derived from inhumation graves at Springhead within two adjacent cemeteries lying upslope to the north-east of the Roman Sanctuary complex (ARC SPH00). The smaller cemetery (300257) was fully excavated but the larger (300258) extended beyond the site limits to the east (see Vol 1, Chap 5). The latter cemetery was subsequently fully excavated in 2007–8 (not as part of the HS1 works), revealing a substantially larger number of graves than was exposed and recorded in 2001.

Results

The methods used for recording and analysing the human bone are set out in McKinley, Vol 3, Chap 1. A summary of the results from analysis is presented in Table 13. Full details are in the archive.

Bone Condition and Survival

The Saxon graves had a similar range (0.02–0.5 m) and average depth (0.18 m) as the Roman graves (Vol 3, Chap 1) and it is unlikely that any bone would have been lost as a result of truncation other than possibly in the five shallowest (<0.06 m; 2616, 2640, 2646, 2649, 2654). There had been no intercutting between graves but 2108 had been disturbed by a later feature which may have resulted in the loss of some bone. The bone is in very poor condition (grade 5–5+), most of the remains surviving after lifting comprising tooth crowns with occasional degraded splinters of long bone shafts. The poor condition of the bone is reflected in the poor skeletal recovery – maximum 42%, average 7%. There is no consistent pattern in the levels of preservation related to obvious intrinsic or extrinsic factors such as the grave depth, presence/absence of grave goods/coffin or the sex of the individual (though the identification of only one female amongst the adults may reflect the preferential destruction of the less robust female bone; see below). As with the Roman burials, the nature of the grave fill –

again comprising the natural brickearth/Thanet Sands – is the major factor affecting bone preservation.

Demographic Data

The assemblage comprised the remains of 30 individuals: 11 (36.6%) immature and 13 (43.3%) adults, with two subadult-adult individuals of *c* 15–20 years and four individuals >13 years. The immature individuals include one infant (4–5 yr), five juveniles (5–10 yr), three infant-juveniles (2–10 yr) and one subadult (15–18 yr). Only six of the adults could be sexed (46.1%), giving a minimum of one female and five males. The graves formed two distinct groups upslope and to the north-east of the Roman occupation area (see Vol 1, Figs 5.2, 5.9, 5.19). The smaller southern cemetery was excavated in its entirety; only seven of the ten graves contained any surviving human bone, including the remains of two infant/juvenile individuals and five adults (minimum one female and one male). The northern group formed only the western portion of a much larger cemetery known to extend to the east (excavated in 2007). Bone survived in 21 of the 26 excavated graves, including the remains of individuals across the age range; the absence of any recognisable females amongst the adults is probably the product of poor bone survival rather than a realistic reflection of the adult population make-up (see above). Both cemeteries appear to have served 'normal domestic' populations, the apparent sub-divisions within the northern cemetery possibly reflecting differing household plots. The grouping of six immature individuals in the central portion of the northern sub-group could reflect deliberate zoning.

The proportion of immature to adult individuals is similar to that from the recently excavated cemetery at Cuxton, Kent (30% immature; Powers 2006), both showing higher proportions than recorded at Saltwood, Kent (24% immature; McKinley 2006a). The median age of adults appears to have fallen in the 25–35 year range, with only one individual conclusively having lived

Table 13 Summary of results from human bone analysis from Saxon Springhead

Context	Cut	Deposit type	Quantification	Age/sex	Pathology
2106	2105	burial	c 2% a.u.l.	adult c 18–35 yr ??male	
2109	2108	?burial	<1% l.	adult >18 yr	
2122	2121	burial	c 22%	subadult c 15–18 yr	mv – max. M2 narrowed
2124	2112	burial	c 2% s.l.	adult c 40–60 yr	
2130	2129	burial	c 25% s.u.l.	adult >35 yr. male	calculus
2133	2134	burial	c 12% s.l.	subadult/adult c 15–20 yr	caries; mv – malformed max. M3, max. I2 medial ridge
2523	2522	burial	c 5% s.l.	adult c 18–25 yr	calculus
2617/8	2616	burial	c 1% s.a.	juvenile c 6–8 yr	hypoplasia
2621	2620	burial	c 42%	adult c 30–40 yr male	calculus; osteophytes – C1-2 anterior facets
2627	2626	burial	c 1 s.	juvenile c 8–10 yr	hypoplasia
2635	2634	burial	<1% s.	subadult/adult >13 yr	
2638	2637	burial	c 2% u.l.	juvenile/subadult c 10–14 yr	
2642	2640	dual burial	c 1% s. <1% s.	1) juvenile c 6–7 yr 2) infant c 4–5 yr	1) mv – max. I2 shovelled
2644	2643	burial	c 2% s.l.	adult c 25–35 yr	
2647	2646	burial	c 1% l.	juvenile c 5–10 yr	
2651	2649	burial	c 5% l.	infant/juvenile c 4–6 yr	
2655	2654	burial	c 8% s.u.l.	adult c 20–30 yr	caries; calculus; hypoplasia; mv – M3s absent
2658	2657	burial	<1% l.	subadult/adult >15 yr	
2664	2662	burial	<1% s.	adult c 18–25 yr	
2784	2783	burial	c 4% s.l.	adult c 25–35 yr ?male	calculus; mv – man. M3 5 cusps
2840	2829	burial	c 1% s.	juvenile c 7–9 yr	hypoplasia
2886	2885	burial	c 1% s.	subadult/adult >13 yr	
2889	2888	burial	c 1% s. a.	subadult/adult c 15–20 yr	
3789	3788	burial	<1% u./l.	infant/juvenile c 2–10 yr	
3818	3816	burial	< 1% s.	infant/juvenile c 4–6 yr	
3907	3903	burial	c 32% s.u.l.	adult c 30–55 yr ??male	
3995	3993	burial	c 30% u.l.	adult >20 yr ??female	
3999	3997	burial	<1% s.u.	adult c 25–45 yr	
4000	3991	burial	c 2% l.	subadult/adult >13 yr	

Key: s = skull; a. = axial skeleton; u. upper limb; l. = lower limb (skeletal areas represented where not all were recovered); mv = morphological variation; C = cervical; bsm = body surface margins

to over 40 years. As was observed for both the aforementioned sites and at Mill Hill, Deal, the proportion of immature individuals is above the average of 21% of the population for Saxon cemeteries nationally, falling in the upper range (Anderson and Andrews, 1997, table 18; McKinley 2006b). The median adult age range is similar to that noted at other contemporaneous Kentish cemeteries, having greater similarities with the figures from Saltwood than from the geographically closer Cuxton, where a higher proportion of adults apparently survived beyond 45 years (McKinley 2006b).

Skeletal Indices and Non-metric Traits

A summary of the indices it was possible to calculate is given in *Table 14* and some non-metric traits/

morphological variations are indicated in Table 13, all other detail is held in the archive. The platymeric index (demonstrating the degree of anterior-posterior flattening of the proximal femur) was calculated for one male, the reading for this falling in the platymeric (broad) range.

The platycnemic index (illustrating the degree of meso-lateral flattening of the tibia) was calculated for two individuals, one male and one female. Where the bones from both sides were measured there was little difference between them. All the bones (both sexes) fall in the eurycnemic range.

Variations in skeletal morphology may indicate population diversity or homogeneity, but the potential interpretative possibilities for individual traits is complex and not, as yet, readily definable. Various tooth crown variations were observed within the assemblage (Table 13 and archive), but no matches between traits were evident.

Pathology

Pathological changes were observed in the remains of nine individuals. Table 13 contains a summary of the pathological lesions observed and the bones affected.

Dental disease

All or parts of 12 erupted permanent dentitions were recovered (Table 15). Dental calculus (calcified plaque/tartar) was observed in five (including three male) of the dentitions. Slight-mild deposits were most commonly observed. Deposits were slightly more common on the maxillary molars and mandibular canines-premolar than on other teeth but both the distribution and severity could be misleading since calculus deposits are commonly disturbed and lost during excavation and post-excavation processing.

Dental caries, resulting from destruction of the tooth by acids produced by oral bacteria present in dental plaque, was recorded in between one and three teeth from two unsexed dentitions (Table 15). The majority of lesions were in the molar teeth. The overall rate is the same as the that for the HS1 Stage I sites of this date (McKinley 2006b, table 3), both being lower than the average of 4.2% for the period given by Roberts and Cox (2003, table 4.14), though several other sites in their sample show similarly low rates. Both affected individuals were less than 30 years of age.

Slight dental hypoplasia (developmental defects in the tooth enamel reflective of periods of illness or nutritional stress in the immature individual; Hillson 1979) was observed in four dentitions (33% including unerupted permanent dentitions). Lesions were seen in

Table 15 Springhead: Saxon human bone, summary of permanent dentitions by sex

Dentitions	Teeth	Socket position	Caries
Male (3)	34	17	–
Total (inc. 9 unsexed)	164	17	4 (2.4%)

1–6 tooth crowns, predominantly the canines from three juveniles (unerupted teeth) and one unsexed adult.

Joint disease

Parts of three spines (including two male) were present in the assemblage. Extra-spinal joints were recovered from six (including three male and one female) subadult/adult individuals. The generally low number of lesions recorded and individuals affected is due to poor bone survival and the preferential destruction of trabecular bone, predominantly those areas affected by joint disease. Lone osteophytes often appear to be a 'normal accompaniment of age', reflective of 'wear-and-tear' (Rogers and Waldron 1995, 25–26). Lesions were recorded in one Saxon spine (Table 13).

Discussion

It is difficult to gain an overall view of the health, lifestyle and potential status of the population at Springhead due to the very poor condition of the bone. However, the condition of the Saxon teeth is very similar to that of the surviving Roman population suggesting a comparable diet (Vol 3, Chap 1).

Chapter 6

The Saxon Animal Bone from Northfleet and Springhead

by Jessica Grimm and Fay Worley
with a contribution by Sheila Hamilton-Dyer

The vast majority of the Saxon faunal assemblage came from Northfleet, with only a very small proportion from Springhead. A total of 4237 fragments (66.9 kg) of animal bone was hand collected from contexts dating to the Saxon period; a further 2453 fragments (0.4 kg) of animal bone was recovered from sieved sample residues. Virtually all of this material is of early Saxon date, with very small quantities from mid- and late Saxon contexts.

Condition and Preservation (Hand Collected Assemblage)

The condition of the Saxon assemblage was generally good to excellent for the Northfleet assemblage and moderate for the Springhead assemblage (*Table 16*). Despite being in good condition, 14% of the Northfleet bone fragments and 26% of the Springhead bone

Table 17 Quantification and taxa identified in each Saxon assemblage presented as total number of fragments (NISP) collected by each recovery method

| | Taxon | Northfleet | | | Springhead | | | Total |
		Hand	Sieved	Total	Hand	Sieved	Total	
Domestic mammals	Cattle (*Bos taurus*)	410	–	410	116	3	119	529
	Equid (cf. *Equus caballus*)	43	–	43	1	–	1	44
	Sheep (*Ovis aries*)	3	–	3	2	1	3	6
	Sheep/goat (*Ovis/Capra*)	140	4	144	62	13	75	219
	Pig (*Sus domesticus*)	219	7	226	126	9	135	361
	Dog (*Canis familiaris*)	5	–	5	–	–	–	5
	Cat (*Felis catus*)	1	–	1	–	–	–	1
Wild mammals	Red deer (*Cervus elaphus*)	40	–	40	–	–	–	40
	Roe deer (*Capreolus capreolus*)	3	–	3	4	–	4	7
	Deer (Cervidae)	17	55	72	–	–	–	72
	Hare (*Lepus* sp.)	–	–	–	2	–	2	2
	House mouse (*Mus musculus*)*	–	2	2	–	–	–	2
	Rabbit (*Oryctolagus cuniculus*)	1	1	2	–	–	–	2
	Vole (*Arvicola* sp.)	–	2	2	–	–	–	2
Indet. mammals	Large mammal	1542	14	1556	86	10	96	1652
	Medium mammal	483	451	934	80	121	201	1135
	Small mammal	–	3	3	–	–	–	3
	Micro mammal**	–	4	4	–	–	–	4
Birds	Diver (*Gavia* sp.)	1	–	1	–	–	–	1
	Domestic fowl (*Gallus gallus* dom.)	2	–	2	2	1	3	5
	Mallard/duck (*Anas platyrhynchos* (dom.))	1	–	1	–	–	–	1
	Woodpigeon (*Columba palumbus*)	–	–	–	1	–	1	1
	Bird (Aves)	5	5	10	–	–		10
Fish	Fish (Pisces)	1	6	7	14	10	24	31
Anura	Common frog (*Rana temporaria*)	–	25	25	–	–	–	25
	Common toad (*Bufo bufo*)***	–	4	4	–	–	–	4
	Frog/toad (*Rana/Bufo*)	1	65	66	–	–	–	66
Unidentified	Unidentified	823	1637	2460	–	–	–	2460
All taxa	Total	3741	2285	6026	496	168	664	6690
	Weight (kg)	63.9	0.3	64.2	3.0	0.1	3.1	67.3

All skeletons were counted as NISP = 1 (actual element numbers can be found in the text)
* Inc probable identification, ** inc rodent, *** inc common toad and toad sp

fragments exhibited root etching. Of the animal bone fragments discovered at Northfleet 30% had new breaks, whereas only 3% of the Springhead bone fragments exhibited new breaks.

The condition of the bone fragments allowed the recognition of surface modification including scavenger gnawing, butchery marks and pathological lesions. Evidence from gnaw marks suggests that a small proportion (1% of the Northfleet fragments and 2% of the Springhead fragments) of the assemblage was accessible to scavenging animals. All gnawing had probably been inflicted by carnivores (probably canids). Butchery marks were identified on 351 bone fragments from Northfleet and a further six from Springhead. Pathological lesions were identified on 131 fragments from Northfleet and on one fragment from Springhead. Both butchery and pathology are discussed by taxon below. A small proportion of the assemblage (3% Northfleet; 2% Springhead) comprised burnt bone fragments, the majority of which were fully calcined.

Species Identified

The animal bone assemblage comprised both domestic and wild mammals, birds, anura and fish (Table 17). Domestic mammals included cattle, pig, sheep/goat, equid (probably horse), dog and cat. No specimens were identified as goat. Wild mammals included hare, house mouse, rabbit, red deer, roe deer and vole. Bird species identified comprised domestic fowl, mallard/duck, woodpigeon and a diver. Other taxa identified in the deposits include common frog, common toad and fish (see Hamilton-Dyer, below).

Relative Proportions of Taxonomic Groups

In both Saxon assemblages, the vast majority of the identifiable animal bone fragments comprised the remains of domestic mammals (Table 17). The proportion of bird remains is low, at around 1%. The proportion of wild mammals is greater at Northfleet with 11% in the assemblage compared to the 2% in the Springhead assemblage. Within the domestic mammal assemblage, the relative proportion of cattle, sheep or goat and pig also varied. The Northfleet assemblage is dominated by cattle, whereas the smaller Springhead assemblage is dominated by pig. This difference might

be real and not related to sample size as the Saxon remains from Northfleet are probably slightly earlier in date (5th–6th centuries) than those from Springhead (6th–7th centuries).

Domestic Mammals

Cattle
Size/type
No evidence for un-horned cattle was found. A total of 68 cattle specimens were measured, representing 53% of all measured bones in the assemblage. The most frequently measured cattle elements were first phalanges (n = 14), second phalanges (n = 8) and astragali (n = 7). The cattle metric data allows limited investigation of the size of the animals. Withers heights were calculated for eleven Saxon cattle specimens (all from Northfleet). The data shows that cattle stood at 1.06–1.28 m (mean = 1.19 m).

Age-at-death and sex
No cattle specimens could be sexed through dimorphic criteria and insufficient metric data was available to conclusively investigate sex through animal size. The cattle mortality data (Fig 9; *Table 18*) indicates that cattle were killed at a range of ages from very young to senile. In addition to the mandibles, four cattle long bones were from neonatal or foetal individuals; the long bones were from two contexts and represent a minimum of one individual. The cattle mortality profile indicates that with 53% of ageable cattle mandibles deriving from young adults or older animals, cattle were most likely used for traction, breeding or milking prior to slaughter.

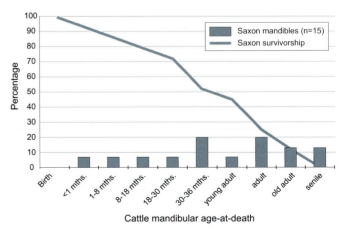

Figure 9 Cattle mortality profile (after Halstead 1985)

Health

Cattle bones exhibited more pathologies or non-metric traits than any other taxa, with 79 Saxon specimens identified (all from Northfleet). The majority of these (n = 58) comprised or included calculus deposits on teeth (included here as a pathological condition following Baker and Brothwell 1980). Three additional oral pathologies included *ante mortem* loss of a mandibular second premolar and maxillary fourth premolar, both of which showed evidence of the tooth sockets having remodelled after the tooth loss. *Ante mortem* mandibular tooth loss was also interpreted from a maxillary tooth with extreme irregular tooth wear.

The Saxon cattle bones showed evidence for nine arthropathies including one tentatively identified as osteoarthritis and two as spavin. All the arthropathies can be interpreted as evidence that the animals were used for draught purposes, although many of the conditions can also develop as a result of old age rather than traction work. Spavin was tentatively identified on two os centrotarsals, one with lipping of an articular facet and one with a bone callus fusing it to two adjacent tarsals. Spavin can be caused by use of the animal for traction (Baker and Brothwell 1980; De Cupere *et al* 2000) but is also found in dairy cattle, particularly those kept in confined conditions (Holmberg and Reiland 1984). Lipping of the proximal articulation of a metacarpal, two first phalanges and a second phalanx may similarly have been a result of traction work (see De Cupere *et al* 2000 for comments on changes in phalanges). These phalanges represent 11% and 13% of all Saxon first and second phalanges identified. Osteoarthritis was identified on a cattle atlas which had severe eburnation of its cranial articular facets with associated lipping and active bone on its ventral side (Pl 9). It was hypothesised that this pathology may have resulted from the animal wearing a yoke, but no

evidence could be found in the zooarchaeological literature to assess this hypothesis. The degree of bone change in this specimen suggests that there would have been associated soft tissue involvement and pain. The osteoarthritis might have ended the animal's useful working life and led to its slaughter. Despite the injury, this portion of the carcass was still butchered.

The remaining arthropathies were identified on a pelvis and a scapula. Both bones had lipping of the socket joints and extra bone growth, surrounding the glenoid cavity in the case of the scapula and peri-acetabular, between the ilium and pubis on the pelvis. These pathologies indicate stresses to the hip and shoulder joints which may be a result of traction work or may be age-related. In addition, a proximal metacarpal had very well defined muscle attachments suggesting that it was a well muscled animal, and the distal condyles of a metacarpal were flared which may also result from draught activity. The remaining identified pathological conditions comprised osteomylitis in the medullary cavity of a femur fragment and a probable ossified haematoma on the medial proximal diaphysis of a metacarpal (Pl 10). The Saxon assemblage also included non-metric creases and lesions identified on a cattle axis (Pl 11), three metacarpals, an os centrotarsal and a first phalanx.

Table 19 Element representation for cattle using NISP and MNE

Element	NISP		MNE	
	North-fleet	Spring-head	North-fleet	Spring-head
Horncore	7	–	1	–
Skull	38	13	6	1
Hyoid	–	1	–	1
Mandible	34	15	23	1
Tooth	68	6	–	–
Atlas	2	–	2	–
Axis	5	–	5	–
Thoracic vert	–	1	–	1
Lumbar vert	–	1	–	1
Costa	–	51	–	22
Scapula	24	8	12	4
Humerus	22	1	15	1
Radius	23	1	12	1
Ulna	17	–	12	–
Metacarpal	23	–	21	–
Pelvis	15	3	10	1
Sacrum	1	–	1	–
Femur	11	8	5	2
Tibia	20	6	14	3
Astragalus	12	–	11	–
Calcaneum	11	–	11	–
Tarsal	9	–	9	–
Metatarsal	19	2	15	1
Carpal/tarsal	3	–	2	–
Metapodial	18	–	–	–
Phalanx (I)	19	–	18	–
Phalanx (II)	8	2	8	2
Phalanx (III)	1	–	1	–
Total	410	119	214	42

0   10cm

Plate 9 Cattle atlas with eburnation of its cranial articular facets, associated lipping and active bone on its ventral side, possibly resulting from a yoke. Context 10537, SFB 16635

Plate 10 Probable ossified haematoma on the medial proximal diaphysis of a cattle metacarpal. Context 10272, SFB 16638

Plate 11 Cattle axis showing non-metric creases and lesions. Context 30086, SFB 30107

Element representation and butchery

All areas of the skeleton were present but elements of the head were the most common elements represented (Table 19). Considering the minimum number of elements (MNE) data, the forelimb, particularly metacarpals, is better represented than the hind limb, with femora particularly infrequent. The element representation does not exclusively focus on meat bearing elements. Between 12% of the Northfleet and 4% of the Springhead cattle bone elements exhibited butchery marks including all major appendicular bones. This frequency is higher than that seen in the pig and sheep or goat bone assemblages and probably reflects a greater need to divide the larger cattle carcasses for preparation and consumption. The butchery marks were dominated by cleaver chops and knife cuts. One saw mark was identified on a horn core. The butchery marks included evidence for skinning, dismemberment, disarticulation, filleting meat and removal of horncores.

Sheep and goats

Size/type

No skulls with the horn core area were recovered and it is thus unknown if the Saxon sheep from Northfleet and Springhead were horned or naturally polled. A radius from Northfleet allowed the calculation of a height at the withers of *c* 0.58 m. Although less reliable, two calcanea from Springhead produced heights at the

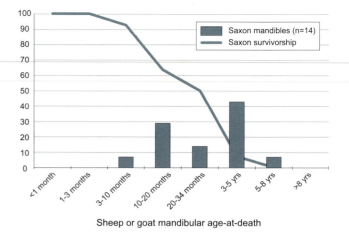
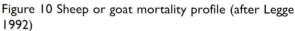

Figure 10 Sheep or goat mortality profile (after Legge 1992)

withers of *c* 0.58 m and 0.59 m. These are normal values for the Saxon period.

Age-at-death and sex

The mortality profile in Figure 10 can be used to suggest that the sheep or goats were kept for their meat (peak at 10–20 months) and for their milk, wool and manure (peak at 3–5 years) (*Table 20*). None of the pelves were sufficiently preserved to determine their sex.

Health

Twenty-one sheep or goat specimens exhibited pathological lesions or non-metric traits (all from Northfleet). The majority of the pathologies (n = 18) comprised or included calculus deposits on the teeth. The other pathologies were an exostosis on the lateral condyle of a right sheep humerus (Pl 12) and evidence of infection (osteomyelitis) in the medullary cavity and on the surface of the diaphysis of a second sheep or goat humerus. The exostosis is consistent with that diagnosed elsewhere as 'penning elbow' (Baker and Brothwell 1980), a pathological bone growth which may be caused by knocking the elbow joint as sheep are put through races or pens, but may also be age-related. One mandible had an extra non-metric foramen on the buccal surfaces below the second premolar.

Element representation and butchery

All regions of the skeleton are present and mandible fragments and loose teeth dominate the assemblage (Table 21). There are few femora, astragali and calcanea, but the presence of metatarsals indicates that the hind feet were present on site. The scarcity of phalanges may be due to the mainly hand collected nature of the assemblage, but only one phalanx was recovered from processed samples. When the data are quantified by

0   100mm

Plate 12 Right sheep humerus with 'penning elbow', an exostosis on the lateral condyle. Context 10179, SFB 16635

MNE, mandibles, radii and tibiae are particularly well represented. This is likely due to their greater resilience and the fact that these elements are readily identifiable in fragmented assemblages.

Twelve sheep or goat bones in the Northfleet assemblage and one in the Springhead assemblage exhibited butchery marks. Butchery marks were only identified on a restricted range of disarticulated sheep or goat elements: a lumbar vertebra, two metatarsals, one metapodial, three radii, four tibiae and two astragali. The butchery marks represent longitudinal chopping of a lumbar vertebra, disarticulation and portioning of the forelimb using cuts and chops at the elbow, disarticulation of the hind foot with cuts to the distal astragalus and cuts and chops on the proximal metatarsal. The assemblage

Table 21 Element representation for sheep/goat using NISP and MNE

Element	NISP		MNE	
	North-fleet	Spring-head	North-fleet	Spring-head
Skull	4	7	2	1
Hyoid	–	1	–	1
Mandible	23	9	13	4
Tooth	34	7	–	–
Atlas	1	–	1	–
Axis	1	–	1	–
Costa	–	27	–	11
Thoracic vertebra	–	3	–	2
Lumbar vertebra	–	2	–	2
Vertebra	–	2	–	–
Scapula	6	1	3	1
Humerus	5	–	4	–
Radius	12	4	10	2
Ulna	6	1	4	1
Metacarpal	8	3	7	2
Pelvis	5	2	3	1
Femur	1	1	1	1
Tibia	14	5	11	4
Astragalus	2	–	2	–
Calcaneum	3	2	3	2
Metatarsal	10	–	7	–
Metapodial	9	1	–	–
Phalanx (I)	2	–	2	–
Phalanx (II)	1	–	1	–
Total	147	78	75	35

also exhibited longitudinal splits and helical fractures which may represent utilisation of radial and tibial bone marrow. One metatarsal had over 58 cuts on the lateral and anterior/medial diaphysis, perpendicular to the long axis of the bone. These were probably inflicted as the leg was skinned.

Pigs

Size/type

Twenty-five suid bones were measured. Suid osteometric data can sometimes be used to assess the presence of wild boar in animal bone assemblages, provided that the analysis takes into account age and sex related variability. Astragali may be particularly useful as they display only limited late growth (Payne and Bull 1988). A total of three suid astragali could be compared to known size ranges for archaeological and modern wild boar and pigs. Their measurements were compared to the size range of early medieval pig measurements held on the ABMAP metrical archive (http://ads.ahds. ac.uk:81/abmap accessed 15/12/2006) and Magnell's (2006) measurements for modern Polish wild boar and Mesolithic Swedish wild boar (Fig 11). The data suggest that one astragalus (from context 10179) is most likely to be wild boar rather than domestic pig while the other two astragali are probably from domestic pigs. Although the scapulae measurements suggest large animals as well, none fell into Magnell's (2006) wild boar range.

Age-at-death and sex

Mandibular tooth wear (Fig 12) and epiphyseal fusion (*Table 22*) can be used to suggest that Saxon pig husbandry strategy involved the slaughter of juvenile to adult individuals. The appearance, texture and epiphyseal fusion of one pig tibia suggest that neonatal pigs were also killed. The Northfleet assemblage included six sexable pig mandibles (two female and four male), and nine sexable canine teeth (one female and eight male). Two of the male mandibles were from the same context and may have been from one individual. The Springhead assemblage included a male maxilla, a male and a female mandible and four male canines. The presence of a large proportion of adult animals as well as the presence of both sexes makes on-site pig breeding a possibility.

Health

A non-metric trait, four oral pathologies and an indeterminate pathological lesion were identified in the Saxon pig bones. The non-metric trait was a crease in the

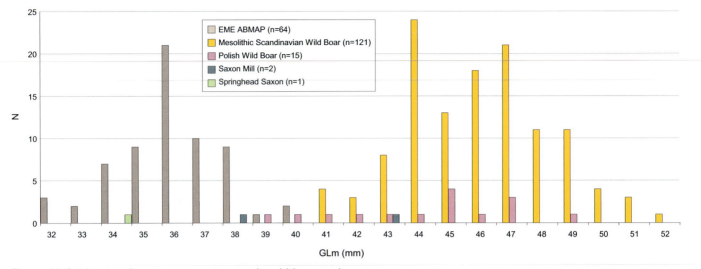

Figure 11 Suid astragalus size comparison with wild boar and contemporary pigs

trochlea of a humerus which would have had no effect on the living animal. The oral pathologies comprised two cases of linear enamel hypoplasia (LEH) manifested as a series of pits on two second mandibular molars (Pl 13), a pig tooth which had been worn down to the root, and the distal part of a canine in a boar mandible penetrating the mandibular bone on the buccal side. The LEH may be used to indicate that the pigs were under nutritional stress during the first winter of their lives (following Dobney and Ervynck 2000). The indeterminate pathology was a series of rounded sub-linear pits above the orbit of a pig frontal bone (Pl 14). There were no associated changes in the internal surface of the skull. It is not clear whether the pits have resulted from a well healed trauma, an infection, other bone disease or are non-metric. Like the arthritic cattle axis, this pig's head was butchered and presumably eaten.

Element representation and butchery

All regions of the skeleton are represented indicating that complete carcasses were present on site (Table 23). Cranial elements (skull, mandible and loose teeth) predominate and phalanges are under-represented. The under representation of phalanges may be due to the hand collected nature of the bone assemblage. However, since canid scavenging was attested from gnawing

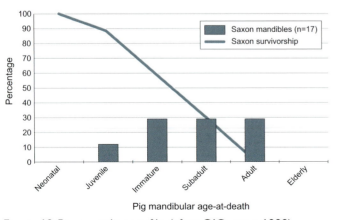

Figure 12 Pig mortality profile (after O'Connor 1988)

Table 23 Element representation for pig using NISP and MNE

Element	NISP		MNE	
	North-fleet	Spring-head	North-fleet	Spring-head
Skull	30	15	2	3
Mandible	40	14	18	6
Tooth	46	16	–	–
Atlas	2	–	1	–
Axis	1	–	1	–
Cervical vert	–	2	–	2
Thoracic vert	2	1	2	1
Lumbar vert	–	5	–	3
Vertebra	–	6	–	–
Costa	–	36	–	12
Scapula	11	–	11	–
Humerus	10	1	8	1
Radius	8	2	7	2
Ulna	9	2	9	2
Metacarpal	9	5	9	5
Pelvis	5	–	5	–
Femur	4	9	3	6
Tibia	14	5	14	2
Fibula	11	3	10	3
Astragalus	3	1	3	1
Calcaneum	–	1	–	1
Metatarsal	9	5	9	5
Metapodial	5	–	–	–
Phalanx (I)	6	1	6	1
Phalanx (II)	–	3	–	3
Phalanx (III)	–	2	–	2
Unidentified	1	–	–	–
Total	226	135	118	61

0   100mm

Plate 13 Pig mandible showing linear enamel hypoplasia manifested as a series of pits on the buccal side of the second molar, context 15001, SFB 15003

0   10cm

Plate 14 Pig frontal bone with pits above the orbit. Colluvial layer 10090

marks, it is likely that at least some of these smaller bones were completely digested. Butchery marks were recorded on eleven of the Northfleet and none of the Springhead suid bones. The butchered bones comprise skull, atlas, scapula, humerus, and radius specimens. The three butchered skulls include one with cuts on the occipital process and one which had a chop through the occipital condyles. These butchery marks were probably inflicted during decapitation. The third skull had been split sagittally to process the head meat or offal, as seen in the sheep bone assemblage. Butchered scapula and radius specimens indicate portioning of the forelimb at either end of the humerus using a cleaver. A dorsal atlas exhibited a longitudinal cut which may relate to filleting meat. Similarly cuts on the medial and lateral diaphysis of a humerus may indicate that the meat had been filleted.

Equids

Size/type

Equids were the third most common taxon identified with 12 Saxon specimens. Withers heights were calculated for three, giving heights of 1.29 m, 1.40 m and 1.41 m (12.3, 13.3 and 14 hands respectively).

Age-at-death and sex

Tooth development and wear indicated that one specimen was 8.5–11.5 years old, one 9.25–11.5 years,

Table 24 Element representation for equids using NISP and MNE

Element	NISP		MNE	
	North-fleet	Spring-head	North-fleet	Spring-head
Skull	4	–	1	–
Mandible	3	–	2	–
Tooth	8	1	–	–
Cervical vert	1	–	1	–
Radius	2	–	1	–
Ulna	2	–	2	–
Metacarpal	5	–	4	–
Pelvis	2	–	2	–
Patella	1	–	1	–
Tibia	2	–	1	–
Metatarsal	2	–	2	–
Metapodial	6	–	–	–
Phalanx (I)	2	–	2	–
Phalanx (II)	1	–	1	–
Phalanx (III)	2	–	1	–
Total	43	1	21	–

one 11–15.5 years and one over 15.5 years old at death. No sufficiently complete mandibles or pelves were found for sexing.

Health

A cervical vertebra had considerable active bone on the ventral centrum and in the transverse foramina. This active bone was probably due to an infection. A set of three maxillary molars (left first and second, right first) displayed an unusual polish on the lingual surface of the teeth, particularly the first molars (Pl 15). The teeth were probably all from a single skull. It is hypothesised that this may relate to the diet of the animal, although foreign objects in the animal's mouth may also have produced this result. In addition, calculus deposits were noted on one isolated equid tooth and the teeth in one Saxon skull.

Element representation and butchery

No butchery marks were seen on the Saxon equid bones. The 43 equid bones include most regions of the skeleton, although no humeri or femora were identified (Table 24).

0   100mm

Plate 15 Horse molars, showing polished enamel on the lingual surface. Alluvial deposit 12205

Dogs and cats

Five dog bones and one cat bone were recovered from the hand collected assemblage at Northfleet. No dog or cat bones were recovered from sieved deposits or from Springhead. The dog bones come from a minimum of one dog. The cat bone was the proximal half of a radius.

Size/type

Two dog mandibles and one tibia were measured. It is not possible to calculate an accurate withers height from any of these measurements but the tibia's greatest length was in excess of 165 mm indicating a dog over 0.49 m tall at the shoulder, approximately the size of a modern border collie. As the proximal end of the tibia was missing, we do not know whether the animal was mature. The lengths of the two measured mandibles indicate a medium sized dog, with skulls also approximately the size of a modern border collie (Von den Driesch 1976 measurement '5' being 100 mm and 118 mm). These dogs are an appropriate size for working animals. The cat bone provided no evidence for size or type of animal. The cat may have been domestic or wild.

Age-at-death and sex

The dog bones probably all derive from adult animals. The cat was over 10 months old at death (following Habermehl 1975).

Element representation and butchery

No dog or cat bones exhibited evidence of butchery (and no pathological dog bones were found). Dog bone element representation included cranial and long bone elements.

Wild Mammals, Birds and Microfauna

Despite the dominance of domestic mammals in the Saxon animal bone assemblage, some hunted wild mammals were identified. The assemblage included hare, rabbit, red deer, roe deer and probably wild boar.

Red and roe deer

The 119 deer remains predominantly comprise antler fragments, but other elements were also identified. The assemblage included 40 antler fragments (25 identified as red deer), at least three fragmented skulls (recorded as n = 6 in the bone database and NISP counts), four loose teeth, two mandibles, a radius, two metacarpals, two tibiae, two metatarsals and two phalanges. One skull, one radius, both tibiae and all metapodials were roe deer

while all the other elements came from red deer. The deer bones were recovered from seven sunken-featured buildings (SFBs) at Northfleet, the vast majority from SFB 30057. The representation of deer specimens in the SFBs is considered below.

SFB 30057 included 31 fragments of antler, two loose red deer teeth and at least three fragmented red deer skulls (recorded as six skull fragments in the database and NISP counts, but these refitted from more than 50 fragments). At least one red deer skull had shed its antlers, but antlers were present on the skulls of the second and third individuals. Providing the red deer were killed rather than the skulls collected after death, and that the assemblage was deposited contemporaneously, this indicates that the animals died in spring, probably around April. The presence of the red deer skulls may indicate that the area was used for storage, if the antler resource was being kept, but the presence of a skull which had shed its antlers might indicate that this was some kind of foundation or ritual deposit. One isolated antler fragment and one skull had been butchered.

SFB 30107 contained five fragments of red deer antler including one attached to a portion of skull, fragments from two right red deer mandibles (MNI = 2) and two red deer maxillary teeth. The antler fragments included one refitted from over 20 fragments. At least one antler fragment had been sawn off at an oblique angle.

SFB 16635 and 16638 each contained a roe deer metapodial fragment which had been butchered. SFB 16636 contained a fragment of butchered radius which was probably red deer rather than cattle; SFB 16699 a red deer third phalanx, and SFB 30119 a red deer first phalanx.

The presence of antler attached to regions of deer skull in so many of the SFBs suggests that either the site had a craft function with antler working occurring in many of the buildings (supported by the fact that many of the antler fragments had been partially worked) or that there was a ritual aspect to their deposition, or a combination of these factors.

The assemblage included a red deer first phalanx with exostosis on the abaxial condyle. In a similar fashion to the 'penning elbow' identified in the sheep remains, this pathology may have resulted from knocking this relatively exposed joint of the foot.

Wild boar

Osteometric data suggest that at least one wild boar was present in the assemblage from Northfleet (an astragalus; see above). Cut marks on the distal end of the anterior and medial faces of the astragalus were probably inflicted in disarticulating the foot.

Lagomorphs (rabbits and hares)

The third phalanx of a rabbit and a fragment of a lagomorph tibia were recovered from SFB 16635 at Northfleet. Part of a hare pelvis and tibia were recovered from a late Saxon (probably 9th century) crop dryer at Springhead. None of the bones exhibited butchery marks. The rabbit bone is probably intrusive as it is thought that the Normans introduced the rabbit (Yalden 1999).

Birds

A layer (11509) on the waterfront at Northfleet contained a partial mallard/duck skeleton comprising left and right humeri, radii, ulnae and femora, left carpometacarpus and the synsacrum. The right ulna exhibited slight active bone growth around the foramen which may indicate osteomylitis. The location of the skeleton on the foreshore suggests that it was a natural casualty, possibly weakened by bone infection, and was not utilised by the people occupying the site. It shows no evidence of scavenging and so was probably buried soon after death.

Occasional domestic fowl were identified in the assemblage. Furthermore, the partial skeleton of a mallard or duck (elements were quite large) and single bones of woodpigeon and a diver were also present.

No bird remains could be sexed and no juvenile bones were identified. Only the partial duck skeleton and the woodpigeon tibiotarsus could be measured.

In addition to the pathological duck skeleton (see above) a domestic fowl femur had extra bone growth inferior to the head. Neither bone had been butchered.

No butchery marks were identified on bird bones. Too few skeletal elements were recovered to consider any implications of skeletal representation.

Microfauna

The mouse and vole species present in the assemblage would have inhabited grassland and scrubland surrounding the site. House mouse had become established in Britain by the Roman period (Yalden 1999) and these may have inhabited the mill at Northfleet. Anuran bones are frequent in the sample residues and include both common toad and common frog.

Conclusions

The data suggests that Saxon animal utilisation centred around domestic mammal stock (cattle, sheep and pig) with horses, dogs and cats also present in the assemblage. Taken as a proportion of the total number of cattle, sheep and/or goat and pig bone fragments, cattle bones were the most frequent at Northfleet, whereas pig bones were most frequent at Springhead. The relative proportion of the species at Northfleet is similar to that identified at Mucking Saxon settlement in Essex, but shows reversed significance of ovicaprids and pigs from several other settlement sites in southern and eastern England (Table 25).

Cattle probably would have contributed the most meat to the diet. However, the age-at-death of the cattle mandibles suggests that meat production was not the animals' only function as they probably also contributed milk and labour to the economy. This is supported by evidence of pathological lesions, including individuals

Table 25 Comparison of relative proportions of taxa at some Saxon sites from southern and eastern England

Site	Cattle		Sheep/goat		Pig	
	NISP	%	NISP	%	NISP	%
Northfleet Saxon assemblage	410	53	143	19	218	28
Springhead Saxon assemblage	119	36	78	23	135	41
Mucking, Essex* (Done 1993)	512	63	130	16	176	21
Wicken Bonhunt, Suffolk (Crabtree 1996)	5138	17	3858	13	20,954	70
Ipswich, Suffolk** (Crabtree 1996)	4282	45	2206	23	3130	33
Brandon, Suffolk (Crabtree 1996)	13,441	28	24,652	52	9121	19
Melbourne Street, Hampshire** (Bourdillion & Coy 1980)	23,896	53	14,606	32	6953	15
Yarnton, Oxfordshire (Mulville & Ayres 2004)	366	57	191	30	90	14
Creswell Field, Oxfordshire (Mulville & Ayres 2004)	199	56	106	30	48	14
Pennyland & Hartigans, Bedfordshire (Holmes 1993)	1170	49	894	37	330	14
West Stow, Suffolk (Crabtree 1996)	26,012	41	28,399	45	9192	14

*combined proportions frags from SFB assemblages with at least 100 bone frags** urban settlement

suffering from spavin and osteoarthritis which may have both developed as a result of heavy traction work. Element representation indicates that all regions of the carcass were present on site and the occurrence of neonatal bones in some contexts suggests that breeding took place in the vicinity.

The age-at-death data for sheep and goat indicates that primary and secondary products were both important. The evidence does not support the practice of sheep breeding on site in the Saxon period as no neonatal bones were recovered in the assemblage. Since all regions of the carcass were represented, the animals at least arrived on site on the hoof rather than as dressed carcasses or meat joints.

Pigs were bred and died on site. Evidence for this comes from the presence of all regions of the skeleton and neonatal individuals. Linear enamel hypoplasia on pig teeth indicates that pig husbandry may have been stretched, causing nutritional deficiency during the animals' first winters.

The horse bones were from animals of approximately 1.29–1.41 m height at the shoulder, typical for horses of the period (Rackham 1995). No butchery was identified on horse or dog bones and it is likely that they were kept as working animals rather than considered as a food. The majority of equid skeletal elements were present in the assemblage, but the animals were not recovered as complete carcasses suggesting that their remains were not generally accorded any special treatment, rather they were disposed of with the refuse from other domestic stock. However, a substantially complete skull was recovered from one context and may represent special treatment of some of the equid remains. One use of the horses and dogs may have been in hunting.

The presence of wild bird species, hare, deer and probably wild boar attests to hunting and wild fowling in the Saxon period, although game probably made only a limited contribution to the diet. The occurrence of antlered red deer skulls in the SFBs suggests that they were of importance at the site, providing antler for working, though other interpretations are possible.

Fish Bone from Springhead and Northfleet
by Sheila Hamilton-Dyer

Fish Bone from Springhead

The 34 bones from the Saxon phase at Springhead (ARC SPH00) were recovered from three contexts. The bones include at least five species, all marine. A flatfish caudal vertebra was recovered from context 5810 and a haddock (*Melanogrammus aeglefinus*) cleithrum from context 3233. All the other bones were recovered from context 3190.

Haddock and cod (*Gadus morhua*) were recovered by hand collection while bones of whiting (*Merlangius merlangus*) and a dentary of herring (*Clupea harengus*) were recovered from a sieved sample. Other remains could not be identified to species, two are either of whiting or of small cod but could not be reliably distinguished between the two. The five haddock bones consist of four cleithra and one post-temporal. This is a typical finding as these bones are large, tend to be hyperostosed and more robust than others in the skeleton and are therefore more likely to survive and be collected.

Fish Bone from Northfleet

Seven fish bones and a crustacean from Northfleet (ARC EBB01) claw were submitted for analysis. A precaudal vertebra of a large salmon (*Salmo salar*) (over 70 cm GL) was recovered from layer 19424. Samples from SFB 30107 produced two caudal and three precaudal vertebrae matching saury (*Scomberesox saurus*) and a further precaudal fragment that could not be identified with certainty.

The claw of a large edible crab (*Cancer pagurus*) was recovered from the backfill of lime kiln 10275, but this deposit may be modern.

Discussion

These are all marine species, although the salmon can also be caught in rivers. The saury or skipper is not a commonly identified fish in British assemblages but was also found in the Roman assemblage at Springhead (see Vol 3, Chap 2). Apart from the saury the species are common and have all been found at other Saxon sites. It is perhaps surprising that the ubiquitous eel is not also present but these are very small assemblages.

Edible crabs can be found on sandy and rocky shores but those of good size are most likely to be found at depths up to 50 m and today are caught in the familiar crab/lobster pot.

Chapter 7

Post-Roman Sedimentary Sequences and Landscape

A similar approach to analysis was taken for post-Roman (predominantly Saxon) deposits to that adopted for late Iron Age and Roman deposits. Few deep sequences of this date exist at the sites, though whether this is due to stabilisation of the landscape or subsequent erosion is unclear. Most post-Roman layers were found to be thin and colluvial in nature, the remains they contained necessarily of mixed taphonomy and thus preventing meaningful analysis. However, useful waterlogged deposits were found, particularly associated with the Saxon mill and mill pond, and are reported below.

Northfleet Sediments and Soils

by Elizabeth Stafford

The broad sedimentary architecture of Northfleet has been covered in detail in the Roman sediment report (Bates and Stafford, Vol 3, Chap 3) and will not be repeated here. Suffice to say, the Wetlands excavation area and Saxon mill are located in a low-lying area immediately north of the gravel 'spur' or promontory occupied by Northfleet villa (see Vol 3, Chap 3, Fig 15). The mill structure itself appears to have been constructed on a sand bar, with the main Ebbsfleet channel to the north, and the area between the sand bar and gravel 'spur' a sheltered backwater area (see Vol 1, Fig 6.1). It was this backwater area that was modified by the building of a series of revetments and clay banks for the construction of the mill pond (Vol 1, Chap 6). The character of the alluvial sequence related to the mill and mill pond is consistent with the 'Upper Clay Silt' unit identified in the master off-site sequences (BH7 and Trench 9, STDR400), associated with environments of middle and upper saltmarsh (see Bates and Stafford, Vol 3, Chap 3). These alluvial deposits largely comprise bluish or brownish grey minerogenic silty clays. Very few contexts could be truly described as organic, although many contained small quantities of organic detrital material and occasional woody fragments. The taphonomic problems associated with radiocarbon dating material from such deposits, where a significant proportion of material may have been reworked, has

resulted in much of the dating relying mainly on stratigraphical relationships. Sequences for analysis have been targeted where sedimentary relationships with archaeological remains could be clearly demonstrated.

Twenty-four profiles were sampled from nine open sections. A total of 41 monoliths and 12 smaller kubiena samples were collected. Initial assessment of the sampled profiles identified a number of key sequences that had the potential to provide data on the local environment of the mill before, during and after its use. Fourteen representative profiles were selected for detailed geoarchaeological and palaeoenvironmental analysis (Table 26). For descriptive purposes these profiles have been divided between the following five groups:

1. Pre-mill deposits.
2. The Ebbsfleet channel.
3. The mill leat.
4. The mill undercroft (wheelhouse).
5. The mill pond.

It should be noted, however, that a large part of all of the sequences investigated, by inference, post-date the use of the mill. Deposits examined that probably accumulated during the lifetime of the mill or immediately after its abandonment have been identified as follows:

1. Banked up against revetment 19319 in the mill leat (Monolith 12217, Fig 13).
2. In the base of the mill pond directly in front of the penstock (monolith 12025, context 12205, Fig 14) below the level of the sluice gates (< +1.0 m OD).
3. At the very base of the mill undercroft (monolith 12085, context 12538, Vol 1, Fig 6.7).

Methods

The methodology for investigation has been outlined in the Roman sediment report (Barnett, Norcott and Stafford, Vol 3, Chap 3). A summary of the sequences investigated with accompanying figure numbers is

Table 26 Summary of environmental analysis of samples from Saxon mill contexts

Feature	Section illus	Comments on sequence	Analyses undertaken
Pre-mill sequences	Vol. 1, fig. 6.8	Profile through sand bar, pre-mill deposits (intercalated silt-clays & humic horizons) & clay make-up of western millpond barrage	Sediment descriptions M12251–2 (micro-morphology, pollen, WPR, diatoms, radiocarbon dating)
	Vol. 1, fig 6.7	Profile through sand bar & pre-mill deposits, truncated by construction cut for wheelhouse	Sediment description M12085 (pollen, ostracods, foraminifera, diatoms)
Ebbsfleet Channel	Fig. 13	Profile through minerogenic alluvial deposits. Inc basal humic silt with large dumped flint clasts/gravel = truncated BA land surface	Sediment descriptions M12201, M12000 (pollen, diatoms, ostracods, foraminifera)
	Fig. 13	Profile through minerogenic alluvial deposits	Sediment description M12003 (pollen, diatoms, ostracods, foraminifera)
	Fig. 13	Profile through minerogenic alluvial deposits adjacent to mill revetment 19318	Sediment description M12204 (pollen, diatoms, ostracods, foraminifera)
	Vol. 1, fig. 6.8	Profile through minerogenic alluvial deposits abutting western mill barrage	Sediment descriptions M12293–4
Mill leat	Fig. 13	Profile through laminated minerogenic alluvial deposits banking up against revetment 19319	Sediment description M12217 (pollen, diatoms, ostracods, foraminifera)
Mill undercroft	Vol. 1, fig 6.7	Profile through minerogenic alluvial deposits infilling mill undercroft. Inc localised build up of bedded organic peaty deposits in front of nozzle block at one end of penstocks	Sediment descriptions M12085–6 (pollen, diatoms)
	Vol. 1, fig 6.7	Profile through backfill deposits & alluvial sequence through centre of undercroft	Sediment description M12091–3 (pollen, diatoms, waterlogged plant remains, insects, ostracods, foraminifera)
Millpond	Fig. 14	Profile through mill pond deposits in front of pentrough, associated with wattle panel 'filter'. Basal part of sequence poss deposited during lifetime of mill. Upper parts likely to relate to later silting of mill pond poss post-abandonment	Sediment descriptions M12024–5 (ostracods, foraminifera, insects)
	Fig. 14	Profile through alluvial deposits directly on front of pentrough behind wattle panel 'filter'	Sediment description M12034
	not illus	Profile minerogenic alluvium infilling mill pond	Sediment description M12323
	Fig. 14	Profile minerogenic alluvium infilling mill pond	Sediment description M12313 (waterlogged plant remains, insects)
	Vol. 1, fig. 6.8	Profile through alluvial deposits of mill pond abutting western mill barrage	Sediment descriptions M12295–6

included in Table 26. The detailed sediment descriptions are tabulated in *Tables 27–31*, and summarised and interpreted in this report. A general discussion of the changes in marine environment, landscape, and vegetation at Northfleet during the Saxon and medieval periods can be found in Vol 1, Chap 5.

Feature-Related Soils and Sediments

Pre-mill deposits

Two sample sequences were examined in detail from deposits pre-dating the construction of the mill. One of these sequences, from section 18549 (P2), was preserved beneath the man-made clay bank of the western mill pond barrage (monoliths 12251 and 12252;

Vol 1, Fig 6.8). The other sequence, from section 11850 (P5), was truncated by the construction cut for the mill undercroft (monolith 12085; Vol 1, Fig 6.7). Both profiles demonstrated a broadly similar sequence of deposits comprising a complex of bedded fine-grained alluvial clay silts, silty clays and more humic horizons.

During the excavations it was assumed that these deposits, particularly the upper part of the sequences, related to the period immediately prior to the construction of the mill. However, four radiocarbon dates from the sequence from beneath the mill barrage confirm that the sequence dates primarily to the Early and Late Bronze Age. This suggests truncation at the interface between the natural sequence and the clay bank of the barrage, probably during the construction of the mill pond.

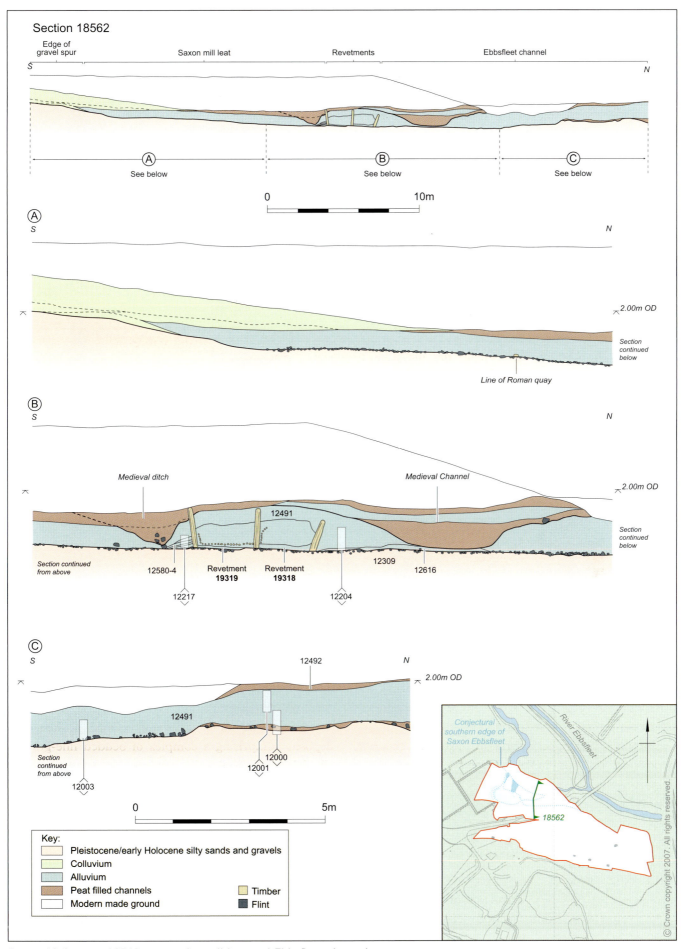

Figure 13 Section 18562 across the mill leat and Ebbsfleet channel

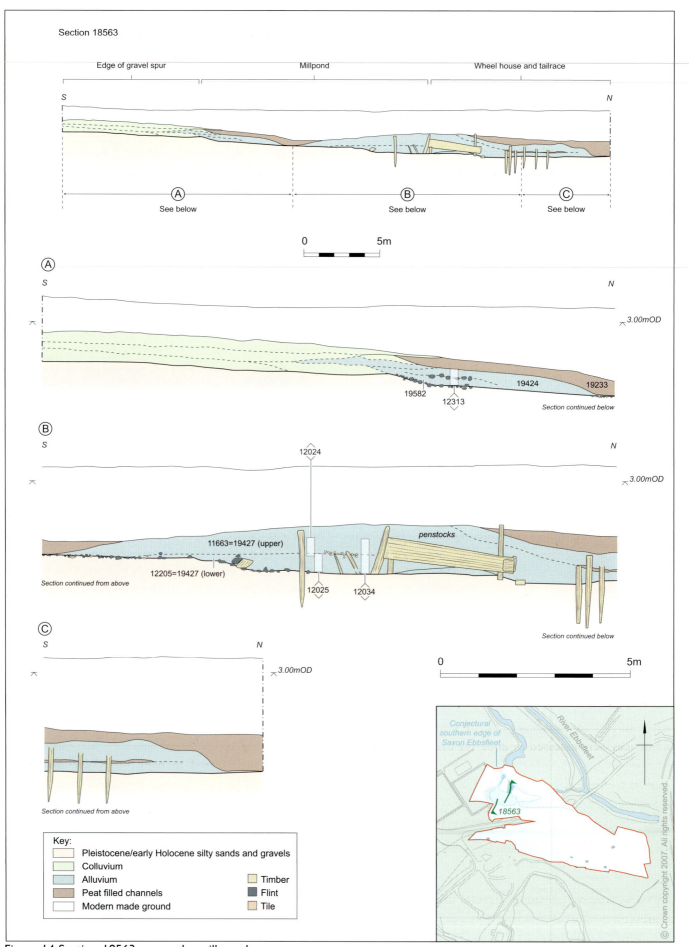

Figure 14 Section 18563 across the mill pond

Micromorphological analysis of the sequence beneath the mill barrage confirmed these deposits are consistent with over-bank flooding and backwater sedimentation (Macphail, this chapter). There is evidence of fluctuating water tables in an estuarine environment by the occurrence of rooting zones, pyrite, gypsum and iron mottling. Stabilisation horizons were identified within these sequences by *in situ* 'peaty' or humic horizons. Overall this suggests that the environment at this location at the time of deposition was rather marginal to any major channel system. The overlying clay bank of the mill barrage was identified in the field, and through further sediment description of the monoliths, as a series of rather mixed or disturbed alluvial clays with clasts of redeposited peat. Although not entirely conclusive, the micromorphology suggests the deposits are consistent with muddy dumps of silty clay and clay with evidence of minor soft sediment deformation and structural collapse of essentially slaked sediments.

The sequence associated with the mill undercroft was assessed in 2002 for the preservation of various categories of palaeoenvironmental remains, and the sequence beneath the mill barrage in 2007. Unfortunately no ostracods or foraminifera were preserved (see Whittaker, this chapter) and waterlogged plant remains were very poor. Pollen and diatom analysis was undertaken on the barrage sequence. Given the prehistoric date of these deposits, details of the analysis are referenced in the Prehistoric Ebbsfleet Principal Study (Bates *et al* in prep).

The Ebbsfleet channel

Three profiles were examined from alluvial deposits located in the eastern area of excavations, north of the sand bar occupied by the mill structure (monoliths 12000–12004). These profiles were sampled from a series of sections forming a north–south transect. The sequences were assessed in 2002 for the preservation of various categories of palaeoenvironmental remains (pollen and diatoms: Haggart 2002, and ostracods and foraminifera: Whittaker, this chapter).

At the base of the northernmost profile, recorded in monolith 12000, a thin gravelly organic silt was recorded (context 19011) directly overlying late Pleistocene or early Holocene sand. Although undated, the elevation and stratigraphical position suggests this unit is likely to represent an eroded prehistoric deposit, similar to that identified beneath the mill barrage. This interpretation is supported by the pollen assemblages which contained a high proportion of tree pollen, and the notable abundance of *Tilia* grains is consistent with a Bronze Age rather than a historical date. The gravel component of the deposit, however, is likely to be a post-depositional feature related to the dumping of large pebbles and cobbles of flint and chalk to consolidate the river bed/edge. Similar extensive gravel deposits were noted across the Wetlands excavation area and are associated with the construction of the Roman quay (see Vol 1, Chap 3).

A large part of the sampled sediment sequences comprised bluish-grey minerogenic silty clay alluvium (context 12491), often with frequent iron mottling but with little sign of any bedding structures. Although environmental material was variably preserved within these deposits, overall the evidence unsurprisingly suggested a relatively open environment of estuarine saltmarsh, with herbs the dominant pollen taxa (Haggart 2002; Whittaker this volume). There is no direct dating evidence for the alluvial sequence, although stratigraphically the majority of the sequence presumably relates to the silting of the channel after the mill structure was abandoned.

Although not represented in the sampled sequence, the minerogenic alluvium is overlain by a further unit of peat (context 12492), which is in turn capped by variable thicknesses of modern made-ground. This peat is correlated with the freshwater 'Upper Peat' unit (identified in the off-site master sequences) which begins to form in the mid- to late Saxon period, with accretion continuing into the medieval period (see Bates and Stafford, Vol 3, Chap 3).

The mill leat

One profile was examined from monolith 12217 from the sequence infilling the mill leat (Fig 13). The sampled sequence was relatively short at 25 cm and comprised a series of bedded minerogenic silty clays and more humic deposits that appeared to bank up against revetment 12217. It is assumed that that this sequence of sediments may well have accumulated during the lifetime of the mill. Evidence from the ostracods and foraminifera assemblages from this sequence was particularly informative, suggesting a local environment of brackish intertidal flats and creeks in the lower part of the sequence, followed by the development of high saltmarsh (Whittaker, this chapter).

The mill undercroft (wheelhouse)

Several monoliths (12085, 12086, 12091–12093) were extracted from the alluvial deposits infilling the mill undercroft (Vol 1, Fig 6.7). The deposits at the edges of the feature primarily comprised redeposited material resulting from backfill or slumping after the superstructure was removed (see Vol 1, Chap 6).

In the centre of the feature deposits comprised minerogenic silty clays deposited by natural alluvial processes, presumably after the structure was abandoned. Context 12538, a yellowish-grey silty clay recorded in the base of monolith 12085, probably represents deposition immediately after abandonment. This deposit is overlain by a localised build-up of bedded organic material (contexts 12532–35, +0.56–+0.85 m OD) which accumulated directly in front of the pentroughs. This material probably represents episodic accumulation of organic detritus overflowing through the disused pentroughs from the mill pond.

The overlying deposits recorded in monoliths 12086 and 12091–3 largely comprised homogeneous minerogenic alluvium, although a darker lens (context 12525) suggests ephemeral lower energy deposition or a stabilisation horizon. The uppermost part of the alluvial sequence was not sampled in the monoliths. However, it appears that the gradual infilling of the undercroft continued with alluvial deposits 12524 and 12523, and a sequence of subsequent dryer episodes denoted by thin organic layers 12522, 12521, and 12520.

A further layer of peat above context 11167 had been removed during machine excavation. Broadly these deposits occur at similar elevations to the 'Upper Peat' in the off-site sequence and may be related to a general period of marine regression dated to the mid–late Saxon period (see Bates and Stafford, Vol 3, Chap 3). Palaeoenvironmental analysis of deposits from the mill undercroft (see Whittaker, Scaife and Cameron, this chapter) suggest initially relatively open environments of tidal creeks and mudflats developing into saltmarsh. Higher up the sedimentary profile the diatom assemblages indicated a period where freshwater input increased.

The minerogenic alluvial layers (12526 and 12525, +0.84–+1.06 m OD) contained high numbers of freshwater diatoms, and in particular opportunistic early colonisers are common such as *Fragilaria* spp. A more diverse group of freshwater diatoms from more stable habitats are present, albeit in small numbers in the slightly organic layer 12525.

The mill pond

Several profiles were examined through the fills of the mill pond. As with many of the sequences examined from the Wetlands, the deposits were primarily composed of homogeneous minerogenic silty clays with varying amounts of organic detrital material, although siltier facies tended to occur towards the base of the sequences. The fine-grained nature of the deposits suggests a low-energy riverine environment, marginal to major channel activity. However, occasional laminations noted within these deposits indicate regular higher water conditions.

The most informative sequence was located immediately in front of the penstocks in monoliths 12024 and 12025 (Fig 14). The lowest deposit, context 12205, comprised a mottled brown, very soft silty clay with occasional organic flecking. More organic lenses were noted at the top of this unit at a similar level to the sluice gates of the pentroughs (+1.0 m OD), and coincidentally with deposit 12525 in the undercroft (see above). The sample sequence was capped by a deposit of dark grey laminated silty clay that contained abundant fine organic detritus (context 11167). A further layer of peat above context 11167 had been removed during machine excavation and was not sampled.

Paleoenvironmental analysis of this sequence revealed a similar sequence to that of the undercroft. Initially, at the base of the sequence, the environment was relatively open with tidal creeks, mudflats and developing saltmarsh. As the mill pond silted up there is evidence of increased freshwater input, towards the top of the sequence (Whittaker and Cameron, this chapter). Similar to the upper sequence of deposits in the undercroft, the upper sequence in the mill pond (above +1 m OD) may be correlated to the 'Upper Peat' in the off-site sequences and post-dates the use of the mill.

Pollen from Northfleet
by Robert Scaife

This sample set was taken from the sediment infill of the mill undercroft (see Vol 1, Fig 6.7). It is thought that this sequence may post-date the use of the mill itself, although the basal context (12538) possibly relates to the phase of final abandonment. The pollen assemblages are dominated by herb taxa but with some representation of trees and shrubs. Poaceae (grasses) dominate the herbaceous group along with cereal pollen and associated weeds of disturbed and arable ground, grassland/pastoral elements and from the local grass/sedge fen. Pollen data are presented in Figure 15.

The Pollen Data

As no local pollen assemblage zones have been recognised which denote changes in the vegetation and environment, the broad vegetation groups identified are described as follows.

2.a.) *Trees and shrubs*: *Corylus avellana* type (hazel) and *Quercus* (oak: to 19%) are the most important elements. The latter has higher values in the lower contexts (12538) and upper levels (12524). In addition, there is a moderately diverse range of trees that occur in small numbers. These include *Betula*, *Pinus*, *Alnus glutinosa* and occasional occurrences of *Ulmus*, *Tilia*, *Fraxinus*, *Fagus sylvatica*, and *Picea* (in the top level at 48 cm). Shrubs, as noted, are dominated by *Corylus avellana* type (to 28% at 96 cm) with occasional *Salix*, *Juniperus*, *Prunus* type, *Sorbus/Crataegus* type and *Calluna*.

2.b.) *Herbs*: Poaceae (non-cultivated grasses) are dominant throughout with high percentage values (to 75% at 60 cm) with cereal type (17% at 108 cm). The latter is of greater importance between 105 cm (12535) and 85 cm (12532). In addition the pollen assemblages contain a very diverse range of other herb taxa which include grassland/pasture types along with cereal associated taxa and wetland/marsh elements. Indicators of the former include a range of taxa that include *Plantago lanceolata* (4%). Cereal pollen comprises largely *Triticum-Hordeum* type with occasional *Secale cereale*. Indicators of arable and disturbed ground include *Sinapis* type, Chenopodiaceae, *Papaver*, *Polygonum* spp., *Plantago major* type, Ranunculaceae, and Asteraceae types.

Cannabis sativa type is important at 95–106 cm (4%). This may be attributed to hemp or hop. The former is suspected because there is little evidence for the typical fen carr habitat of the latter (hop) and also the (Saxon) age of the sediments.

2.c.) *Marsh and aquatic taxa*: Fen herb types include Cyperaceae, *Typha angustifolia/Sparganium* type, *Potamogeton* type, *Lemna* and *Callitriche*. Cyperaceae is of greater importance in the lower context (12538) at 108–132 cm (to 12%) also with higher values of *Potamogeton* type (1%), *Typha angustifolia* type and *Typha latifolia*. Occasional cysts of freshwater algal *Pediastrum* occur throughout.

2.d.) *Spores*: Where these are present, they include largely *Pteridium aquilinum* (12538) peaking at 112 cm. Occasional monolete forms (*Dryopteris* type) and *Sphagnum* moss spores were also recorded.

The Saxon–Medieval Vegetation

The nature of this site suggests that the taphonomy of the pollen in these sediments might be complex. This is the case, and at first appearance the pollen data suggested that the region in proximity to the sample site was a strongly arable habitat, as attested by the quantities of cereal pollen (wheat/barley and rye) and weeds regarded as characteristic of such habitats. However, it is possible that this may be of secondary, derived origin coming from local crop processing. Pollen trapped in cereal inflorescence may be liberated during crop processing (winnowing and threshing) and may be present in waste chaff remains, which are disposed of in a multitude of contexts (Robinson and Hubbard 1977). Given the character/use of this site, this would appear to be the most likely interpretation of these relatively high pollen numbers. Cultivation and use of cereals is, however, clearly demonstrated at this time. Wheat and barley and rye are indicated. Associated pollen of segetals may also be trapped and present in resulting pollen assemblages. Here, spurrey (*Spergula*), goosefoots and oraches (Chenopodiaceae), poppy (*Papaver*), black bindweed (*Fallopia convolvulus*) and other less diagnostic taxa may come from this source. Such numbers of secondary/derived pollen will also have a depressing effect on pollen from primary sources. Cereal pollen attains greatest importance in context 12535 at 105 cm.

Cannabis type (hemp) is present, peaking at 105 cm (12535). Whilst this pollen may derive from hop (which has similar pollen morphology), it is most probably from cultivation of hemp which is diagnostic of the Saxon to medieval period when it was widely grown for fibre.

In addition to the arable component, there is a background of tree and shrub, grassland/pasture elements and wetland taxa. The range of tree taxa present is diverse but total pollen numbers are generally small. Oak (*Quercus*) is the most important tree with

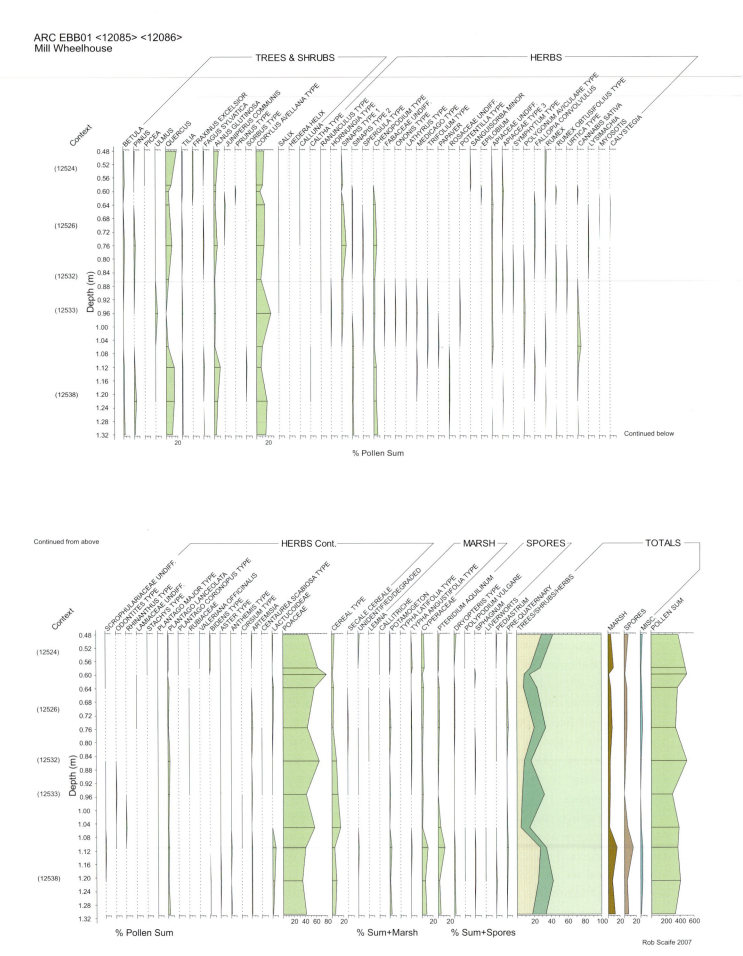

Figure 15 Pollen diagram for samples from sediment infill of the mill undercroft

higher values in the basal context 12538 and upper levels of context 12524.

This similarly applies to alder (*Alnus glutinosa*). The latter is, however, a high pollen producer (anemophilous) and values obtained here do not reflect any substantial local growth. There are occasional occurrences of birch, pine, elm, lime, ash, and beech. These are interpreted as pollen derived from the region as a whole although it is not, of course, possible to delimit the pollen catchment. In the case of lime, ash, beech, and willow these are not generally well represented in pollen spectra and may be of more local origin. Hazel (*Corylus avellana*) is the dominant shrub with highest values at 95 cm (12533) and it is suggested that there was local growth. Spruce (*Picea*) is an interesting record. Being non-native, this occurrence is attributed to planting of exotics probably within the near region. In recent years there has been an increasing number of records of this conifer from the late historic period after its introduction into parks and gardens (Scaife 2000b).

Juniper (*Juniperus*) is similarly an unusual record for this late period. This pollen may have originated from natural growth of juniper on calcareous soils of the chalk interfluves and North Downs or similarly from introduced planting.

Grasses (Poaceae) are the dominant pollen taxa in all samples from this sequence with high pollen values. This pollen may derive from various habitats from arable, pastoral, and local fen. However, ribwort plantain (*Plantago lanceolata*) and a range of other taxa (buttercups, medicks, vetches, docks, and Asteraceae types) are strongly indicative of important areas of local grassland (probably pasture). Although the herb assemblages are diverse, it is, unfortunately, not possible to identify taxa to a lower taxonomic level that would allow clearer designation of plant communities to be made.

A significant part of the pollen assemblages include fen/marsh taxa from the on-site community. Reed swamp taxa include sedges (Cyperaceae), reedmace or bur reed (*Typha angustifolia* type). Sedges are of greater importance in the basal context 12538. Evidence of standing water comes from pondweed (*Potamogeton* type), water starwort (*Callitriche*) and duckweed (*Lemna*).

Summary and Conclusions

This analysis of the mill wheelhouse sediments has produced diverse assemblages of pollen taxa that have a complex taphonomy. The assemblages derive from the on-site/near site fen, pastoral habitats, near and extra-local woodland elements, and a strong secondary (derived) arable component.

Soil Micromorphology from Northfleet
by Richard I. Macphail

Undisturbed monolith samples from alluvial sequences associated with the Saxon mill were submitted for the analysis of soil micromorphology. Five undisturbed samples were chosen to test the field interpretation of a depositional sequence associated with a mill. These comprise Pleistocene/early Holocene sands, later silts, clays, silty clays, peat and possible ephemeral soil horizons, and a Saxon dumped 'clay bund' (see Vol 1, Fig 6.8).

Samples and Methods

Most samples had been taken across boundaries within and between contexts (19495, 19496, 19496, 19547, 19548, and 19549), and the five samples studied were thus able to characterize a series of layers identified in Section 18549 (Vol 1, Fig 6.8).

Samples M2–M6 were impregnated with a clear polyester resin-acetone mixture; samples were then topped up with resin, ahead of curing and slabbing (*Tables 32 and 33*) for 50 mm wide thin section manufacture (Goldberg and Macphail 2006; Murphy 1986). Thin sections (Figs 16–17) were cleaned and given a final polish using fine carborundum paper, and analysed using a petrological microscope: under plane polarised light (PPL), crossed polarised light (XPL), oblique incident light (OIL) and using fluorescent microscopy (blue light – BL), at magnifications ranging from x1 to x200/400. Thin sections were described, ascribed soil microfabric types (SMTs) and microfacies types (MFTs) (see *Tables 32 and 33*) and counted according to established methods (Bullock *et al* 1985; Courty 2001; Courty *et al* 1989; Goldberg and Macphail 2006; Macphail and Cruise 2001; Stoops 2003). Local

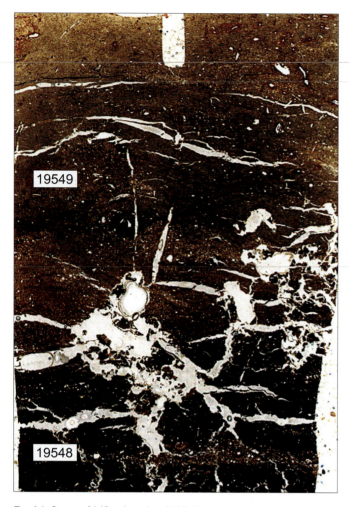

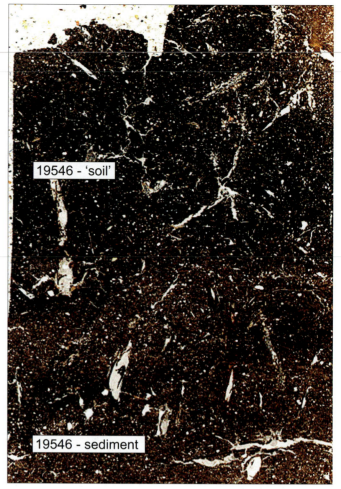

Fig 16: Scan of M2; silty clay (19549) sediments over iron stained humified peat (19548). Width is ~50 mm.

Fig 17: Scan of M5 (19546); bioworked 'soil' layer over humic silty sediment. Width is ~50 mm.

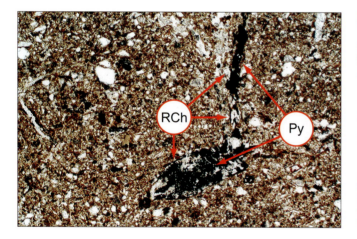

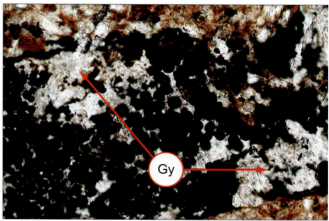

Fig 18: Photomicrograph of M6 (19495); humic silty alluvium with root channels (RCh) partially infilled with pyrite (Py). Plane polarised light (PL), frame width is ~4.6 mm

Fig 19: Detail of Fig 18, root channel part infilled with spherical pyrite framboids and gypsum (Gy). PPL, frame width is ~1.06 mm.

Figures 16–19 Soil micromorphology thin sections

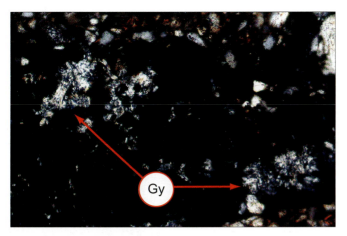

Fig 20: As Fig 19, under crossed polarised light (XPL) showing first order grey birefringence of gypsum (Gy).

Fig 21: As Fig 19, under oblique incident light (OIL); note typical brassy colour of pyrite.

Fig 22: Burned flint in humic alluvium (19495). OIL, frame width is ~4.6 mm.

Fig 23: Charcoal in alluvium (19495). OIL, frame width is ~4.6 mm.

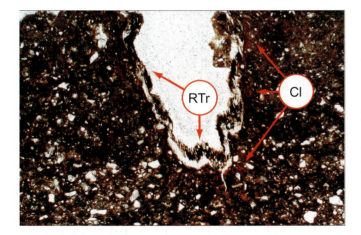

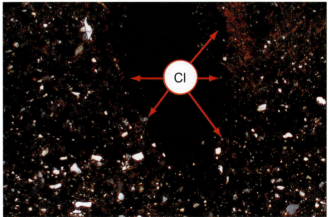

Fig 24: Photomicrograph of M4 (19497); root trace (RTr) forming vertical channel; note associated localised inwash of mobilised dusty clay (Cl). PPL, frame width is ~4.6 mm.

Fig 25: As Fig 24, under XPL showing oriented dusty clay textural pedofeatures–void coatings and associated intercalations.

Figures 20–25 Soil micromorphology thin sections

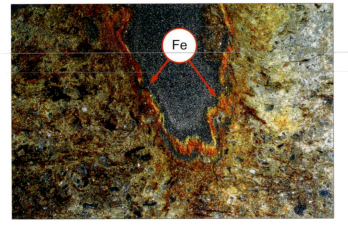

Fig 26: As Fig 24, under OIL; note dark brown organic inclusions and red ferruginised (Fe) root remains.

Fig 27: Photomicrograph of lower part of M5 (19496) (see Fig 17); thin peaty organic laminae in humic silts. PPL, frame width is ~4.6 mm.

Fig 28: Detail of Fig 27, showing laminae of coarse silt, detrital and amorphous organic matter. PPL, frame width is ~1.06 mm.

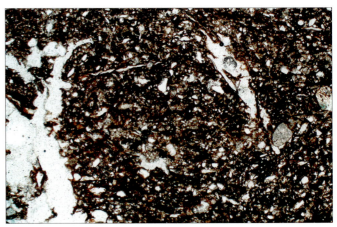

Fig 29: Photomicrograph of upper part of M5 (19496) (see Fig 17); broad burrow in weakly subangular structured 'soil' layer. PPL, frame width is ~4.6 mm.

Fig 30: Detail of Fig 29, showing finely fragmented organic matter and homogenised 'soil' in burrow. PPL, frame width is 1.06 mm.

Fig 31: Photomicrograph of M3 (19548); peat formed from layered organic fragments (monocotyledonous organs). PPL, frame width is ~4.6 mm.

Figures 26–31   Soil micromorphology thin sections

Fig 32: Photomicrograph of M2 (19548) (see Fig 16); humified (silty) peat. PPL, frame width is ~4.6 mm.

Fig 33: As Fig 30, under OIL, showing 'blackened' humified peat and yellow ferruginisation (lepidocrocite?).

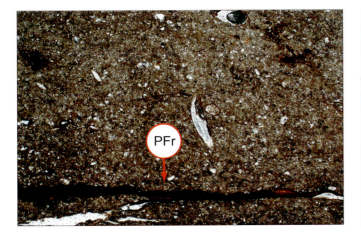

Fig 34: Photomicrograph of M2 (19549) (see Fig 16); dumped layers of silty clay sediment that include long horizontally oriented plant fragment (PFr). PPL, frame width is ~4.6 mm.

Figures 32–35 Soil micromorphology thin sections

Fig 35: As Fig 30, under XPL; note birefringence (Bir) patterns associated with partially collapsed voids and root channels (intercalations) from dumping of wet sediment/ minor soft sediment deformation.

soil studies from north Kent, and both UK and international analogues have been utilised in this investigation (Avery 1990, 325–8; Jarvis *et al* 1984, 281–4; Miedema *et al* 1974; Reineck and Singh 1986, 295–7).

Results

Layer 19495

This context is a well sorted moderately humic dominant coarse silt, with both detrital organic matter and rare fine charcoal; an example of burned flint was noted (Figs 18–23). There are fragmented and part-pyritised root traces alongside trace amounts of dusty clay grain coatings resulting from slaked burrow fills. Secondary pyrite, gypsum and iron staining (see Figs 24–6) occur. These massive well-sorted humic silty

alluvial sediments represent moderately low energy deposition where episodic alluviation (flooding?) allowed plant growth and burrowing by mesofauna. This resulted in mixing and re-wetting that homogenized any of the original fine bedding; a typical finding for accreting flood plain deposits (Barclay *et al* 2003; Goldberg and Macphail 2006, 95–9). Background activity by human groups is recorded in the field (Section 18549) and by the presence of fine charcoal and a burnt flint fragment (Figs 22–3); the early Mesolithic for example produced large amounts of background charcoal in southern England (Lewis *et al* 1992). The formation of pyrite (FeS_2) framboids (Wiltshire *et al* 1994) associated with relict roots is most commonly related to hydromorphic soils formed in marine sediments (Bullock *et al* 1985, 67; Miedema *et al* 1974), and at Ebbsfleet is consistent with the proximity of estuarine deposits. The possibly later formation of gypsum ($CaSO_4$) is also typical of such soil-sediments and relates to the weathering of pyrite and the availability of calcium (Avery 1990, 325–8; Bullock *et al* 1985, 71).

Layer 19496

The lower part of M5 records weakly layered, dominantly humic coarse silts, with horizontally oriented detrital (some charred and humified) organic matter, and clay and fine charcoal-rich laminae (Figs 27–8). There is both rooting and root mixing of the sediments, and later gypsum and iron impregnations along root channels (the presence of fungal body concentrations here and above in the sequence is enigmatic, but may be associated with rooting). Here, well-sorted humic silty clay alluviation is interdigitated with weak organic fine silty clay deposition, indicative of back-swamp flooding and developing peat formation. The junction between these laminated sediments and the upper part of M3 is characterised by very broad (5 mm) burrowing, with the overlying layer being sufficiently homogenized and broadly burrowed enough to form a weakly subangular blocky structured 'soil' (Figs 17, 29–30).

Soil formation in these presumably once-layered organic and fine charcoal-rich silts was noted in the field (Stafford, pers. comm.). Later medium rooting, gypsum formation and iron staining are also recorded. This thin layer within context 19496 is evidence of short-lived subaerially biological working (Dinç *et al.* 1976) of 'peaty' silts forming an 'incipient soil' layer in sediments where background activity by humans is recorded. Again, this fits the model of Duchaufour (1982, 186–7) for the formation of a hydromorphic alluvial soil in swampy ground.

Layer 19497

Sample M4 is composed of generally well-bedded humic silty clay and clays, with detrital organic matter, but little charred organic matter. Secondary rooting, and pyrite, gypsum and iron staining microfeatures are also present, along with textural pedofeature evidence of wet sediment disruption (Figs 24–6). The layering noted in the field does not seem to relate to any periods of incipient soil formation, but rather to the laminated deposition of silty clay and clayey muds, as evidence of both low and very low energy humic silts and clay sedimentation. This may indicate ponding under undisturbed conditions, at a time when there is little background (fine charcoal) evidence of human activity.

Layer 19547

The uppermost part of 19547 in M3 is composed of finely bedded clay and silty clays containing little organic matter, but rare amounts of fungal material. Textural pedofeatures associated with bedding and root disturbance, traces of pyrite and much iron staining also occur (see Figs 18–21, 24–6). These deposits again probably result from low energy muddy sedimentation.

Layer 19548

The lowermost (M3) and uppermost (M2) levels of context 19548 were examined. In M3 the finely bedded organic silty clays develop upwards into a plant layered peat (Fig 31). Both *in situ* fleshy roots and compressed roots testify to *in situ* peat formation. M3 thus records undisturbed natural peat formation by mono-cotyledonous semi-aquatic plant growth. Higher up in M2, humified silty peat, intercalated peat and detrital organic matter is present alongside intercalated silty clay sediments (Figs 32–3). Both samples show iron impregnation with later gypsum and pyrite formation.

19548 thus shows a period of peat formation and associated high water table, and later probable fluctuating water tables. The latter led to subaerial humification of the uppermost peat layers, and iron impregnation to form a very weak 'bog iron'-like deposit (Landuydt 1990) where the original peat and silty clay laminae are still visible (*cf* Boxgrove layer 5a; (Macphail 1999)). Unlike the 'soil' layer in context 19496, no faunal working took place (see above).

Layer 19549

Generally 'bedded' poorly humic poorly sorted (impure) silty clay and clays, with detrital organic matter and peat fragments at the base were observed in this layer (Fig 16); there are also wet sediment disruption/soft sediment features resulting from collapse of voids (Figs 34–5). The layer also shows occasional very broad burrow mixing at the base, minor rooting and weak secondary pyrite and iron staining. Although not totally unequivocal, the deposit characteristics are consistent with muddy dumps of silty clay and clay that include sandy, peat and large plant fragment inclusions. The first dump of sediment comprised fragments of weakly ferruginised peat from 19548, as well as anomalous large plant inclusions (Figs 34–5). Muddy dumping led to minor soft sediment deformation and structural collapse of the essentially slaked sediments. These deposits seem to form the base of the Saxon bund/dam (see Vol 1, Fig 6.8), where ubiquitous secondary rooting, pyrite, and iron staining from later water table fluctuations and ground water effects can also be observed.

Conclusions

A waterlain sequence of sediments was investigated from the Ebbsfleet Saxon mill site. All are low energy silts, silty clays, and clays, consistent with over bank flooding and back-swamp sedimentation, which also produced both humic silts and peats. Generally the deposits were waterlogged, but fluctuating water tables and the likely influence of estuarine waters and minor weathering permitted rooting, pyrite, gypsum, and iron staining to affect the sediments. Evidence of occasional burrowing by mesofauna is also present, and a distinct drying-out phase and ephemeral soil formation episode is recorded at the top of 19496. Clayey muds testify to 'ponding', while peats are evidence of *in situ* organic matter accumulation rather than simple detrital organic matter deposition. At the top of the natural sequence the peat became partially humified and iron-impregnated, presumably just prior to burial by the Saxon bund/dam, as little faunal working occurred.

Local human activities are represented by inputs of very fine charcoal, which can be quite concentrated in the lower contexts. Both 19495 and the 'soil' layer in 19496 include examples of burned flint. Fine charcoal becomes increasingly sparse upwards in layers 19547, 19548 and 19549, presumably, with the deposition of clay and peat, possibly indicating little human disturbance locally.

Diatoms from Northfleet
by Nigel Cameron

Twenty-three samples were prepared for diatom analysis from alluvial sequences associated with the Saxon mill. These samples were evaluated and, where possible, analysed for diatoms in order to reconstruct past water quality characteristics. Of particular interest for the geoarchaeological investigation here are possible variations in salinity indicated by the diatoms. Samples taken from three sequences have been selected for diatom analysis. These are: Section 18549, the pre-mill alluvial/peat sequence (Vol 1, Fig 6.8); Section 11850, the mill wheelhouse (Vol 1, Fig 6.7); and Section 11830, the mill pond.

Methods

Diatom preparation followed standard techniques: the oxidation of organic sediment, removal of carbonate and clay, concentration of diatom valves and washing with distilled water (Battarbee 1986). Two coverslips, each of a different concentration of the cleaned solution, were prepared from each sample and fixed in a mounting medium of a suitable refractive index for diatom microscopy (Naphrax). Slides were scanned and counted at magnifications of x400 and x1000 under phase contrast illumination.

Diatom floras and taxonomic publications were consulted to assist with diatom identification; these include Hendey (1964), Werff and Huls (1957–1974), Hartley *et al* (1996) and Krammer and Lange-Bertalot (1986–1991). Diatom species' salinity preferences are discussed using the classification data in Denys (1992), Vos and de Wolf (1988; 1993) and the halobian groups of Hustedt (1953; 1957, 199), these salinity groups are summarised as follows:

1. Polyhalobian: >30 g l-1
2. Mesohalobian: 0.2–30 g l-1
3. Oligohalobian–Halophilous: optimum in slightly brackish water
4. Oligohalobian–Indifferent: optimum in freshwater but tolerant of slightly brackish water
5. Halophobous: exclusively freshwater
6. Unknown: taxa of unknown salinity preference.

Diatom data were manipulated and plotted using the C2 program (Juggins 2003).

Results and Discussion

The results of diatom species analysis and summaries of the diatom halobian groups in this sequence (excluding the prehistoric sequence in section 18549) are shown in Figures 36 and 37.

Diatoms are present in 21 of the 23 samples that were assessed from the mill sequences. The good to moderate quality of diatom assemblages allowed diatom counting and analysis to be carried out for 18 samples. Diatom numbers and the quality of preservation within the 18 countable samples were variable. In five samples diatoms are either absent or the number of diatom valves was very low. Where diatoms were present there was a

Figure 36 Diatom diagram from section 11850 the mill wheelhouse

high degree of diatom valve breakage and silica dissolution (Flower 1993; Ryves *et al* 2001), and species diversity was low. It was not therefore possible to carry out diatom counting for these five samples, but where diatoms were present it is possible to comment on the partial assemblages present.

Section 18549: the pre-mill alluvial/peat sequence

A bulk peat sample from context 19458 at 38–39 cm, immediately overlying the uppermost diatom sample (41 cm depth), has an uncalibrated radicarbon age of 3367±30 BP placing this level in the early Bronze Age. Samples from the top and bottom of peat context 19497 at 53 cm (depth from top of sequence) and 62 cm have late Bronze Age (2767±30 BP) and early Bronze Age (3263±30 BP) dates respectively. Lastly a peat sample from context 19496 (68–69 cm from top of section 18549) has an uncalibrated radiocarbon age of 3568±30 BP, placing it in the early Bronze Age.

The diatom assemblages in the pre-mill sequence are of low diversity with a total of only 30 taxa identified. The diatom flora is consistently dominated by estuarine, benthic, epipelic (mud-surface) taxa, indicating shallow-water, and tidal conditions. In particular *Diploneis interrupta*, *Navicula peregrina*, *Nitzschia navicularis*, *Nitzschia granulate*, and *Diploneis smithii* represent this habitat. Marine plankton such as *Paralia sulcata* is relatively uncommon, as is estuarine plankton such as *Cyclotella striata*. The decline in *Nitzschia navicularis* (maximum 20% at the base, absent at the top) from the base of the sequence and increase in *Diploneis interrupta* (from 20% to 75%) suggests that the site of deposition became drier. *Diploneis interrupta* is a marine/brackish aerophilous diatom. Along with the relatively low percentages of marine-brackish plankton this reflects an environment that had some shelter, eg, mud or creeks in middle to high marsh zones beyond the range of neap tides. The accumulation of sediment through time would also have had the effect of decreasing tidal exposure. Freshwater diatoms are also represented in the assemblages, and in particular the aerophilous diatom *Pinnularia major* (maximum 10%, minimum less than 1%) has a consistent presence along with other freshwater aerophiles such as *Ellerbeckia arenaria*. It is notable that all the marine, brackish and freshwater species that are preserved are robust, heavily silicified taxa that have survived complete breakage and dissolution where other more delicate taxa will have been dissolved and broken beyond recognition. In the sample from 0.46 m depth differential preservation has

resulted in the presence of only two identifiable diatom valves. These were *Nitzschia navicularis* and a fragment of the central area of *Cyclotella striata*. Though a count was not therefore possible, these diatoms are consistent with the tidal conditions and environment indicated elsewhere in the sequence. The basal sample from 0.73 m depth has no diatoms. A small number of diatoms was present at 0.66 m depth; these include five valves of *Nitzschia navicularis* and single examples of *Diploneis interrupta*, *Diploneis smithii*, *Aulacoseira* sp., and an indeterminate centric girdle band.

Section 11850: the mill wheelhouse

The diatom assemblages in the mill wheelhouse sequence, section 11850 (Fig 36), are moderately diverse with a total of 91 taxa recorded in nine samples. Diatoms are absent from the organic level at 0.85 m depth in context 12532, and a single valve of *Navicula rhyncocephala* was identified in an extensive scan of the sample from 0.95 m depth in context 12533.

In the lower part of the sequence (contexts 12538 and 12535) the diatom flora is dominated by mesohalobous and polyhalobous taxa comprising over 70% of the total diatoms whilst freshwater and halophilous diatoms represent 10–15% of the total. Both epipelic (*Nitzschia navicularis*) and planktonic (*Cyclotella striata*) mesohalobous taxa are present along with a significant number of (allochthonous) polyhalobous plankton (*Paralia sulcata*, *Rhaphoneis* spp., *Podosira stelligera*, *Cymatosira belgica*, *Dimmeregramma minor*) and some marine non-plankton (*Achnanthes longipes*, *Trachyneis aspera*). In context 12538 a decline in the benthic diatom *Nitzschia navicularis* is accompanied by increases in the proportions of plankton (*Paralia sulcata* and *Cyclotella striata*) reflecting slightly increased water depth and tidal transport of planktonic valves to the site. Overall there is a small increase in polyhalobous diatoms and decline in mesohalobous species in 12538. In context 12535 the flora is dominated by the mesohalobous, epipelic aerophile *Diploneis interrupta* which comprises 49% of the total diatom assemblage. Polyhalobous and polyhalobous to mesohalobous diatoms in 12535 decline to approximately 10% of the total, whilst the overall proportion of mesohalobous diatoms is at a maximum of almost 70% of the total flora (*Nitzschia navicularis*, *Cyclotella striata* in addition to *Diploneis interrupta*). The dominance of the aerophilic species in 12535 reflects the lithostratigraphy (dry and desiccated organic sediments) and subsequent poor preservation in 12533 and 12532 (see above). Again

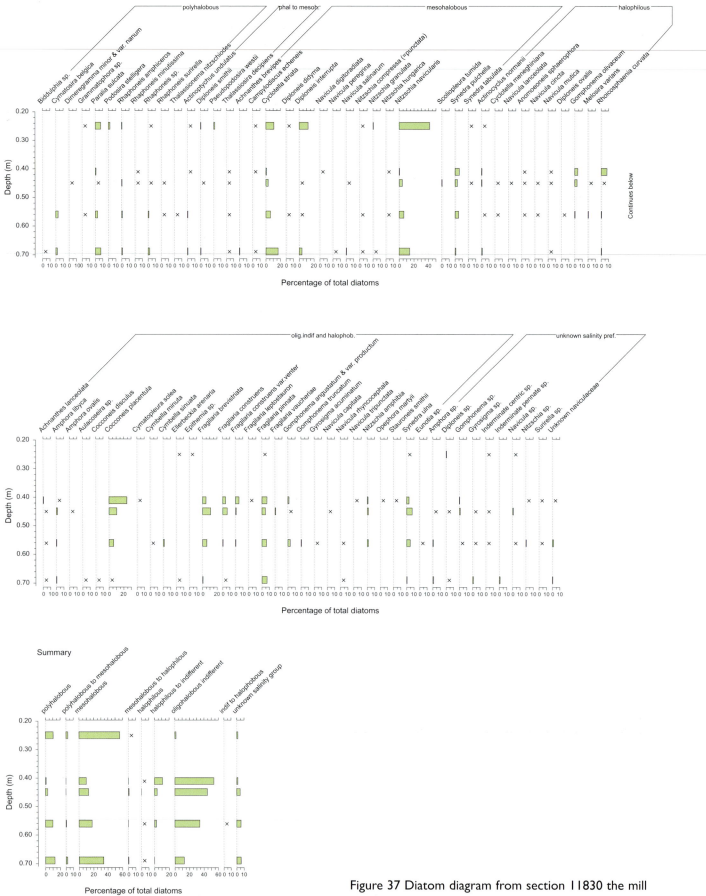

Figure 37 Diatom diagram from section 11830 the mill pond

freshwater diatoms in 12535 represent only about 10% of the total, reflecting the dominance of water from the estuary.

In contexts 12526 and 12525 there is a return to clay deposition with increasing percentages of mesohalobous plankton (*Cyclotella striata*) and benthos (*Nitzschia navicularis*) (minimum 30%, maximum 50%). At the same time there is a decline in polyhalobes from around 20% to 10%. However, high numbers of oligohalobous indifferent (freshwater) diatoms are evident in 12526 and 12525, and in particular opportunistic early colonisers are common such as *Fragilaria* spp. with wide salinity tolerance (but with optimal growth in freshwaters). These non-planktonic, shallow water, freshwater diatoms include *Fragilaria brevistriata* and *Fragilaria pinnata*. They are often associated with less stable conditions and rapidly changing environments. It is noticeable that a more diverse group of freshwater diatoms from more stable habitats are present, albeit in small numbers, at 0.60 m in context 12525 (*Amphora libyca*, *Caloneis schumanniana*, *Cocconeis disculus*, *Cocconeis placentula*, *Cymbella minuta*).

In the two upper levels of the 11850 sequence from context 12524, oligohalobous indifferent diatoms decline from 25% to about 2% of the total. At the same time the percentages of mesohalobous to halophilous, meso-halobous and polyhalobous diatoms increase. There is a diverse mixture of species; the dominants are again marine species *Paralia sulcata*, *Podosira stelligera*, *Rhaphoneis* spp. with estuarine plankton *Cyclotella striata* and epipelon *Nitzschia navicularis*. Both increasing salinity and water depth are indicated by these changes.

Section 11830: the mill pond

The diatom sequence from the mill pond sequence is relatively diverse with 78 taxa present (Fig 37). Despite the homogenous appearance of the lithostratigraphy the diatom assemblages show some variation through the monoliths. At the base (0.69 m) mesohalobous diatoms are dominant, forming about 35% of the diatoms with both epipelic (*Nitzschia navicularis*, *Diploneis didyma*) and planktonic (*Cyclotella striata*) marine-brackish diatoms common. Marine plankton (*Paralia sulcata*, *Cymatosira belgica* and *Rhaphoneis* spp.) represent less than 15% of the flora whilst non-planktonic, freshwater diatoms (*Fragilaria* spp., *Synedra ulna*, *Amphora libyca*) and halophiles (*Rhoicosphaenia curvata*) comprise about 15% of the diatoms.

There is a steady increase in the percentage of oligohalobous indifferent and halophilous to indifferent taxa from the base of the sequence to 0.41 m depth.

Freshwater diatoms become dominant and comprise approximately 55% of the assemblage and halophilous to indifferent over 10% of the total at 0.41 m depth. At the same time there is a decline of mesohalobous and polyhalobous diatoms (and the intermediate polyhalobous to mesohalobous salinity group). Mesohalobous diatoms reach a minimum of just over 10% at 0.41 m depth whilst polyhalobous diatoms have declined to around 2% of the total. The main oligohalobous taxa that are increasing in this phase are *Cocconeis placentula*, which is generally an epiphyte, and a range of *Fragilaria* spp. (*F. brevistriata*, *F. construens*, *F. construens* var. *venter*, *F. pinnata*) and *Synedra ulna*. The halophilous taxa that increase in this part of the sequence include *Gomphonema olivaceum* and *Rhoicosphaenia curvata*, both attached species of shallow water. These changes indicate a decrease in tidal influence and salinity and decreasing water depth.

In the top samples at 0.25 m depth there is a significant decline in oligohalobous indifferent taxa (their cumulative percentage is about 3%) and disappearance of halophiles. In this sample mesohalobous diatoms (represented by epipelic diatoms such as *Nitzschia navicularis*, *N granulata* and the aerophile *Diploneis interrupta*; and also the planktonic *Cyclotella striata*) are dominant, comprising approximately 57% of the total. Polyhalobous diatoms (including *Paralia sulcata*, *Podosira stelligera*, *Rhaphoneis* spp) increase to approximately 12% of the total diatoms and there is a slight increase in the percentage of the intermediate polyhalobous to mesohalobous group (benthic *Diploneis smithii* and planktonic *Pseudopodosira westii*). These changes represent a return to more saline conditions and deeper water with a mixture of autochthonous mesohalobous attached or motile species and a component of allochthonous marine and estuarine plankton.

Conclusions

Diatom counting has been carried out for 18 of the 23 samples prepared. Diatoms are absent from two samples and in three samples small numbers of poorly preserved valves and fragments were present.

The pre-mill sequence is of an early date (Bronze Age) relative to the construction of the mill. The diatom assemblages are dominated by marine-brackish epipelon with a relatively low proportion of marine-brackish plankton and increasing numbers of marine-brackish

Table 34 Northfleet: results of ostracod and foraminiferal assessment undertaken in 2002 (productive contexts only; see archive for further details)

Feature	Context	Sample	m OD	Wt (g)	O	F	Taxa
Ebbsfleet Channel	11589	12138	+0.80	200	-	x	Agglutinating brackish foraminifera (*Balticammina pseudomacrescens* Brönnimann, Lutze & Whittaker, *Haplophragmoides* sp., and *Jadammina macrescens* (Brady))
	12616	12137	+0.40	200	x	x	Rare freshwater ostracods and common brackish agglutinating foraminifera (*Balticammina pseudomacrescens* Brönnimann, Lutze & Whittaker, *Jadammina macrescens* (Brady) and *Tiphotrocha comprimata* (Cushman & Brönnimann))
Mill leat	12584	12140	+0.90	200	x	x	Few freshwater ostracods and the brackish agglutinating foraminifer *Jadammina macrescens* (Brady)
	12584	12139	+0.50	200	x	x	Both brackish (*Cyprideis torosa* (Jones)) and freshwater ostracods, and common brackish and brackish/marine foraminifera (*Haplophragmoides* sp., *Jadammina macrescens* (Brady), *Tiphotrocha comprimata* (Cushman & Brönnimann), *Ammonia* sp., and *Haynesina germanica* (Ehrenberg))
Mill undercroft (wheelhouse)	12526	12102	+0.87	150		x	Common brackish agglutinating foraminifera (*Balticammina pseudomacrescens* Brönnimann, Lutze & Whittaker, *Haplophragmoides* sp., *Jadammina macrescens* (Brady) and *Tiphotrocha comprimata* (Cushman & Brönnimann))
	12536	12115	+0.30	100	x	x	Rare freshwater ostracods and common brackish agglutinating foraminifera (*Balticammina pseudomacrescens* Brönnimann, Lutze & Whittaker, *Haplophragmoides* sp., *Jadammina macrescens* (Brady) and *Tiphotrocha comprimata* (Cushman & Brönnimann))

Key: x = present; O = ostracods; F = foraminifera

aerophilous diatoms. The diatom assemblages indicate shallow water with some shelter from the sea and increasing dry periods. The quality of preservation is variable, with differential dissolution and breakage throughout the diatom assemblages.

The diatom assemblages from the mill wheelhouse sequence 1 1850 show a sequence of variations reflecting changes in salinity and water depth. Initially marine plankton increases to dominate, followed by a drier context with mesohalobous aerophiles. Diatoms are poorly preserved in the organic contexts. With a return to clay deposition polyhalobous and meso-halobous taxa recover, but there are significant numbers of early colonising freshwater species. At the top of the 11850 sequence, increasing salinity and water depth are reflected by the increase in polyhalobous and mesohalobous diatoms and decline in the salt-tolerant freshwater element of the flora.

The diatom sequence from the mill pond shows a gradual increase in the number of freshwater and halophilous diatoms from the base at 0.69–0.41 m depth. Mesohalobous and polyhalobous diatoms decline at the same time. The salinity optima and lifeforms of these diatoms show that salinity and water depth were declining during this period. In the uppermost sample from 0.25 m depth there is an abrupt decline in freshwater diatoms and loss of halophiles. Meso-halobous benthic and planktonic diatoms reach a maximum and there are higher numbers of alloch-thonous polyhalobous diatoms again. These changes at the top of the mill pond sequence show that there was a return to more saline conditions with greater water depth and tidal influence.

Foraminifera and Ostracoda from Northfleet

by John Whittaker

Twenty samples from seven profiles through alluvial deposits associated with the Saxon mill at Northfleet (ARC EBB01) have been examined for ostracods and foraminifera. Fourteen samples from six profiles were initially assessed for preservation levels in 2002, whilst the excavations were ongoing (Table 34). The results of this assessment, which have been incorporated into this

Table 35 Results of ostracoda and foraminifera analysis from the Northfleet Saxon mill pond

Section			18563			
Monolith	12024			12025		
Context	11667			12205		
m OD	+1.25/1.19	+0.70/0.68	+0.68/0.65	+0.68/0.60	+0.55/0.50	+0.40/0.35
Brackish foraminifera	–	x	x	x	x	x
Brackish ostracods	–	–	–	–	–	x
FORAMINIFERA						
Jadammina macrescens/ Haplophragmoides sp.	–	+	+	+	+++	+++
Tiphotrocha comprimata	–	–	–	+	+	+
Ammonia sp. (small)	–	–	–	–	+	+
OSTRACODA						
Leptocythere porcellanea	–	–	–	–	–	+
ECOLOGY	Weathered?	Mid–high saltmarsh				Saltmarsh & mudflats

Key: x = present, + = several specimens, ++ = common, +++ = abundant

report, concluded the preservation of assemblages was quite variable between profiles but that targeted sampling, particularly of the mill pond deposits, offered good potential for further detailed analysis. In 2007 a further sequence of six samples from the fill of the mill pond, directly in front of the penstocks, was examined in detail as part of the post-excavation analysis (Table 35). The primary aim of the analysis was to determine categorically whether the mill had been a watermill using water only from the River Ebbsfleet, or a tidal mill ponding the incoming tide and running the water through penstocks to drive the horizontal wheel at low tide (for overall discussion of tidal conditions see Vol 1, Chap 5).

Methodology

Samples from the original assessment phase in 2002 included a profile through the pre-mill sand island which included several possible buried soils predating the mill (see Vol 1, Fig 6.7). Four profiles, located along a north–south transect in the eastern part of the Wetland excavation area (see Fig 13 above), and associated with the main channel of the Ebbsfleet and the Saxon mill leat were also examined, along with deposits from the mill undercroft (see Vol 1, Fig 6.7). The sequence selected for analysis in 2007 from the mill pond was also located in the western area of excavation (see Fig 14 above).

Each sample was weighed and put in a ceramic bowl and, first, thoroughly dried in the oven. Boiling water was then poured on the sample and a little sodium carbonate added to help remove the clay fraction on washing. It was then left to soak overnight. Next, it was washed through a 75 μm sieve with hot water and the resulting residue decanted back into the bowl for drying back in the oven. As most of these sediments were plastic clays and very organic this process had to be repeated several times to achieve a satisfactory breakdown. When finally broken down and dry, the sample was stored in a labelled plastic bag. Picking was undertaken under a binocular microscope. First the residue was put through a nest of dry sieves (>500, >250 and >150 microns) and the foraminifera and ostracods picked out with a fine camel-haired brush from a tray, a fraction at a time. They were stored on 3 x 1 inch faunal slides for record purposes. Both the foraminiferal and ostracod species are listed by sample. Those from the mill pond (Table 35) were recorded semi-quantitatively. Detailed sediment descriptions of the profiles examined are presented in the sediment report (see Stafford above).

Results and Discussion

Pre-mill landsurface
Two samples from contexts 12554 and 12553, adjacent to monolith 12085 (Vol 1, Fig 6.7), were examined from a sequence of sediments pre-dating the construction of the mill. Unfortunately both samples were completely barren of ostracods or foraminifera.

The main Ebbsfleet channel
Of the profiles taken through the main channel section (see Fig 13 above), the first two (adjacent to monoliths 12000/12001, and 12003 respectively) were completely barren of ostracods and foraminifera. What little

evidence there was, chitinous valves and ephiphia (egg-cases) of cladocerans (water-fleas), suggests freshwater habitats. However, lack of preservation of freshwater ostracods is puzzling unless the sediments had been subjected to decalcification. If brackish or even marine, calcareous foraminifera and ostracods would not have survived, but brackish agglutinating foraminifera (so common elsewhere on the site) are usually preserved under such circumstances.

Two samples from a third profile (adjacent to revetment 19319 and monolith 12204), however, contained brackish agglutinating foraminifera typical of high saltmarsh, covered only by spring tides (*Balticammina pseudo-macrescens*, *Jadammina macrescens*, *Haplophragmoides* sp. and *Tipohotrocha comprimata*; see Murray 2006). There were a few freshwater ostracods (that can tolerate low salinities) that may have been washed in, or living in pools within the saltmarsh community.

The mill leat

The sediments from the mill leat (south of revetment 19319 and adjacent to monolith 12217) offer perhaps the most interesting environmental scenario (see Fig 13 above). The lower of the two samples, at +0.5 m OD (sample 12139, context 12584), contained not only brackish saltmarsh foraminiferal species, but also others (common *Ammonia* sp. and rare *Haynesina germanica*), in association with the ostracod *Cyprideis torosa*, that clearly indicate brackish intertidal flats and creek development.

The upper sample at +0.9 m OD (sample 12140, context 12584), on the other hand, contained only agglutinating foraminifera, suggesting high saltmarsh had overtaken the intertidal flat or creek. This could indicate a fall in marine influence or, perhaps, explains why the revetment was built in the first place, that is to shore up an area in danger of being eroded by an encroaching intertidal creek. Interestingly, the same association occurred in the lowermost samples of monoliths 126 and 175 (evaluation trench 3818 TT, ARC ESG00), nearby, followed by a similar, subsequent growth of high saltmarsh (Whittaker 2002).

The mill undercroft

Two samples from deposits infilling the base of the mill undercroft (Vol 1, Fig 6.7) provided unequivocal evidence for high to medium saltmarsh. Sample 12102 from context 12526 at +0.87 m OD contained common brackish agglutinating foraminifera (*Balticammina pseudomacrescens* (Brönnimann, Lutze and Whittaker), *Haplophragmoides* sp., *Jadammina macrescens* (Brady) and *Tiphotrocha comprimata* (Cushman and Brönnimann)). Sample 12115 from context 12536 at +0.3 m OD contained rare freshwater ostracods and common brackish agglutinating foraminifera (*Balti-cammina pseudomacrescens* (Brönnimann, Lutze and Whittaker), *Haplophragmoides* sp., *Jadammina macrescens* (Brady) and *Tiphotrocha comprimata* (Cushman and Brönnimann)). The site of the mill immediately following abandonment, therefore, was clearly tidal for at least medium and high water spring tides.

The mill pond

Six samples were analysed in detail from monoliths 12024 and 12025 from the infilled mill pond (Table 35; see Fig 14 above). Brackish foraminifera were found in all but the uppermost sample at +1.25 to +1.19 m OD (context 11667), and brackish ostracods occurred in the lowest sample at +0.40 to +0.35 m OD (context 12205).

Many of the brackish foraminifera found in the Ebbsfleet Valley deposits have already proved of great interest (Whittaker 2007). The agglutinating foraminifera, in particular, are important ecological marker species for low, mid and high saltmarsh (Murray 2006). They have a shell (test) of accumulated mineral grains in an organic cement and thus are preserved in even the most acid of sedimentary environments. Their tests are small, quite flexible and tend to collapse, however, thus making study difficult. They are also hard to spot against a background of the organic residue, and thus very careful picking is required. Dependent on the type of coiling they exhibit, they can belong to several genera. Suffice to say, the Northfleet mill pond species seem to contain the following: a low trochoid species with a primary, interiomarginal aperture plus multiple areal apertures (*Jadammina macrescens*); and a planispiral form with a single, interiomarginal aperture (*Haplophragmoides* sp.). In Table 35 these two have been grouped together as they are difficult to tell apart at a cursory level. The third agglutinating foraminifer in the samples is *Tiphotrocha comprimata*. All three are herbivores and detrivores living epifaunally and infaunally and are widespread on mid to high saltmarsh (Murray 2006). The final foraminifer, a very small species of *Ammonia* needs further careful study. A preliminary analysis of the present material seems to indicate that it is not *A. limnetes sensu stricto*, but is instead a juvenile or low brackish form of *A. aberdoveyensis* (a common estuarine species).

Table 36 SWLI index calibrated for MHWST showing when the mill pond could be expected to have been fillied

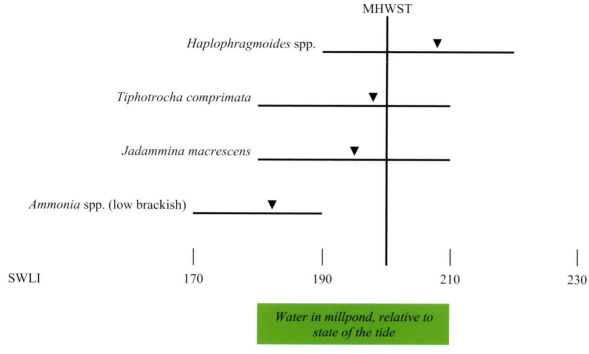

MHWST: Mean High Water Spring Tides
SWLI: 'Standardised Water-level Index'
Horizontal lines show tolerances of each species against the SWLI; arrows indicates their optima

Although all the sediment samples were quite organic, the lowermost two samples, perhaps significantly, were more silty and it is therefore not surprising that in the lowest one, at +0.40 to +0.35 m OD (context 12205), brackish ostracods indicative of creek and mudflats were found, albeit preserved as pyrite casts and easy to miss. It was not too difficult, however, because of their shape to recognise them as belonging to *Leptocythere porcellanea*. This species had been common in the STRD400, borehole 7 samples at Ebbsfleet (Whittaker 2007).

Without doubt, the ostracod and foraminiferal assemblages provide evidence that the Northfleet mill was a tidal mill. Its mill pond was accessible, especially initially to medium and high spring tides and made use of this ponded water, running it through the mill wheel at low tide. Through time the mudflats exposed at low tide became vegetated by encroaching saltmarsh vegetation and by silting. Perhaps the mill became less efficient. The uppermost sample from the mill pond was barren of microfossils. This could be due in part to weathering of the sediments, but may significantly indicate the mill pond was now totally silted up and the mill inoperable or abandoned.

Foraminifera do not live in freshwater, but it was rather surprising not to find a single freshwater ostracod within any of the mill pond sediments. This could be partly related to decalcification, as the brackish ostracods are preserved only as molds, and in the lowermost sample at that, so the sediment would seem not to be too conducive for the preservation of calcareous matter. However, no (organic-walled) cladoceran ephiphia (egg-cases) were noted, which are a clear sign of a freshwater habitat. One is tempted to state, therefore, that freshwater input into the mill pond, even at low tide, was relatively insignificant.

Horton *et al* (1999), formulated a training set from various locations in the UK to determine past sea-levels at sites, especially in Eastern England. From a complex calculation, a 'standardised water-level index' (SWLI) was devised which is shown on Table 36, calibrated to Medium High Water Spring Tides (MHWST). On this is added proxy data (provided by Horton *et al* 1999) from the four foraminiferal species found in the Northfleet mill pond, the horizontal lines being the tolerances, the arrows indicating the optima, in terms of the SWLI, for these species. Put somewhat simply and crudely, it can be seen that the ecological requirements

Table 37 Waterlogged plant remains from the Northfleet Saxon mill chute

		Sample 12278	12272
		Group/section s 18544	s 18544
		Feature	wicker fishtrap?
		Context 19488	19403
		Size (L) 1.00	1.00
		WL flot 250	200
Waterlogged	*Common name*		
Triticum spelta (glume base charred)	Spelt wheat glume base	–	est.27
Triticum aestivum (grain charred)	Free-threshing wheat	1	–
Cereal indet. (coleoptiles charred)	Cereal sprout	–	1
Species	*Common name*		
Caltha palustris	Marsh marigold	16	est.24
Ranunculus subg. *Ranunculus arb*	Buttercup	–	28
Ranunculus sardous	Hairy buttercup	35	est.93
Ranunculus subg. *Batrachium*	Water-crowfoot	20	est.295
Papaver sp.	Poppy	1	est.11
Fumaria sp.	Fumitory	–	2
Urtica dioica	Common nettle	20	est.172
Betula sp. (seeds)	Birch	5	
Chenopodium cf. *vulvaria*	Stinking goosefoot	–	est.87
Chenopodium cf. *vulvaria/album*	Stinking goosefoot/fat-hen	2	
Chenopodium album	Fat-hen	–	est.125
Atriplex sp.	Orache	17	est.85
Atriplex cf. *prostrata/littoralis*	Spear/grass-leaved orache	–	1
Atriplex littoralis	Grass-leaved goosefoot	6	–
Caryophyllaceae (indet.) v. small	Pink-family	–	1
Lychnis flos-cuculi	Ragged-robin	–	1
Silene vulgaris	Bladder campion	–	4
Polygonum aviculare	Knotgrass	–	14
Fallopia convolvulus	Black bindweed	–	1
Rumex sp.	Dock	20	est.170
Rumex acetosella	Sheep's sorrel	–	est.11
Rumex crispus (fruit/tepals)	Curled dock	17	1+cf.5f
Hypericum sp.	St John's wort	1	est.21
Malva sp.	Mallow	–	2
Barbarea vulgaris	Winter cress	–	1
Brassica oleracea/nigra	Wild cabbage/wild black mustard	–	est.28
Raphanus raphanistrum	Wild radish	–	1
Anagallis sp.	Pimpernel	–	1
Rosaceae thorn	Bramble/rose type thorn	–	3
Rubus sp.	Bramble	–	est.24
Potentilla sp.	Cinquefoil	–	2
Aphanes arvensis	Parsley-piert	–	1
Epilobium sp.	Broad-leaved/hoary willowherb	85	est.50
Apiaceae large (>2.5mm)	Carrot family indet. seed.	+	1
Oenanthe sp.	Water-dropwort	–	1
Conium maculatum	Hemlock	1	3
Apium cf. *graveolens*	Wild celery	80	est.394
Torilis japonica/arvensis	Hedge-parsley	–	1
Hyoscyamus niger	Henbane	–	est.43
Solanum sp.	Nightshade	–	est.5
Verbena officinalis	Vervain	–	est.10
Lamiaceae	Dead-nettle family	–	2
Lamium sp.	Dead-nettle	–	4
Ajuga reptans	Bugle	–	1
Prunella vulgaris	Self-heal	1	–
Origanum vulgare	Wild marjoram	1	–
Lycopus europaeus	Gypsywort	1	est.6
Mentha sp.	Mint	1	est.12
Callitriche cf. *stagnalis*	Common water-starwort	22	est.20
Sambucus nigra	Elder	1	3
Valerianella sp. *rimosa/dentata*	Broad/narrow-fruited cornsalad	1	–
Asteraceae indet.	Daisy family	–	est.10
Asteraceae indet. small	Daisy family	2	–
Cirsium/Carduus	Thistles	1	3
Onopordum acanthium	Cotton thistle	–	6
Lapsana communis	Nipplewort	–	1
Leontodon autumnalis	Autumn hawkbit	3	est.5

Table 37 Waterlogged plant remains from the Northfleet Saxon mill chute (continued)

		Group/section	s 18544	s 18544
		Feature		wicker fishtrap?
		Context	19488	19403
		Size (L)	1.00	1.00
		WL flot	250	200
Sonchus oleracea	Smooth sow-thistle		1	1
Sonchus asper	Prickly sow-thistle		3	1
Aster tripolium	Sea aster		cf.2	1
Anthemis cotula	Stinking mayweed		–	1
Chrysanthemum segetum	Corn marigold		–	2
Triglochin maritimum	Sea arrowgrass		9	–
Potamogeton sp.	Pondweed		6	9
Zannichellia palustris	Horned pondweed		3	7
Juncus sp.	Rush		1	1
Juncus gerardii	Saltmarsh rush		–	est.240
Cyperaceae (small <2mm)	Sedge family		–	1
Eleocharis palustris	Spikerush		2	6
Schoenoplectrus lacustris/tabernaemontani	Common/grey club rush		8	est.116
Carex sp.(lenticular)	Sedge		20	est.26
Carex sp.(trigonous)	Sedge		3	est.34
Poaceae/Cereal culm node	Grasses/cereal stems		1	–
Sparganium erectum	Bur-reed		–	25
Seed indet. <1mm reticulate cell	Indet. seed		–	est.4
Bud indet.	Indet. Bud		–	3

of the foraminifera can tell us when the mill pond could be expected to be filled, relative to MHWST. It would appear to have been a pretty viable tidal mill pond.

Waterlogged Plant Remains from Northfleet

by Chris J. Stevens

Waterlogged samples relating to the Saxon environment were taken from the mill wheelhouse (section 11850, 12557), and the sequences from the chute (section 18544, 19488) and mill pond (section 18545, 19426) (see Vol 1, Chap 6).

Such remains are often derived from local vegetation so can address those aspects of the project aims concerning changes in the local environment during the Saxon period, especially those relating to sea-level.

Methods

All waterlogged samples were of 1 litre. Samples were processed by laboratory flotation. The resultant flot was decanted onto a 250 μm mesh sieve and the residues fractionated to 0.5 mm. Prior to analysis, the flots were sieved in order to facilitate sorting and identification of the plant remains. This was carried out using a stack of granulometric sieves (2 mm, 1 mm, 0.5 mm and 0.25

mm). Recovery and identification was by the use of a low power stereo-binocular microscope with magnifications between x6.4 and x40. Identification of more unusual taxa was made with reference to the Seed Atlas (Cappers *et al* 2006) and modern reference material at the Institute of Archaeology, University College, London. The results are presented in Tables 37–39. Nomenclature follows that of Stace (1997). Ecological information upon the species comes from Stace (1997), Clapham *et al* (1965; 1987), Rodwell (1991a; 1991b; 1992; 1995; 2000) and Horwood (1919).

Results

Both the lower contexts from the chute fill (section 18544, context 19403) and the mill pond (section 19427, context 12331) contained quite high numbers of charred spelt glumes and in the latter case waterlogged glume bases as well. By comparison the upper context from the mill pond (section 18545, context 19426) contained only two charred glume bases, while that from the chute fill (section 18544, context 19488) contained no glumes and a single charred grain of free-threshing wheat (*Triticum aestivum*). Other crop remains included single seeds of flax from the upper part of the mill pond sequence.

The lower parts of the sequences were in general richer than the upper parts, with the lowest chute fill

Table 38 Waterlogged plant remains from the Northfleet Saxon mill pond

		Sample Group/section Feature Context Size (L) WL flot	12316 s 18545 19426 1.00 80	12331 s 18545 Column B2 19427 1.00 20
Waterlogged	*Common name*			
Hordeum vulgare (rachis fragment)	Barley rachis		–	1c
Triticum spelta (glume base charred)	Spelt wheat glume base		2	26c+18wl
Triticum dicoccum/spelta (grain charred)	Spelt wheat grain		–	2c.
Avena sp. (charred)	Oat grain		–	4c.+1wild fb
Cereal indet. *(*culm node)	Cereal straw node		–	1c.
Species	*Common name*			
Musci	Bog moss CHK		–	1
Ranunculus subg. *Ranunculus arb*	Buttercup		3	2+2f.
Ranunculus sardous	Hairy buttercup		1	3
Ranunculus subg. *Batrachium*	Water-crowfoot		60	11
Papaver sp.	Poppy		–	9
Fumaria sp.	Fumitory		–	1
Urtica dioica	Common nettle		12	9
Chenopodiaceae	Goosefoot		–	1
Chenopodium sp.	Goosefoots		–	1
Chenopodium cf. *rubrum*	Red goosefoot		3	–
Atriplex sp.	Orache		7	–
Atriplex cf. *prostrata/littoralis*	Spear/grass-leaved orache		–	1
Atriplex littoralis	Grass-leaved goosefoot		1	–
Stellaria graminea	Lesser stitchwort		–	1
Stellaria cf. *uliginosa*	Bog stitchwort		–	1
Silene vulgaris	Bladder campion		1	–
Polygonum aviculare	Knotgrass		–	2
Rumex sp.	Dock		7	11+1c.
*Rumex cripus/longifolius*fruiting tepals	Curled/northern dock		–	1
Rumex crispus (fruit/tepals)	Curled dock		1f.	2
Raphanus raphanistrum	Wild radish		–	1seed?
Reseda sp.	Mignonette		1	–
Linum usitatissimum (seed)	Flax		1	–
Linum catharticum	Fairy flax		–	3
Apiaceae large (>2.5mm)	Carrot family indet. seed.		1	–
Conium maculatum	Hemlock		–	+
Apium cf. *graveolens*	Wild celery		1w spines	2
Hyoscyamus niger	Henbane		–	1
Lycopus europaeus	Gypsywort		–	2
Mentha sp.	Mint		–	1
Callitriche cf. *stagnalis*	Common water-starwort		3	–
Plantago major	Greater plantain		1	1
Sambucus nigra	Elder		1	1
Asteraceae indet. small	Daisy family		–	3
Arctium sp.	Burdocks		–	1
Cirsium/Carduus	Thistles		–	1
Sonchus asper	Prickly sow-thistle		1	1
Anthemis cotula	Stinking mayweed		6	–
Alisma cf. *plantago-aquatica*	Water plantain		2	20
Triglochin maritimum	Sea arrowgrass		–	65
Potamogeton sp.	Pondweed		2	–
Zannichellia palustris	Horned pondweed		–	3
Juncus sp.	Rush		–	1
Juncus gerardii	Saltmarsh rush		–	28+
Juncus gerardii (capsule)	Saltmarsh rush (capsule)		–	1
Eleocharis palustris	Spikerush		1	–
Scirpus sylvaticus	Wood club-rush		1?	–
Schoenoplectus lacustris/tabernaemontani	Common/grey club rush		55	–
Carex sp. *(lenticular)*	Sedge		5	3
Carex sp. *(trigonous)*	Sedge		1	1
Poaceae/Cereal culm node	Grasses/cereal stems		–	2
Poaceae (small)	Grasses		2	1
Bromus sp.	Brome grass		–	2c

Table 39 Waterlogged plant remains from the Northfleet Saxon mill wheelhouse

		Sample	12171	12121
		Group/section	s 11850	s 11850
		Context	12557	12561
		Size (L)	1.00	1.00
		WL flot	80	50
Species	*Common name*			
Musci	Bog moss CHK		++++	–
Ranunculus subg. *Ranunculus arb*	Buttercup		–	2
Ranunculus subg. *Batrachium*	Water–crowfoot		1	7
Fumaria sp.	Fumitory		1	–
Urtica dioica	Common nettle		–	1
Betula sp. (seeds)	Birch		1	–
Chenopodium sp.	Goosefoots		–	1
Chenopodium cf. *rubrum*	Red goosefoot		–	1
Atriplex sp.	Orache		–	2
Rumex acetosella	Sheep's sorrel		1	–
Hypericum sp.	St John's wort		–	1
Rubus sp.	Bramble		1	3
Potentilla sp.	Cinquefoil		–	2
Torilis japonica/arvensis	Hedge–parsley		1	–
Sambucus nigra	Elder		3	2
Triglochin maritimum	Sea arrowgrass		1	–
Juncus sp.	Rush		1	–
Eleocharis palustris	Spikerush		–	1
Schoenoplectrus lacustris/tabernaemontani	Common/grey club rush		–	1
Carex sp. *(lenticular)*	Sedge		2	–
Carex sp. *(trigonous)*	Sedge		–	1
Sparganium erectum	Bur–reed		–	1

deposit (section 18544, context 19403) being the richest in waterlogged plant remains overall. The samples from the mill wheelhouse were generally poor, although they contained a similar array of species to those seen in the other samples.

Most of the species present are those associated with water bodies, wetlands, and marshlands. Species found in standing, shallow water or the edges of such water-bodies were represented by seeds of water-crowfoot (*Ranunculus* subgenus *Batrachium*) present in all the sequences, along with rush (*Juncus* sp.), sedge (*Carex* sp.), water-plantain (*Alisma plantago-aquatica* and water-starwort (*Callitriche*), the latter absent from the wheelhouse sequence. Those of wetlands in general, especially marshland, included common/grey club (*Schoenoplectus lacustris/tabernaemontani*), spikerush (*Eleocharis palustris*), and bur-reed (*Sparganium erectum*).

Of some interest were seeds of several species associated with saltmarsh and coastal areas. These included saltmarsh rush (*Juncus gerardii*), wild celery (*Apium* cf. *graveolens*), hairy buttercup (*Ranunculus sardous*) and spear/grass-leaved orache (*Atriplex* cf. *prostrata/littoralis*), while horned pondweed (*Zannichellia palustris*) is commonly found within brackish as well as freshwater.

Other plants, such as sea aster (*Aster tripolium*) and sea arrowgrass (*Triglochin maritimum*), are more strongly indicative of saltmarsh and brackish inlets, while wild cabbage/mustard, either black mustard (*Brassica nigra*) or wild cabbage (*Brassica oleracea*), are also common within coastal areas. Many seeds of willowherb (*Epilobium* sp.) were recovered from the chute fill, which potentially may be of hoary willowherb (*Epilobium pariviflorum*), that along with marsh willowherb (*Epilobium palustre*), is recorded from strandlines, shingles, dunes and to a lesser extent coastal marshes (Rodwell 2000). It might be noted that several species of pond-weed (*Potamogeton* sp.) are to be found in similar conditions. Common starwort (*Callitriche stagnalis*) is generally found in fresh-water, but does have a degree of salt-tolerance (Grime *et al* 1988).

It was observed that many of the seeds of *Chenopodium* sp. recovered resembling fat-hen (*Chenopodium album*) were small in size, and at least some from the lower fill of the chute were tentatively identified as stinking goosefoot (*Chenopodium vulvaria*), a species associated with coastal marshes. Several seeds of probable red-goosefoot (*Chenopodium rubrum*, as opposed to *C. urbicum*) were recovered from the wheelhouse and the mill pond. This species, associated with waste ground, is furthermore often found in coastal areas.

Gypsywort (*Lycopus europaeus*), buttercup (*Ranunculus acris/repens/bulbosus*), mint (*Mentha* sp.), winter cress (*Barbarea vulgaris*), thistle (*Cirsium/Carduus* sp.) and hemlock (*Conium maculatum*), the last whose seeds were very common within the mill pond, can all be associated with rough grassland, hedges and open scrub on wetter and damp soils. Water droplet (*Oenanthe* sp.), while not found in arable fields, is associated with disturbed areas of marshland and ditches.

There was generally little indication of woodland within the samples, although a few species point to the presence of some shaded environments, eg, hedgerows or woody scrub. Seeds of birch (*Betula* sp.) were recovered from the upper part of the sequence from the chute fill and the wheelhouse, while seeds of elder (*Sambucus nigra*) were recovered from all of the sequences and can be seen as indicative of hedges or wooded shrub. Marsh marigold (*Caltha palustris*) was present in the chute fill sequence (section 18544) and this species is associated with partially shaded, wet habitats. A single seed of bugle (*Ajuga reptans*) was recovered from the lower part of the chute fill; this species is common within damp woods, but also found in meadows. Seeds and probable thorns of bramble (*Rubus* sp.) were also common in the lower fills of the chute, as well as being recovered from the wheelhouse.

Associated more directly with wet grasslands were seeds of ragged robin (*Lychnis flos-cuculi*), while it is probable that the seeds of Saint John's wort (*Hypericum* sp.) are also of those species commoner in wet grasslands. Associated with grasslands in general were bladder campion (*Silene vulgaris*) and buttercup (*Ranunculus acris/repens/bulbosus*), while vervain (*Verbena officinalis*) is found in rough grassland upon drier, calcareous soils. Docks (*Rumex* sp.), probably curled leaved dock (*Rumex crispus*), can also be associated with rough pasture, although they are also found on wasteland and arable fields.

Several species may be taken as more indicative of arable and wasteland, including poppy (*Papaver* sp.), fumitory (*Fumaria* sp.), black bindweed (*Fallopia convolvulus*), knotgrass (*Polygonum aviculare*), nipplewort (*Lapsana communis*), autumn hawkbit (*Leontodon autumnalis*), sow-thistle (*Sonchus* sp.), narrow-fruited cornsalad (*Valerianella dentata*), hedge parsley (*Torilis japonica/arvensis*) and stinking mayweed (*Anthemis cotula*), the last of which is associated with heavier clay soils. Despite the evidence for wetter soils, several species whose seeds were recovered from the sample are commoner on drier, sandier soils, for example, sheep's sorrel (*Rumex acetosella*) and corn marigold (*Chrysanthemum segetum*).

A single seed of greater plantain (*Plantago major*) from the mill pond is indicative of waste, arable and/or grassland, although it may be that the seeds are of *Plantago major* ssp. *intermedia* which is commoner on damp soils close to the coast. The upper part of the mill pond sequence also contained several seeds of stinking mayweed (*Anthemis cotula*), associated with heavy clay soils, and often the cultivation of such soils.

Seeds of nettle (*Urtica dioica*), orache (*Atriplex* sp.), and fat-hen (*Chenopodium album*) were present and relatively common in all the sequences. As noted above some of the seeds of *Atriplex* and *Chenopodium* may relate to the proximity of saltmarsh; however, these species are also associated with general disturbed waste ground and nitrogen enriched soils common around settlements.

Finally, of some interest were seeds of cotton or Scotch thistle (*Onopordum acanthium*) from the lower part of the chute fill, a species rarely recorded within archaeological samples. The species is generally thought to be a Roman introduction and has been recorded from Roman sites in the Thames Valley (Robinson 1979; 1988; Reid 1908; 1909; 1910). While this species will colonise waste and rough ground, it is today – and was commonly in the past – grown as an ornamental.

Discussion

The presence of numerous spelt glumes in the lower parts of both the mill pond and the chute fill sequences is of considerable interest. Charred material can potentially be reworked, although this material was well preserved. However, despite the numerous waterlogged samples assessed and examined, and despite the fact that the Roman samples were rich in charred glumes of spelt (see W Smith Vol 3, Chap 4), waterlogged glume bases of spelt were only seen to have survived in the mill pond sequence. From the charred material at Northfleet it can be seen that glumes were far more common during the Roman period, although it might be noted that radiocarbon determinations on emmer and spelt wheat provided evidence for this crop in the earliest Saxon period, from the early 5th–6th centuries AD (see Barnett below and W Smith below). It would seem unlikely that this material was reworked and probably indicates that the very lowest deposits are at least late Romano-British/early Saxon in date. There was generally little other evidence for crops, although a single grain of charred free-threshing wheat (*Triticum aestivum* sl.) is perhaps more in keeping with the known cultivation of this crop during most of the Saxon period (see Stevens below and W Smith below).

As might be expected, given the presence of the tidal mill, there is good evidence in the samples for marshland with elements of brackish water and saltmarsh. These elements are however much more prominent within the lower parts of both the chute and the mill pond sequences. There is relatively little evidence for shrub, bar a few seeds of bramble elder and birch, suggesting a generally open landscape.

As also seen for the Roman period there is good evidence for rough grassland, which was possibly grazed, with some patches of barer wasteland. The upper parts of the sequences provided slightly less evidence for disturbed soils than seen in the earlier parts of the sequence, and it might be assumed that the level of activity associated with settlement, for example, middens and trampling by animals, was less in the Saxon period than before. However, it might be noted that the evidence for saltmarsh and brackish species was less noticeable in the upper parts of the sequence compared with lower parts of the sequence and the Roman cistern (see Stevens Vol 3, Chap 4). In the upper part of the sequence general marshland species were better represented, and it may be that the decline in seeds of species of disturbed soils may be related to a general reduction in the area of saltmarsh. This, in turn, may be further related to a reduced tidal influence in the area (see Stafford above).

The seeds of stinking mayweed (*Anthemis cotula*) might be taken as indicating some local cultivation at this time. Further, the ecologically wide range of species generally present within the samples can be seen as reflective of the wide range of soil types within the local area. So along with wetter areas of grassland and marsh, we also find seeds of species that are more commonly found on drier, gravelly or sandy soils, such as wild mustard/cabbage, corn marigold (*Chrysanthemum segetum*), mallow (*Malva* sp.) and sheep's sorrel. It is also interesting to note the presence of vervain (*Verbena*

officinalis), a species associated with drier calcareous chalk soils, although it is only represented by a single seed.

The single seed of flax may relate to its use as a crop, although the species does grow wild. Flax was not recorded from the charred plant remains at either Northfleet or Springhead (see Stevens below and W Smith below) and so this provides the only evidence for its potential use as a crop. Flax has however been recorded for the late Saxon period at Springfield Lyons, Essex (Murphy 1994).

Insects from Northfleet
by David Smith

Insect analysis was undertaken on seven waterlogged samples (12120, 12121, 12171, 12272, 12278, 12335, and 12336) associated with the Saxon mill and mill pond. Samples for analysis were initially selected based on obvious waterlogged preservation and an assessment of the potential for insect analysis undertaken by Chris J. Stevens (Wessex Archaeology). It was hoped that the study of the insect remains from these deposits might provide information on the landscape, and land use, associated with the the Saxon mill.

Methods

The waterlogged samples were processed using the standard method of paraffin flotation as outlined in Kenward *et al* (1980). The weights and volumes of the samples processed are presented in *Table 40*. The insect remains present were sorted from the flots and stored in ethanol. The Coleoptera (beetles) present were identified by direct comparison to the Gorham and Girling Collections of British Coleoptera. The various taxa of insects recovered are presented in *Table 40*. The taxonomy for the Coleoptera follows that of Lucht (1987).

Where applicable each species of Coleoptera has been assigned to one, or more, ecological groupings and these are indicated in the second column of *Table 40*. These groupings are derived from the preliminary classifications outlined by Kenward (1978). The classification used here replicates that used in Kenward and Hall (1995). The groupings themselves are described at the end of *Table 40*. The various proportions of these groups, expressed as percentages of the total Coleoptera present in the faunas, are shown in *Table 41*.

Not all taxa have a coding and some taxa occur in more than one ecological group. As a result percentages do not equal 100%.

Results

Seven insect faunas from Northfleet are from the 'wetlands' area of the site, from three sections through channel deposits that are associated with the Saxon mill (see Vol 1, Chap 6). Samples 12120, 12121 and 12171 are from section 11850 through the millrace associated with the wheelhouse. Samples 12272 and 12278 are from section 18544 through the overflow chute and samples 12335 and 12336 are from section 18545 through the mill pond. In most cases the insect faunas recovered are very similar and therefore will be discussed together.

In all of the samples from the sections examined there is a distinct coastal or estuarine influence (see ecological group 'c' in *Table 41*). This is especially strong in the samples from the Saxon mill pond. The species that indicate this are the ground beetles *Bembidion normannum*, *B. minimum*, *B. iricolor* and *Agonum viduum* and the water beetles *Ochthebius dilatatus* and *O. marinus*, all of which are associated with the clay margins and banks of saline pools and estuaries (Lindroth 1974; Hansen 1986). However, a number of 'elmid riffle beetles' such as *Elmis aenea*, *Esolus parallelepipedus*, *Oulimnius* and *Riolus* species suggest that fast flowing and non-saline waters were also associated with these channels (Holland 1972). One notable factor is that there are very few of the dytiscid or hydreanid water beetles that usually indicate slow flowing and fresh water conditions.

There are indications that water reed (*Phragmites australis* (Cav.) Trin. ex Steud), suggested by the presence of *Odacantha melanura*, *Silis ruficollis* and *Plateumaris braccata*, and sedges (*Carex* spp.), the host plant of *Donacia aquatica* (Lindroth 1974; Koch 1992), grew in the area. Other waterside plants suggested by the beetles are marsh marigold (*Caltha palustris* L. – the host of *Leiosoma deflexum*) and aquatic umbelifers (Apiacae – the host of *Prasocuris phellandrii*).

There is also evidence for pasture and grassland in the area (indicated by ecological groups 'rd' and 'p' in *Table 41*). This is most clearly suggested by the presence of a limited number of *Onthophagus* and *Aphodius* 'dung beetles' which are associated with animal dung, often lying in open pasture (Jessop 1986). Grassland or

meadow is also suggested by several beetle species that indicate the presence of clover (*Trifolium* spp.), such as *Sitona lineatus*, *S. sulcifrons*, *S. flavescens* and *Hypera* spp. Equally, *Mecinus pyraster* and the *Gymetron* species are all associated with ribwort plantain (*Plantago lanceolata* L.). There are also clear indications for the presence of waste ground or disturbed ground. In particular *Brachypterus urticae*, *Cidnorhinus quadrimaculatus* and *Ceutorhynchus pollinarius* are all associated with stinging nettle (*Urtica dioica* L.). Equally, poppies (Papaveraceae) and migonettes (Resedaceae) are indicated by *Ceutorhynchus contractus*.

There are only a few indicators for woodland or trees (often group 'l' accounts for less than 5% in *Table 41*) suggesting that the landscape was essentially clear. Amongst those that are present are the 'longhorn' *Pogonocherus hispidulus* and the 'bark beetle' *Scolytus intricatus* that are associated with a range of hard woods and *Leperisinus varius* that is associated with ash (*Fraxinus excelsior* L.) (Koch 1992). There also appears to have been broom (*Cytisus scoparius* L.) nearby since this is the host of the 'bark beetle' *Phloeophthorus rhododactylus*, which occurs in some numbers. There is also a single individual of *Rhamphus pulicarius* that is often associated with willow (*Salix* spp.). Other species, such as the 'woodworm' *Anobium punctatum* and the 'powder post beetle' *Lyctus linearis* are more probably associated with the timbers of the mill itself, rather than natural woodland.

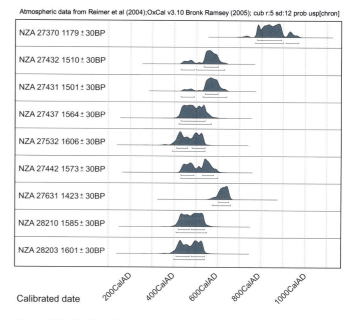

Atmospheric data from Reimer et al (2004);OxCal v3.10 Bronk Ramsey (2005); cub r:5 sd:12 prob usp[chron]

NZA 27370 1179 ± 30BP
NZA 27432 1510 ± 30BP
NZA 27431 1501 ± 30BP
NZA 27437 1564 ± 30BP
NZA 27532 1606 ± 30BP
NZA 27442 1573 ± 30BP
NZA 27631 1423 ± 30BP
NZA 28210 1585 ± 30BP
NZA 28203 1601 ± 30BP

Calibrated date

200CalAD   400CalAD   600CalAD   800CalAD   1000CalAD

Figure 38 OxCal Multiplot of Saxon radiocarbon dates at Springhead and Northfleet

Table 42 Saxon radiocarbon dates for Springhead contexts

Feature type	Sub-group/ feature no	Context	Sample	Material	Lab no	δ¹³C	Result BP	Cal AD date (2σ)	Phase
Sanctuary site (ARC SPH00)									
Corn drier	3475	3481	8091	*Triticum aestivum* grain	NZA 27370	-22.5	1179±30	770–990 (85.5%) 910–970 (9.9%)	mid-/late Saxon
342 watching brief east (ARC 342E02)									
pit related to SFB	105/300855	111	2	*Triticum aestivum* grain	NZA 27432	-23.5	1510±30	430–490 (14.9%) 500–630 (80.5%)	early Saxon
				Corylus avellana nutshell	NZA 27431	-26.8	1501±30	430–490 (8%) 530–640 (87.4%)	early Saxon

Present again are species that indicate the presence of rotting grain such as the 'granary weevil' *Sitophilus granarius*, the 'saw toothed grain beetle' *Oryzaephilus surinamensis*, the 'rust red grain beetle' *Laemophloeus ferrugineus* and 'the small eyed grain beetle' *Palorus ratzeburgi*. Noticeably, these species occurred in some numbers in the samples from the millrace associated with the wheelhouse of the mill.

Radiocarbon Dating
by Catherine Barnett

The radiocarbon submissions for predicted Saxon remains all dated successfully (methods outlined by Barnett in Vol 3, Chap 3), and their δ¹³C‰ values were within the normal expected ranges for the type and terrestrial source of the materials selected (see eg, Coleman and Fry 1991; http://gsc.nrcan.gc.ca/c14/delc13_e.php).

The determinations detailed in Tables 42 and 43 and plotted in Figure 38 show that all but one of the post-Roman buildings and features investigated at both Springhead and Northfleet were of early Saxon date. The calibrated date ranges span a restricted period, of cal AD 420–660. The sunken-featured buildings (SFBs) at Northfleet are shown to be contemporary with each other. The pit dated at Springhead has determinations (NZA 27431/2) statistically indistinguishable from each other. This pit appears slightly later than the SFBs at Northfleet, but the two groups have overlapping calibrated date ranges and can be said to be broadly contemporary.

The piece of vertical wheel rim, timber 25 (context 12279) queried as part of an earlier mill structure, has been dated to cal AD 575–660 (NZA 27631, 1423±30 BP), indeed slightly earlier than the main structure dated by dendrochronolgy to AD 667 (see Tyers below). It appears slightly later than the SFBs but has an overlapping calibrated date range, particularly with the pit at Springhead.

A single feature proved later in date, with a layer of burnt wheat grain in crop dryer 3475 at Springhead (ARC SPH00) dated to the mid–late Saxon period at cal AD 770–970 (NZA 27370, 1179±30 BP), indicating that it is broadly contemporary with a second possible

Table 43 Early Saxon radiocarbon dates for Northfleet contexts

Feature type	Sub-group/ feature no	Context	Sample	Material	Lab no	δ¹³C	Result BP	Cal AD date (2σ*)
Hearth in SFB	16635/10533	10534	11106	Pomoideae: rw charcoal	NZA 27437	-25.2	1564±30	420–570
SFB	30119/30081	30082	31538	1 charred grain @20–22 cm	NZA 27532	-21.2	1606±30	390–540
Posthole of SFB	30107/30087	30090	31537	*Corylus*: rw charcoal	NZA 27442	-26.0	1537±30	430–600
Mill		12279	25	*Quercus*: waterlogged wood	NZA 27631	-25.3	1423±30	575–660
SFB	16638	10272	10272	*Triticum dicoccum*: charred grain	NZA 28210	-24.6	1585±30	410–550
SFB	30107	3971013/ 30086	31114	*Triticum spelta*: charred grain	NZA28203	-22.6	1601±30	400–580

rw = roundwood; *95.4%

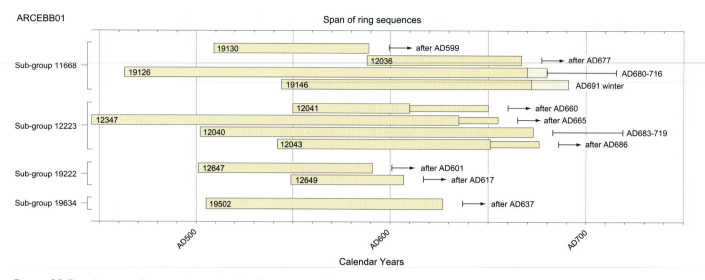

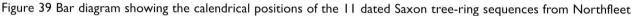

Figure 39 Bar diagram showing the calendrical positions of the 11 dated Saxon tree-ring sequences from Northfleet

crop dryer at the site (feature 3217) which contained a coin of AD 838–877.

Most of the questions addressed relate to site and feature specific enquiries. However, the results add to the overall understanding of the chronology, sequencing and development of the Saxon features and activities at Springhead and Northfleet and, in so doing, they help to put the two sites into a wider chronological framework.

Table 44 Details of the analysed Saxon dendrochronological samples from Northfleet

Context/ sample	Size (mm)	Rings	Sap rings	Date measured sequence (AD)	Intepreted result (AD)
12036	180 x 80	80	–	588–667	after 677
12040	125 x 100	172	H/S	502–673	683–719
12041	175 x 45	61 + *40*	–	550–610	after 660
12043	140 x 65	110 + *25*	–	542–651	after 686
12347/26	310 x 55	190 + *20*	–	446–635	after 665
12647/ 12124	105 x 70	91	–	501–591	after 601
12649/ 12125	90 x 35	59	–	549–607	after 617
19126/20	435 x 70	218	10	463–680	680–716
19130/28	90 x 65	81	–	509–589	after 599
19146/14	355 x 85	148	19 + Bw	544–691	691 winter
19164/29	215 x 50	99	17 + Bs	undated	
19502/ 12297	105 x 100	123	–	505–627	after 637

Key: H/S = heartwood/sapwood boundary; Bw = bark-edge, winter felled; Bs = bark-edge, spring felled
Values in italics in ring column = unmeasured rings

Dendrochronology
by Ian Tyers

Eleven samples of timber from Northfleet were successfully dated to the Saxon period (methods outlined in Tyers, Vol 3, Chap 3), representing the first group of timbers of this date analysed from the county (Table 44; Fig 39). The Saxon samples derive from four different sub-groups (three from the mill structure; see Vol 1, Chap 6) and are discussed below.

Sub-group 11668

Four samples were datable from this sub-group – the Saxon mill. The recent samples provided from this sub-group included two massive planks both with significant amounts of surviving sapwood. One of these (19146) is complete to bark-edge and this timber was felled in the winter of AD 691/2. The plank shows no sign of previous use, and thus provides an accurate building date for the mill. The result of applying sapwood estimates for the other dated sample with incomplete sapwood indicates it was felled between AD 680 and AD 716.

Sub-group 12223

Four samples were datable from this feature, part of a possible sluice gate for the mill. No sapwood is present on these timbers, but one sample ended at the heartwood/sapwood boundary, and applying sapwood estimates to this indicates this was felled between AD 683 and AD 719. One other timber has slightly later heartwood rings, further constraining the date of this sub-group to AD 686–719. This result indicates this feature is contem-poraneous, broadly at least, with the mill.

Sub-group 19222

The are two datable timbers from this sub-group – a line of stakes. These cannot have been felled before AD 617.

However, there is no sapwood on these samples, and there is nothing from the tree-ring analysis that precludes this material also being of later 7th century date.

Sub-group 19634

This sub-group is represented by a single datable timber from an alignment of posts west of the mill. The absence of sapwood means that although it was certainly felled after AD 637, there is nothing from the tree-ring analysis that precludes this material also being of later 7th century date, or later, or re-used.

Chapter 8

Post-Roman Environmental Evidence for Subsistence and Economy

As noted above, deep sedimentary sequences were generally lacking for the post-Roman period at Springhead and Northfleet. However, layers, dumps and fills directly associated with archaeological features were more plentiful and reports on the charred plant remains, charcoal and waterlogged wood are presented below.

Charred Plant Remains

Charred Plant Remains from Springhead
by Chris J Stevens

Twenty-eight samples were taken from Saxon features at Springhead. There were no Saxon features on Springhead Roadside settlement (ARC SHN02), but 17 Saxon samples came from Springhead Sanctuary site (ARC SPH00) and 11 from the watching brief (ARC 342E02). Three of the samples from ARC SPH00 came from an early Saxon sunken-featured building (SFB 5809) that contained some residual Roman pottery. Radiocarbon dating of cereal grains within this SFB confirmed that these were also redeposited and this material is discussed in Vol 3, Chap 3, in the report on the remains from the Roman period.

A total of seven samples were chosen for analysis (Table 45). Of those selected from ARC SPH00, three came from the two late Saxon crop dryers (3227 and 3475) and one from early Saxon pit 2868. Three samples were selected from the watching-brief, two from pit 105 and one from SFB 127.

It was hoped that analysis of the samples could contribute to various aspects of the project aims, in particular the general transition from the Roman administration to the Saxon political and economic landscape and what aspects of this, relating to cereal production and agricultural practices, are seen within the charred evidence.

More specifically, analysis might indicate the nature and use of individual features, particularly the SFBs and the crop dryers, as well as the mill and its implications for agricultural production.

Processing procedures and details of quantification are described elsewhere (see Stevens, Vol 3, Chap 3). In the case of one rich sample, that from crop dryer 3475, it was decided to only examine a 10% sub-sample of the 1 mm and 0.5 mm fractions. These counts were then multiplied by 10, and are shown as 'est.' in Table 45.

Results
Generally, the Saxon samples were poor in charred plant remains, though both crop dryers were much richer, in particular crop dryer 3475, which contained many thousands of items. The predominant cereal was free-threshing wheat (*Triticum aestivum sl*), although barley made up over a third of the identified cereals. While rye (*Secale cereale*) was only just under 10%, given the number of grains there can be little doubt that it was cultivated as a crop rather than representing a weed. Oats (*Avena* sp.) was reasonably well represented, although no floret bases were recovered to ascertain the presence of the cultivated species, and they are as likely to represent the wild weedy type. It might be noted that no cereal chaff was recovered from either crop dryer.

The early Saxon pits 105 and 2868 produced relatively few cereal remains, mainly of free-threshing wheat, but also hulled barley (*Hordeum vulgare sl*). Both pits had occasional unidentified glumes of hulled wheats emmer or spelt (*Triticum dicoccum/spelta*). Only one possible grain of rye (*Secale cereale*) was seen in SFB 127, and a single rachis of free-threshing wheat was identified from this same sample.

The only other crop remains positively identified was that of broad bean (*Vicia faba* var. *minor*), from early Saxon pit 105 and late Saxon crop dryer 3475. This crop dryer also contained two possible grains of lentil (*Lens culinaris*). Fragments of plum or sloe were also identified from both SFB 127 and crop dryer 3475, although no fragment was large enough to distinguish between the cultivated plum (*Prunus domestica*) and the wild sloe

Table 45 Charred plant remains from Saxon contexts at Springhead

		1	2	4	8282	8021	8021	8091
Sample		1	2	4	8282	8021	8021	8091
Site code		ARC 342E02			ARC SPH00			
Phase		Early Saxon			Early Saxon	Late Saxon		
Feature type		Pit		SFB	Pit	Corn driers		
Feature		105		127	2868	3227		3475
Context		109	111	126	2869	3190		3481
Size (l)		20.00	20.00	20.00	20	10	10	20
Flot size(ml)		50.00	175.00	60.00	50	400	300	900
Rooty matter		25.00	8.75	30.00	12.5	20	6	9
Contamination (%)		50.00	5.00	50.00	0.25	0.05	2	0.01
Charcoal relative frequency		++++	++++	++++	+	++++		++++
Percentage sorted (% 1 mm)		100	100	100	100	100	100	10
Percentage sorted (% 0.5 mm)		100	100	100	100	100	100	10
Cereals								
Hordeum vulgare L. *sl* (hulled grain)	Hulled barley	–	15	3	–	–	6	est.6030
Hordeum vulgare L. *sl* (grain)	Barley	–	–	–	–	7	20	3 tail
Triticum sp. L. (grains)	Wheat	2	1	–	–	2	–	–
T. cf. *dicoccum* Schübl./*spelta* L. (grains)	Emmer/spelt wheat		cf.1	–	–	–	–	–
T. cf. *dicoccum* Schübl./*spelta* L. (glume bases)	Emmer/spelt wheat	2	–	–	1	–	–	–
Triticum spelta L. (glume bases)	Spelt wheat	–	–	–	–	–	1	–
T.aestivum L./*durum* Desf./*turgidum* L. (grain)	Bread wheat	2	23	5	–	42	87	est.9712
T.aestivum L./*durum* Desf./*turgidum* L. (rachis frag)	Bread wheat	–	–	1	–	–	–	–
Secale cereale L. (grain)	Rye	–	–	cf.1	–	–	–	est.1616
Cereal indet. (grains)	Cereal	6	10	3	–	23	28	est.1000
Cereal indet. (est. whole grains from frags)	Cereal	–	–	6	–	8	32	–
Cereal indet. (detached coleoptile)	Cereal	–	–	–	1	–	–	–
Other Crop Species								
Corylus avellana L. (frags)	Hazel	8	33	10	–	–	1	22
Prunus sp. L.	Plum type stone	–	–	1	–	–	–	cf.2 +1fruit
Vicia faba var. *minor* L.	Broad bean	1	cf.1		–	–	–	5
Lens culinaris Medik.	Lentil	–	–		–	–	–	cf.2
Vicia sp. L./*Pisum sativum* L.	Pea/bean/large vetch	–	–	2	–	–	–	–
Species								
Chenopodium album L.	Fat hen	–	–	–	–	–	–	est.2600
Atriplex sp. L.	Oraches	–	–	–	–	–	4	est.50
Stellaria media (L.) Vill.	Stitchwort	–	–	–	–	–	–	est.10
Spergula arvensis L.	Corn spurrey	–	–	–	–	–	–	cf.1
Agrostemma githago L.	Corn cockle	–	–	–	–	–	2	est.1280
Silene sp. L.	Campions	–	–	–	–	–	–	est.20
Polygonaceae indet.		–	1m	–	–	–	–	1
Polygonum aviculare L.	Knot grass	–	–	–	–	–	–	est.40
Fallopia convolvulus (L.) Á. Löve	Black bindweed	–	–	–	–	–	–	est.60
Rumex sp. L.	Docks	–	7	1	–	–	–	est.213
Rumex acetosella L.	Sheeps sorrel	–	–	–	–	–	–	est.40
Rumex cf. *crispus* L.	Curled dock	–	–	–	–	–	3	est.150
Malva sp. L.	Mallow	–	–	–	–	–	–	est.10
Brassica sp. L.	Cabbage, wild mustard	–	cf.13m	–	–	–	–	–
Vicia L./*Lathyrus* sp. L.	Vetch/pea	–	–	–	–	–	–	est.224
cf. *Lathyrus* L. sp.	Grass–pea	–	–	–	–	–	–	est.20
Medicago lupilina L.	Black medick	–	–	–	–	–	–	est.10
Trifolium sp. L.	Clover	–	–	–	–	–	–	est.20
Large Apiaceae indet.		–	1	–	–	–	–	–
Torilis sp. Adans.	Hedge parsley	–	–	–	–	–	–	est.10
Prunella vulgaris L.	Self–heal	–	–	–	–	–	–	est.10
Mentha sp. L.	Mint	–	–	–	–	–	–	est.10
Plantago major L.	Greater Plantain	–	–	–	–	–	–	est.10
Plantago lanceolata L.	Ribwort plantain	–	–	–	–	–	–	est.20
Odontities vernus (Bellardi) Dumort.	Red bartsia	–	–	–	–	–	–	est.10
Galium sp. L. small indet.		–	–	–	–	–	–	est.10
Galium aparine L.	Cleavers	–	–	–	–	–	–	est.49
Asteraceae indet. (small)		–	–	–	–	–	–	est.20
Centaurea sp. L.	Knapweed	–	1m	–	–	–	–	–
Lapsana communis L.	Nipplewort	–	–	–	–	–	–	est.20
Anthemis cotula L.	Stinking chamomile	–	–	–	–	–	–	est.470

Table 45 Charred plant remains from Saxon contexts at Springhead (continued)

Sample		1	2	4	8282	8021	8021	8091
Site code		ARC 342E02				ARC SPH00		
Phase		Early Saxon			Early Saxon	Late Saxon		
Feature type		Pit		SFB	Pit	Corn driers		
Feature		105		127	2868	3227		3475
Context		109	111	126	2869	3190		3481
Size (l)		20.00	20.00	20.00	20	10	10	20
Flot size(ml)		50.00	175.00	60.00	50	400	300	900
Rooty matter		25.00	8.75	30.00	12.5	20	6	9
Contamination (%)		50.00	5.00	50.00	0.25	0.05	2	0.01
Charcoal relative frequency		++++	++++	++++	+	++++		++++
Percentage sorted (% 1 mm)		100	100	100	100	100	100%	10
Percentage sorted (% 0.5 mm)		100	100	100	100	100	100	10
Tripleurospermum inodorum (L.) Sch. Bip.	Scentless mayweed	–	–	–	–	–	–	est.20
Cyperaceae indet.	Sedges	–	1	–	–	–	–	–
Schoenoplectus lacustris (L.) Palla	Club–rush	–	1	–	–	–	–	est.10
Carex sp. L. lenticular	Sedge flat seed	–	–	–	–	–	–	est.10
Carex sp. L. triganous	Sedge trigonous seed	–	–	–	–	–	–	est.20
Poaceae (small indet.)	Small grass seed	–	–	–	–	–	–	est.180
Lolium perenne L.	Rye grass	–	–	–	–	–	–	est.290
Avena sp. L. (grain)	Oat grain	–	9	1	–	–	–	est.349
Avena L./*Bromus* L. sp.	Oat/brome	–	–	–	–	–	–	2
Phleum sp. L.	Cat's tails	–	–	–	–	–	–	est.170
Bromus sp. L.	Brome	–	–	–	–	1	–	est.62
Seed indet. large		–	–	–	–	–	stone?	–
Seed indet.		–	–	–	–	–	1	–
Seed indet. small		–	–	–	–	–	–	est.30
Mineralised nodules (large)		–	–	–	9	–	–	–
OTHER								
Conglomerated stems and grains		–	–	–	–	–	–	+++

(*Prunus spinosa*). Hazelnut (*Corylus avellana*) is well represented by fragments in most of the samples.

Weed seeds were scarce in all but the sample from crop dryer 3475 in which they were very well represented. Seeds of fat-hen (*Chenopodium album*) were present in high numbers in this feature, as were those of corncockle (*Agrostemma githago*). Seeds of stinking mayweed (*Anthemis cotula*), perennial rye-grass (*Lolium perenne*), vetches/wild pea (*Vicia*/*Lathyrus* sp.), brome grass (*Bromus* sp.) and oats (*Avena* sp.) were numerous although, as noted above, the latter species may be of the cultivated rather than the wild variety. Seeds of dock (*Rumex* sp.), most probably curled leaved dock (*Rumex crispus*), based on the many well preserved specimens with characteristic 'sharp-edges', were well represented. Small grass seeds were also frequent in this sample, including those of cat's-tail (*Phleum* sp.).

Most of the other species present within the sample are common arable weeds including those of black bindweed (*Fallopia convolvulus*), knotgrass (*Polygonum aviculare*), cleavers (*Galium aparine*), sheep's sorrel (*Rumex acetosella*) and orache (*Atriplex* sp.).

Others species, seen through the presence of one to two seeds, included stitchwort (*Stellaria media*), clover (*Trifolium* sp.), ribwort plantain (*Plantago lanceolata*),

mallow (*Malva* sp.), nipplewort (*Lapsana communis*), scentless mayweed (*Tripleurospermum inodorum*), sedge (*Carex* sp.), campion (*Silene* sp.), black medick (*Medicago* sp.), self-heal (*Prunella vulgaris*) and red bartsia (*Odontites vernus*). Of the other features, late Saxon crop dryer 3227 produced only a few seeds of curled leaved dock (*Rumex crispus*), orache (*Atriplex* sp.), corncockle (*Agrostemma githago*), and brome grass (*Bromus* sp.).

While pit 105 produced a few charred seeds of docks (*Rumex* sp.) and oats (*Avena* sp.), and single seeds of sedge and club rush (*Schoenoplectus lacustris*), it also produced several mineralised seeds including those of probable cabbage/mustard (*Brassica* sp.), as well as knapweed (*Centaurea* sp.) and Polygonaceae.

Discussion
Cultivated crops
The dominance of free-threshing wheat (*Triticum aestivum sl*) and barley (*Hordeum vulgare sl*), with evidence for rye in the later Saxon period, is seen generally from the Saxon into the medieval period across England as a whole (Greig 1991). The dominance of these crops, and the general absence of the hulled wheats emmer and spelt (*Triticum dicoccum*/*spelta*), marks a

significant cultural development accompanying the changing political situation and the arrival of the Saxon peoples from the east.

To what extent this may be related to a changing economic environment is uncertain. Free-threshing cereals require less processing, making them desirable especially where trade and transport are involved (Green 1981; Jones 1981; Hillman 1981). However, they are more susceptible than hulled wheats to loss both in the field and during storage through mould, fungi and insect predation, so that improvements in storage might also lead to them being preferred over spelt.

Of interest were the remains of the hulled wheats emmer and spelt (*Triticum dicoccum/spelta*) which were present in several early Saxon features, and a single glume of probable spelt recovered from one sample within late Saxon crop dryer 3227. The question arises of whether such remains are likely to represent crops grown in the Saxon period, or whether they are in fact reworked or residual (Greig 1991). The answer appears to be both.

Grains of both emmer and spelt from Northfleet were radiocarbon dated to the early Saxon period (see W Smith below), indicating that these crops were probably still cultivated in the 5th–6th centuries. However, radiocarbon dates on spelt wheat from a Saxon SFB (5809) at Springhead indicated a Roman date for this material, showing it to be residual.

Murphy (1985) suggests that spelt was cultivated at West Stow until the 5th century, while finds from the Thames Valley indicate the cultivation of emmer up until the 9th century (Pelling and Robinson 2000). The general absence of hulled wheats from the richer later Saxon deposits at Springhead might indicate that it went out of cultivation prior to the 9th century on this site.

The status of rye is that it appears as a definite crop within a sample from one of the late Saxon crop dryers, but is generally absent within the early Saxon samples from both this site and Northfleet (see W Smith below). Rye is certainly known from early Saxon sites in East Anglia (Murphy 1985), and mid-Saxon London (Carruthers 2004; Davies 2003; Davis and de Moulins 1988), while finds from Saltwood Tunnel, Kent may be mid- or late Saxon in date (Stevens 2006b).

The only other crop identified was broad bean (*Vicia faba*), which as well as being present in the Roman period (see Stevens, Vol 3, Chap 4), has also been recovered in large quantities from late Bronze Age deposits elsewhere in Kent (Stevens 2006b). Two grains of possible lentil (*Lens culinaris*) were recovered from one of the crop dryers, but could not be confirmed. Lentil is known from a number of Saxon sites in southern England, and the circumstance that many of these sites are low-status rural settlements has led to the suggestion that it may have been locally cultivated (Moffett 1988; Grieg 1991; Stevens 1997).

Arable husbandry

Given the small number of weed seeds in the early Saxon samples, little information can be gleaned on the nature of arable husbandry for this period. Most of the seeds are either of docks (*Rumex* sp.) or oats (*Avena* sp.), which ecologically are relatively unspecific. However, the presence of single seeds of sedge and common/grey club rush (*Schoenoplectus lacustris/tabernaemontani*) may indicate that fields with crops extended into areas bordering seasonally flooded marshland. The general absence of weeds in these earlier samples may also indicate that crops were stored relatively clean with most of the waste disposed of in the field, leaving only minimal sorting and sieving to prepare the crop for consumption or use.

The later Saxon samples were generally richer in plant remains, in particular that from crop dryer 3475. A wide range of weed species was recovered from this feature, covering a range of different ecological habitats. This crop dryer also contained a wide range of crops with rye, free-threshing wheat and hulled barley all present. This might imply that rather than a single crop being present, separate crops have become mixed within the feature. However, it is possible that the crops were sown together, as a maslin, although generally rye and wheat are the commoner combination within medieval records, usually cultivated in direct response to land pressure, increasing population and general declining yields (Campbell 1983; 2000).

With regards to the time of sowing today, rye tends to be regarded as a winter crop, and this appears to be true for medieval times (Fitzherbert 1523; Tusser 1580). These same authors also recommend the sowing of barley in spring, although Tusser (1580) provides instructions for the sowing of rye and wheat, along with barley in his entry for tasks conducted in March.

High numbers of seeds of the Chenopodiaceae, as seen in the crop dryer, can be associated with nitrogen-rich fertile soils and/or spring sowing. However, given the use of traditional fertilisers that more strongly rely on the breakdown of nitrates by soil organisms, the association with spring sowing is probably the stronger. Generally, most of the species are either found in spring-sown crops or common in both spring and autumn. The exceptions are nipplewort (*Lapsana communis*), cleavers (*Galium aparine*), vetches/wild pea (*Vicia/Lathyrus* sp.) and rye-grass (*Lolium* sp.), which all tend to be commoner in autumn sown crops.

Ecologically the assemblage shows some variation in the species present, and may provide further supporting evidence of the mixing of crops from different harvests in the crop dryer. Of the more ecologically specific species present, sheep's sorrel (*Rumex acetosella*) and to a lesser extent scentless mayweed (*Tripleurospermum inodorum*) are both common on lighter, drier, slightly acidic soils, while stinking mayweed (*Anthemis cotula*) is commoner on heavier clay soils, as is also nipplewort (*Lapsana communis*). Finally, as stated above, common/grey club rush (*Schoenoplectus lacustris/tabernaemontani*) is commoner in flooded areas. Apart from stinking mayweed (*Anthemis cotula*), many of these elements were relatively scarce, and do not totally preclude the possibility that the assemblage came from a single field.

Seeds of annual species, which can be seen as a general indication of a moderately high level of soil disturbance, were well represented with relatively few seeds of perennials. On the basis of pictorial evidence, the introduction and use of the mouldboard is questionable prior to the 12th century (Blair 1977; Rees 1979). The appearance and gradual increase in stinking mayweed (*Anthemis cotula*) can generally be associated with changing methods of tillage (Jones 1981). The first appearance of this species occurs with the introduction of asymmetrical ploughs and iron coulters in the Roman period, with both becoming notably more common in the later Roman period. Such ploughs would undoubtedly have made the working of clay soils much easier; however, it is notable that such evidence is only largely forthcoming from more Romanised settlements. The increase in this species seen in the Saxon period suggests that along with rye and free-threshing wheat, the Saxons introduced new ploughing technologies to the lower status rural farmer.

Crop dryer 3475

Concerning the use of the crop dryer, it might be noted that, during the processing of the free-threshing cereals (*cf* Hillman 1981; 1984b), threshing separates the grain from the ear, often leaving the rachis relatively intact. Winnowing separates off the lighter paleas and lemmas, and sieving with a coarse sieve removes the still intact rachises and straw, along with weed seedheads, while the grain, grain-sized and smaller weed seeds fall through the sieve. Further, smaller weed seeds are removed with fine-sieving, while grain-size weed seeds are removed in the very final stages by hand.

The absence of rachis fragments, therefore, implies that the crop had at least been threshed and winnowed, with the removal of most of the rachises, before the grains became charred. The dominance of grain over weed seeds is to be expected if the assemblage comprises the crop product being either accidentally charred, or possibly deriving from sweepings of spilt grain during drying. The conditions of preservation and the presence of a large quantity of burnt daub suggest a single charring event.

The exact purpose of such crop dryers is often unclear and, as with the Roman period, it might be assumed that they were used for drying the crop prior to storage, to facilitate processing or to terminate malting.

Hillman (1981, fig 6) lists a number of stages at which the crop may be dried and/or exposed to fire. While crops are dried in the field prior to being threshed, this rarely involves the use of ovens. Rather, they are usually dried back at the settlement in ovens or kilns just prior to being put into storage. Unlike hulled wheats, free-threshing wheats require little further processing and are not subject to heat other than within the cooking process, for example preparation in groats (Hillman 1981, fig 7).

As the final stages of cooking are unlikely to be carried out in bulk, the use of such ovens could only be for malt or for drying prior to storage. That the samples consist predominantly of free-threshing wheat (*Triticum aestivum sl*) would make the former less likely and, unlike the Roman period, certainly no evidence was seen for malting in any of the grains.

This makes drying of the crop prior to storage the most likely function of the crop dryer. If the assemblage is from a single event, then it is notable that no rachis fragments appear in the crop, implying that threshing, winnowing, coarse-sieving and raking were conducted in the field and that such waste generated during these operations was left in the field. The number of small weed seeds was quite high, but the absence of rachis fragments implies that either fine-sieving had not taken place or such fine-sieving as had taken place was not that thorough. Against this interpretation is the fact that the crop dryer seems to have a number of crops mixed within it, and one might expect that unless grown as a maslin they would be harvested, processed, dried and stored separately.

Charred Plant Remains from Northfleet

by Wendy Smith

Of the 247 samples collected from Roman and Saxon features during the excavations at Northfleet villa, 11 samples dated to the Saxon period were selected for full analysis of charred plant remains. The methodologies employed for both assessment and analysis of the samples from Northfleet are outlined in the section covering the Roman period (see W Smith, Vol 3, Chap 4).

Results

The results for the Saxon samples are presented by phase in Tables 46–8 and in Figures 40–1. The Saxon deposits are not as rich as the Roman samples and, in all cases, 100% of the flot was sorted for analysis. Spelt glume bases and spikelet forks are recovered in the 5th–6th century samples; however, spelt chaff is noticeably less frequent in the nine 6th–7th century samples. Hulled barley grain is frequently recovered from Saxon deposits and several samples have produced wheat grains which are clearly compact (small-sized and very rounded in profile).

5th–6th century deposits

Only two samples were fully analysed from this early phase of the Saxon period at Northfleet villa – a sample from within an SFB (sample 11102) and a sample from a hearth (sample 11106) (Tables 46 and *48*, Fig 40). The SFB sample contained a fairly even mixture of cereal grain (27.1%), cereal chaff (39.0%) and weed/wild taxa (9.2%). The hearth sample contained a mixture of cereal grain (26.3%) and weed/wild taxa (39.0%); however, a large number of indeterminate plant remains (n = 111) were

Table 46 Charred plant remains recovered from 5th/6th century Saxon deposits at Northfleet villa

		Sample	11102	11106
		Sub-group	16638	16635
		Feature type	SFB	Hearth
		Feature	10271	10533
		Context	10272	10534
		Proportion sorted (%)	50	25
		Size (l)	40	40
		Flot size(ml)	290	300
		Seeds per litre	14.6	50.5
Cereals				
Hordeum sp. (hulled)	Hulled barley		9	12
Hordeum sp. (hulled germinated)			–	2
Triticum cf. *dicoccum* Schübl.	Emmer wheat		1	–
Triticum dicoccum Schübl./*spelta* L.	Emmer/spelt		1	–
Triticum spelta L.	Spelt wheat		–	1
Triticum aestivum L./*durum* Desf./*turgidum* L. – type	Bread wheat		10	–
Triticum sp. (indet.)	Wheat		–	27
Cereal (indet.)	Cereal		40E	38E
Cereal (indet. germinated)			–	1
Cereal/large Poaceae (indet.)	Cereal/large grass		18	55E
Cereal/large Poaceae (indet. germinated)			1	–
Cereal chaff				
Hordeum sp. (indet. rachis node)			4	–
Triticum spelta L. (spikelet fork)			1 = 1gb + 1r	–
Triticum spelta L. (glume base)			34	2
Triticum spelta L. (glume/lemma frags)			(+)	(+)
Triticum aestivum L./*durum* Desf./*turgidum* L. – type rachis node			2	–
Triticum sp. (spikelet fork)			21E = 33gb	1 = 2gb
Triticum sp. (glume base)			20E	8
Triticum sp. (rachis node)			19	5E
Triticum sp. (awn)			(+)	–
Cereal (indet. rachis internode)			–	13
Cereal/large Poaceae (glume)			–	(+)
Coleoptile/detached embryo				
Cereal/large Poaceae (coleoptile) (estimate m.n.i.)			4	1
Cereal/large Poaceae (detached embryo)			5	21
Other crops				
Vicia faba L. var minor	Broad bean		1E	–
Vicia sp./*Pisum sativum* L.	Bean/pea		2E	–
Tree/shrub				
Corylus avellana L. (nutshell frags)	Hazel		–	1
Weed/wild plants				
Papaver rhoeas L/*dubium* L./*argemone* L.	Field poppy		–	2
Chenopodium sp.	Goosefoot		1	9E
Atriplex spp.	Oraches		3	1
Chenopodium spp./*Atriplex* spp.	Goosefoot/oraches		1	–
Cerastium spp.			1	1
cf. *Agrostemma githago* L. (calyx tip)	Corn cockle		2	–
Polygonum spp./*Rumex* spp./*Carex* spp.(indet. internal structure)			1	3
Fallopia convolvulus (L.) Á. Löve	Black bindweed		–	2
Rumex spp.	Docks		2	2
Malva spp.	Mallow		–	1
Brassica cf. *rapa* L.	Field mustard		–	1
Brassica nigra (L.) W.D.J. Koch	Black mustard		–	16
Vicia spp./*Lathyrus* spp.	Vetch/pea		1	2
Melilotus spp./*Medicago* spp./*Trifolium* spp.	Clovers		–	3
Apiaceae (indet.)			–	1
Euphrasia sp./*Odontites* sp.	Eyebright/bartsia		1	3
Lamiaceae (indet.)			–	2
Galium spp.	Bedstraw		–	1
Lapsana communis L.	Nipplewort		–	2
Anthemis cotula L.	Stinking camomile		1	48
cf. *Anthemis cotula* L./*Tripleurospermum inodorum* (L.) Sch. Bip.	Stinking camomile/Scented mayweed		–	31E
Tripleurospermum inodorum (L.) Sch. Bip.	Scented mayweed		2	–
Asteraceae (indet.)			3	1
Carex spp. (2-sided)	Sedges		–	1
Carex spp. (3-sided)			–	2
Avena sp.	Oat		1	7E

Table 46 Charred plant remains recovered from 5th–6th century Saxon deposits at Northfleet villa (continued)

	Sub-group	16638	16635
	Feature type	SFB	Hearth
	Feature	10271	10533
	Context	10272	10534
	Proportion sorted (%)	50	25
	Size (l)	40	40
	Flot size (ml)	290	300
	Seeds per litre	14.6	50.5
Avena sp. (floret base)		–	3
Avena sp. (awn) (estimate m.n.i.)		1	1
Avena sp./*Bromus* sp.	Oat/Brome	–	23E
Poaceae (indet. small caryopsis)	Grasses	3	3
Poaceae (indet. medium caryopsis)		3	3
Poaceae (indet. large caryopsis)		–	2E
Unidentified (capsule frag)		2	–
Unidentified (mineralised seed)		7	3
Unidentified		7	10
Indeterminate		43	111
Total identifications		292	505

SFB 31118 (68.5%), pit 31520 (72.3%), SFB 31522 (60.4%) and SFB 31527 (71.1%)) were dominated by cereal grain (*Table 49*). The two hearth samples (31516 (50.2%) and 31531 (75.0%)) were dominated by weed/wild taxa. The two remaining SFB samples (31530 and 31534 from SFB 30119) contained a mixture of cereal grain (40.0% and 45.6% respectively), cereal chaff (24.2% and 13.6% respectively) and weed/wild taxa (15.0% and 16.8% respectively). Notably, samples from this phase on site produced little or no spelt spikelet forks or glume bases (Table 47).

recovered, most likely as a factor of fairly poor preservation in this sample, possibly as a consequence of direct exposure to high temperatures. Small quantities of germinated cereal grain, detached embryos and sprouts (coleoptiles) were also recovered in both samples (3.4% and 5.0% respectively).

6th–7th century deposits

Nine samples were fully analysed from this phase of the Saxon deposits at Northfleet villa, including six samples from SFBs (samples 31114 and 31118 from SFB 30107, samples 31522 and 31527 from SFB 30057 and samples 31530 and 31534 from SFB 30119), two hearth samples (31516 and 31531) and one pit sample (31520) (Tables 47 and *48*, Fig 41). Six samples (SFB 31114 (79.2%),

Discussion

The Saxon assemblage recovered from Northfleet was not as rich or as well-preserved as the Roman assemblage. Nevertheless, there are some intriguing results. First, there is a clear continuity of spelt cultivation into the 5th–6th centuries; however, barley grain becomes much more dominant in the later 6th–7th century deposits. Rye, a commonly cultivated Saxon cereal, is absent from the deposits fully analysed here, suggesting that at least at Northfleet, this crop was not widely adopted in the first two centuries of the Saxon period. The weed/wild taxa recovered provide an indication of the variety of soil conditions cultivated and there does appear to be a subtle shift in the taxa recovered between the two Saxon phases.

Continuity and changes in cereal cultivation

Eleven samples were analysed from Saxon phases at Northfleet villa (*Table 48*); however, only two samples dating to the 5th–6th centuries were fully analysed and, therefore, these could be unrepresentative of activity in the period. Nevertheless both samples contain grain and/or chaff remains of spelt and indeterminate glume wheat, suggesting that spelt cultivation continued into the first century of Saxon occupation at Northfleet villa. Although small quantities of spelt or indeterminate glume wheat chaff are present in the nine samples studied from the second phase of Saxon occupation (dating to the 6th–7th centuries), it is clear that hulled barley (*Hordeum* sp.) remains, primarily grain, become much more dominant. With only a few samples from the

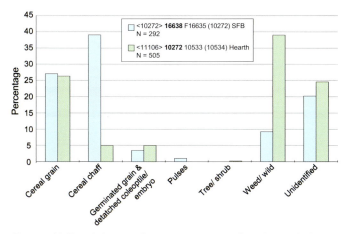

Figure 40 Breakdown of plant categories for charred plant remains from 5th–6th century Saxon deposits from Northfleet villa

Table 47 Charred plant remains recovered from 6th–7th century Saxon deposits at Northfleet villa

Sample	31114	31118	31516	31520	31522	31527	31530	31531	31534
Sub–group	30107	30107	30009	30015	30107	30057	30119	30078	30119
Feature type	SFB	SFB	Hearth	Pit	SFB	SFB	SFB	Hearth	SFB
Feature	3971016/ 30084	3971016/ 30084	30009	30015	30084	30058	30081	30078	30081
Context	3971013/ 30086	3971013/ 30086	30012	30019	30086	30060	30082	30079	30082
Proportion sorted (%)	100	100	100	100	100	100	100	100	100
Size (l)	40	40	40	10	40	10	30	30	40
Flot size(ml)	200	150	125	30	125	25	125	25	100
Seeds per litre	3.6	2.2	33.2	40.5	1.2	32.2	4	5.6	3.1

Cereals

Hordeum sp. (hulled)	Hulled barley	21	7	132	114	6	10	5	–	5
Hordeum sp. (hulled, straight)		–	–	5	–	–	–	–	–	–
Hordeum sp. (hulled, twisted)		–	–	2	–	–	–	1	–	–
Hordeum sp. (hulled germinated)		–	2	–	13	–	–	–	–	–
cf. *Hordeum* sp. (hulled)		2	–	29	–	2	2	6	–	–
Hordeum sp./*Avena* sp.(indet.) Barley/Oat		4	–	–	–	–	–	–	–	–
Hordeum sp./*Triticum* sp. (indet.)		–	–	1	–	–	–	–	–	–
Triticum cf. *dicoccum* Schübl. Emmer		–	–	–	–	–	–	–	1	1
Triticum dicoccum Schübl./ *spelta* L. Emmer/Spelt wheat		–	–	–	–	–	–	–	–	1
Triticum dicoccum Schübl./*spelta* L. (germinated)		1	–	–	–	–	–	–	–	–
Triticum spelta L.		3	–	–	–	–	–	–	–	1
Triticum aestivum L./*durum* Desf./*turgidum* L. – type Bread wheat		–	–	–	–	–	84	–	–	–
Triticum sp. (indet.) Wheat		–	14	–	4	2	10	2	1	23
Triticum sp. (indet., compact variety)		25	1	103	–	–	–	–	–	–
Triticum sp. (indet. tail grain)		1	1	–	–	–	10	–	–	1
Cereal (indet.) Cereal		44	26E	194E	55E	15	13E	15E	8E	13E
Cereal (indet. germinated)		–	–	–	8	–	–	–	–	–
Cereal/large Poaceae (indet.) Cereal/grasses		14E	12E	111E	120E	4	100E	19E	3E	12E

Cereal Chaff

Hordeum sp. (indet. rachis node)		–	–	–	–	–	–	1	–	1
cf. *Hordeum* sp. (rachis node)		–	–	–	–	–	–	–	–	1
Triticum dicoccum Schübl./*spelta* L. (glume base)		–	1	–	–	–	–	–	–	–
Triticum spelta L. (glume base)		–	–	1	–	–	–	2	1	1
Triticum aestivum L./*durum* Desf./*turgidum* L. – type rachis node		–	–	–	–	–	–	1	–	2
Triticum sp. (spikelet fork)		–	–	–	–	1 = 2gb	–	–	–	1 = 2gb
Triticum sp. (glume base)		1	1	1	–	1	–	9	–	5
Triticum sp. (rachis node)		1E	1	–	–	–	–	10	1	1
Triticum sp. (glume/lemma frags)		(+)	(+)	–	–	–	–	–	–	–
Cereal (indet. rachis internode)		–	–	1	–	1	–	6	–	3
Cereal/large Poaceae (culm base)		–	–	–	–	–	–	–	–	1
Cereal/large Poaceae (culm node)		–	–	–	1	–	1	–	–	–

Coleoptile/detached embryo

Cereal/large Poaceae (coleoptile (est. mni)		–	1	–	29	–	1	1	–	–
Cereal/large Poaceae (detached embryo)		–	1	30	9	–	36	4	–	3

Other crops

Vicia faba L. var minor Broad bean		1	–	–	–	–	–	–	–	–
Vicia sp./*Pisum sativum* L. Bean/Pea		6E	1	–	–	2E	1	2	–	4E

Tree/shrub

Corylus avellana L. (nutshell frags) Hazel		2	–	–	–	–	–	–	–	–

Weed/wild plants

Chenopodium sp. Goosefoot		–	2	307	2	–	10E	3	–	1
Atriplex spp. Oraches		–	–	23	1	–	–	–	–	–
Chenopodium spp./*Atriplex* spp.		–	–	260	2	–	–	–	–	–
Persicaria sp. Knotweed		–	–	1	–	–	–	–	–	–
Polygonum aviculare L. Knotgrass		–	–	2	–	–	–	–	–	–
Polygonum spp.		–	–	2	–	–	–	–	–	–
Polygonum spp./*Rumex* spp./*Carex* spp. (indet. internal structure)		–	–	–	–	–	1	–	1	–
Fallopia convolvulus (L.) Á. Löve Black bindweed		–	–	–	–	–	1	–	–	–
Rumex spp. Docks		–	–	3	1	–	–	–	–	–
Malva spp. Mallow		–	–	3	–	–	2	1	7	–
cf. *Thlapsi arvense* L. Penny cress		–	–	–	–	–	1	–	–	–

Table 47 Charred plant remains recovered from 6th–7th century Saxon deposits at Northfleet villa

		30107	30107	30009	30015	30107	30057	30119	30078	30119
Sub–group		SFB	SFB	Hearth	Pit	SFB	SFB	SFB	Hearth	SFB
Feature type Feature		3971016/ 30084	3971016/ 30084	30009	30015	30084	30058	30081	30078	30081
Context		3971013/ 30086	3971013/ 30086	30012	30019	30086	30060	30082	30079	30082
Proportion sorted (%)		100	100	100	100	100	100	100	100	100
Size (l)		40	40	40	10	40	10	30	30	40
Flot size(ml)		200	150	125	30	125	25	125	25	100
Seeds per litre		3.6	2.2	33.2	40.5	1.2	32.2	4	5.6	3.1
Rubus spp. section Rubus	Bramble	–	–	1	–	–	–	–	–	–
Vicia hirsuta (L.) Gray	Hairy tare	–	1	–	–	–	–	–	–	1
Vicia spp./*Lathyrus* spp.	Tare/Pea	–	–	10	–	2E	–	1	2	3E
Melilotus spp./*Medicago* spp./ *Trifolium* spp.	Clovers	–	–	–	–	–	–	–	9	1
Apiaceae (indet.)		–	–	–	–	–	–	–	1	–
Solanum nigrum L.	Black nightshade	–	–	–	–	–	–	–	5	–
cf. *Solanum nigrum* L.		–	–	–	–	–	–	–	4	–
Plantago media L./*lanceolata* L.	Plantain	–	–	–	–	–	–	–	–	1
Lamiaceae (indet.)		–	–	–	–	–	–	–	3	–
Galium cf. *mollugo* L. – type	Hedge bedstraw	–	–	1	–	–	–	–	–	–
Lapsana communis L.	Nipplewort	–	–	8	–	–	–	–	–	–
Anthemis cotula L.	Stinking mayweed	–	–	3	–	–	1	1	–	1
Juncus spp.	Rushes	–	–	–	–	–	1	–	–	–
Eleocharis palustris (L.) Roem. & Schult./*uniglumis* (Link) Schult.	Spikerush	–	–	1	–	–	–	–	–	–
Schoenplectus spp.	Club rush	–	–	2	–	–	–	–	–	–
Carex spp. (3–sided)	Sedges	–	–	7	–	–	–	1	32	–
Cyperaceae (indet.)		1	–	–	1	–	–	–	–	–
Briza media L./*minor* L.	Quaking grass	–	–	–	–	–	–	–	33	–
Briza cf. *maxima* L.	Greater quaking grass	–	–	–	–	–	–	–	25	–
Avena sp.	Oat	–	–	5	1	–	3	–	–	–
Avena sp. (floret base)		–	–	–	–	–	1	–	–	–
Avena sp. (awn (est. mni)		–	–	(+)	–	–	–	1	–	1
Avena sp./*Bromus* sp.	Oat/Brome	2	2	14	–	3	8	9	1	5
Bromus sp.	Brome	–	–	2	–	–	–	–	–	–
Poaceae (indet. small caryopsis)	Grasses	–	–	2	4	1	1	–	3	2
Poaceae (indet. medium caryopsis)		–	1	7	–	–	–	–	–	–
Poaceae (indet. large caryopsis)		1E	3	1	–	1	6E	1	–	5E
Poaceae (indet. rachis node)		–	–	1	–	–	–	–	–	–
Poaceae (indet. culm node)		1	–	–	–	–	–	–	–	–
Unidentified (capsule frag)		–	–	–	–	–	–	–	–	–
Unidentfied (mineralised seed)		9	9	–	–	–	–	–	–	–
Unidentified (seed coat/pod (frags)		–	–	3	–	–	7	1	–	–
Unidentified		–	2	45	10	–	2	2	25	1
Indeterminate		5	–	4	30	6	9	15	2	22
Total identifications		144	89	1328	405	48	322	120	168	125

first Saxon phase, it is difficult to make much of this data, although it suggests that patterns of Roman spelt cultivation are maintained in the earliest phase of Saxon activity at Northfleet but shift to barley cultivation in the 6th–7th centuries.

Continuity and changes in weed taxa

The changes observed in cereal cultivation can also be detected in the weed/wild taxa recovered (*Table 48*). Common weed taxa in the Roman period such as scentless mayweed (*Tripleurospermum inodorum*) appears in the first Saxon phase but is absent from the 6th–7th century deposits. Stinking chamomile (*Anthemis cotula*) has a very interesting result. This taxon is found in low quantities in the early–middle Roman phases but in fairly large concentrations in the late Roman and first

Saxon phase. Stinking chamomile occurs frequently on heavy clay and clay-loam soils and, although less common on 'medium texture' soils, can usually be found in poorly drained situations (Kay 1971, 625). The shift from scentless mayweed – a plant typical of medium to light texture, well-drained soils (Kay 1994, 682) – to stinking chamomile may simply be happenstance, since stinking chamomile is very 'plastic' and occurs in a wide range of habitats (Kay 1971, 623). Stinking chamomile typically produce between 100–160 capitula (seed heads) and can produce as many as 2700 achenes (*ibid*, 629 and 632). In addition in both the late Roman and the first phase of the Saxon occupation only a few samples were studied (five in the Late Roman and two in the first Saxon phase), which may not be truly representative of the full range of weed/wild taxa present

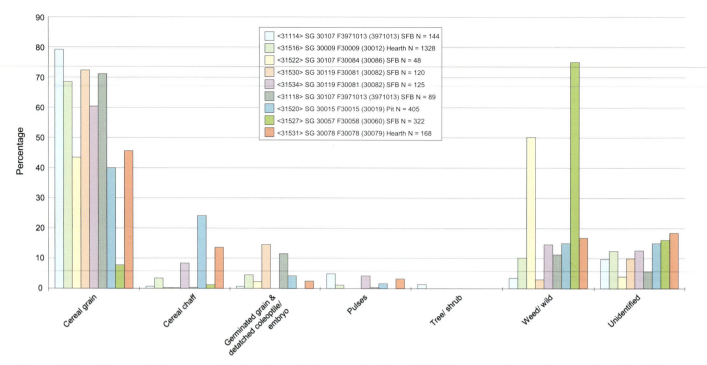

Figure 41 Breakdown of plant categories for charred plant remains from 6th–7th century Saxon deposits from Northfleet villa

at the time. Nevertheless, this change is coupled with an increase in the range and number of taxa typical of wet or damp habitats, such as common/slender spike-rush (*Eleocharis palustris/uniglumis*), club-rush (*Schoenoplectus* spp), knotweed (*Persicaria* spp.), rush (*Juncus* spp.) and sedge (*Carex* spp.), suggesting cultivation of heavier and damper soils than those cultivated in the Roman period. This does not necessarily indicate cultivation of new soils; it is possible that Roman field drainage systems were beginning to fail by the 6th–7th centuries AD.

Rye – a significant absence?

Rye (*Secale cereale*) was adopted as a cultivated cereal crop in the Saxon period (eg, Green 1994); however, not in all regions and not instantly. The absence of significant quantities of rye in all of the Saxon samples studied does suggest that at Northfleet villa, at least, rye was not widely in use in the 5th–7th centuries.

The Saxon weed flora

The majority of weed/wild taxa recovered typically occur as weeds of arable crops or on cultivated/disturbed ground (*Table 48*). Many of the taxa recovered in the Roman period are still present in the Saxon phases, possibly suggesting some continuity in the land under cultivation. As discussed above, there are subtle shifts in the range of taxa between the first and second Saxon

phases. Certainly the range of taxa typical of damp to wet conditions has increased.

One result of note is that hearth sample 31531 produced a quantity of quaking grass/lesser-quaking grass (*Briza media/minor*) and possible greater quaking grass (*Briza cf. maxima*) caryopses. Quaking grass (*Briza media*) is typical of calcareous soils and can occur in quite damp to dry conditions (Dixon 2002, 738–9), but lesser-quaking grass (*Biza minor*) and possible greater quaking grass (*Briza cf. maxima*) typically occur as arable weeds, with lesser-quaking grass considered possibly native and greater quaking grass considered a Mediterranean introduction to the British Flora (Stace 1997, 856). Their recovery is limited to this hearth sample and may simply reflect the gathering of dry grasses as kindling.

Comparison with other Saxon sites

Charred plant macrofossil assemblages from Kent are limited, and only three sites from Section 1 of the HS 1 excavations have produced Saxon period assemblages. Both Cuxton (Davis 2008a) and Little Stock Farm (Stevens 2008c) have produced a few small assemblages; however, ten Saxon period samples were studied by Stevens (2008a) from North of Saltwood Tunnel. The ten Saltwood Tunnel samples all produced spelt and indeterminate glume wheat grain and chaff remains, again suggesting continuity with the Roman cultivation of spelt at that site, a feature also seen with the first phase of Saxon occupation at Northfleet villa. In addition, Saltwood tunnel produced broad bean (*Vicia faba*) identifications, as was seen at Northfleet villa. However, unlike Northfleet villa, rye (*Secale cereale*) grain was present in small numbers in a few of the Saltwood Tunnel samples. This may suggest that rye was a contaminant of the spelt and/or barley crops, rather than a main cultivar (as was interpreted for the rye from Roman deposits at Northfleet). Certainly, it suggests that although rye was available, it was not the main cultivated cereal in use in this area of Kent during the 5th–7th centuries. Unlike Saltwood Tunnel, however, compact forms of wheat were observed at Northfleet villa. Compact wheat (identified as *Triticum aestivo-compactum*) has been observed at the Peabody Museum Site, London, where it was considered the main variety of wheat cultivated in these mid-Saxon deposits (de Moulins 1989, 134).

Conclusions

Saxon deposits at Northfleet villa were less rich than the Roman, and not particularly well-preserved. Nevertheless, they provide some evidence for a continuity of spelt cultivation into the 5th–6th centuries AD. Ultimately, however, spelt cultivation appears to be superseded by cultivation of hulled barley at Northfleet villa.

Wood Charcoal
by Catherine Barnett

Wood Charcoal from Springhead

Two samples were analysed from late Saxon contexts at Springhead (ARC SPH00), both crop dryers (3227 and 3475) (see Vol 1, Fig 5.2). The taxa identified are listed in *Table 49*. A larger number of fragments were recovered from feature 3227 than 3475, but a similar range of taxa was identified in both assemblages. Field maple (*Acer campestre*), silver/downy birch (*Betula pendula/pubescens*) and particularly hawthorn-type pomaceous fruits (Pomoideae, *Crataegus* sp.) were common in both, while alder (*Alnus glutinosa*) occurred only in 3475 and hazel (*Corylus avellana*) only in 3227 where it formed 35% of the assemblage.

The range of deciduous tree and shrub types indicates local collection and a willingness to use semi-natural resources for use as fuel rather than targeting or managing particular tree types.

Wood Charcoal from Northfleet

The nine Saxon (-medieval) samples chosen for Northfleet (ARC EBB01) come from domestic, agricultural and food preparation contexts. The taxa identified are listed in *Table 50*.

Pit 15965
A range of taxa (a minimum of eight) was identified from this pit, including oak (*Quercus* sp.), field maple, hazel, blackthorn (*Prunus spinosa* type) and 50% hawthorn-type pomaceous fruits. Mature, roundwood and twigwood were represented, and this and the range of taxa are suggestive of a 'natural life' assemblage with a source of open scrub or hedgerow, providing a useful picture of the environment at this time.

Contexts 10271, 10809, 20242, 30111, 30084, 30085 and 30081
These posthole fills, occupation deposits and backfills are presumed to relate to use and immediate disuse of the SFBs at Northfleet (see Vol 1, Figs 5.7 and 5.8). The backfill of 10271 (SFB 16638) contained field maple, hazel, ash (*Fraxinus excelsior*), blackthorn, willow/aspen (*Salix/Populus*) and pomaceous fruits, but oak and an equal number of oak roundwood fragments formed 37% of the assemblage. The same taxa were common in feature 10809 (SFB 16699), but oak was less important and the assemblage also included a number of dogwood roundwood fragments and a piece of holly (*Ilex aquifolium*). The fill of posthole 30111 (SFB 30119) comprised only oak and probably represents the post charred *in situ*. However, the fill of posthole 20242 (SFB 20186) additionally contained hazel, beech (*Fagus sylvatica*) and pomaceous fruit wood, the assemblage likely deriving from domestic activity post-dating the decay or removal of the original post. The small, fragmentary assemblage from feature 10809 (SFB 16699) comprised mainly field maple, hazel and pomaceous fruit.

The three assemblages from occupation deposits in the SFBs (30081 in SFB 30119; 30084 and 30085 from SFB 30107) were all dominated by mature hazel and oak wood, with common field maple, pomaceous fruits and ash. The upper fill 30085 also contained a number of lesser taxa including elm (*Ulmus* sp.), willow/aspen, alder and a single fragment *cf.* alder blackthorn (*Frangula alnus*), its only occurrence in this analysis. This taxon is particularly prized in modern times as prepared charcoal for its quality and consistency of burn (Edlin 1949). One fragment of another species of the buckthorn family, *Rhamnus cathartica*, was found in context 30060 (lower fill of SFB 30057).

Conclusion

Use of a wide range of locally available tree and shrub taxa from open woodland, scrub and hedgerows has been identified for domestic contexts at Northfleet, similar to that observed for the same broad period at Springhead. Management or targeting of particular taxa for fuel has not been demonstrated for this period, although hazel and oak continued to be in common use (see also Waterlogged Wood, Barnett, below). Most of the woody taxa identified tolerate a range of environmental conditions but ash and field maple, both of which occurred in a large proportion of the assemblages, and also beech, particularly thrive on calcareous soils, reflecting the chalk geology of the area. Conversely, the buckthorns and alder found in small numbers of samples grow on base-poor, wet, peaty soils (Stace 1997) as would have occurred on the margins of the River Ebbsfleet.

Discussion of the Saxon Wood Charcoal

Well-dated environmental sequences that cover the end of the Roman Empire to Saxon times are limited for the south-east (*cf* Rackham 1990; Murphy 1994), with most remains coming from urban centres (*cf* Dark 2000). The scant pollen data available has sometimes been used to suggest woodland regeneration after the 6th century AD (Turner 1981), with some reduction of agricultural land (eg, at Bignor, Sussex (Waton 1982)). Conversely, however, other areas are thought to have shown continued use or even had further clearance and cultivation (Dark 2000). Rackham (1986) suggested there was no widespread forest regeneration of secondary woodland in the Saxon period on the basis of documentary evidence and place names and Murphy (1994), on consideration of the palaeoenvironmental evidence from a number of sites in East Anglia and Essex, also concluded that there is no evidence for large-scale reversion to woodland. There was a marked decrease in cereal pollen/arable agriculture at Michelmere lake basin by the Roman fort of Pakenham following its decline, yet an open landscape continued, likely maintained by grazing (Murphy 1994). Overall, no clear widespread trend in landscape change is apparent, but it may be suggested that the few changes that have been observed in the few sequences available relate specifically to the local decline of Roman estates and a shift in geographical focus for activity.

The data from the analysis of 11 Saxon charcoal samples from Springhead and Northfleet does provide some small supplement to this evidence, for in contrast to the late Roman charcoal findings, some vegetation recovery and re-establishment of secondary woodland is indicated for the Saxon period at Springhead and Northfleet, leading to a reversion in use of a wide range of deciduous tree and shrub types. Management and use of large quantities of managed stands as a fuel source is less apparent than previously, however continuation of such stands or large-scale importation of a very restricted range of taxa for structural use in the mill is indicated by the waterlogged wood findings (see Barnett below).

No published charcoal reports exist for Saxon material in this region. A little comparable data comes from the results of charcoal analysis of six mid-Saxon pits at Anderson's Road, Southampton (Saxon *Hamwic*). These were found to contain a range of woody taxa, dominantly native deciduous types, with alder, oak, hazel, ash, cherry types, birch and willow/aspen important (Chisham 2006). Likewise, a similar assemblage though with somewhat less species variety was also found at the nearby St Mary's Stadium site (Gale 2005). The scarcity of charcoal and other environmental analyses for the period increases the importance of the assemblages at Springhead and Northfleet in adding to current knowledge of the vegetation history and economic, industrial and domestic selection and use of wood.

Waterlogged Wood from Northfleet
by Catherine Barnett

Substantial quantities of artefactual/worked waterlogged wood were found at Northfleet, in the main associated with the Saxon mill (see Vol 1, Chap 6). A number of other possible structural pieces were recorded, including elements of a revetment or trackway, sealed within waterlogged middle Bronze Age to early Iron Age contexts at the site; these are reported under the Prehistoric Ebbsfleet Study. No waterlogged wood was recovered from the excavations at Springhead, where a lowering of the water table has occurred as a result of the de-watering of nearby chalk quarries in the mid-20th century.

Selected pieces were chosen for identification in order to inform on the availability, selection, management and use of wood for buildings and other structures. Details of the working of the wood and the techniques employed in construction are reported by Hardy, Watts and Goodburn (Vol 1, Chap 6).

Methods

Selected wood samples were identified in their entirety, with a fine slice taken from each fragment along three planes (transverse section (TS), radial longitudinal section (RL) and tangential longitudinal section (TL)) using a razor blade. The pieces were mounted in water on a glass microscope slide, and examined under bi-focal transmitted light microscopy at magnifications of x50, x100 and x400 using a Kyowa ME-LUX2 microscope. Identification was undertaken according to the anatomical characteristics described by Schweingruber (1990) and Butterfield and Meylan (1980). Identification was to the highest taxonomic level possible, usually that of genus, and nomenclature is according to Stace (1997). A species list for the site is given in Table 51 and the full results in *Table 52*.

Results

Nine taxa were identified from the worked wood assemblage associated with the Saxon mill. The findings, as detailed in *Table 52*, are described by type of worked piece as follows.

The mill chute
The chute itself was suggested to be formed of mature oak during excavation, and the single piece from context 19508 submitted for identification supports this.

Pegs and bungs
Hazel was normally used to create pegs and bungs associated with the mill chute, although two were of oak

Table 51 Species represented in the Saxon worked wood assemblage

Taxon	Common name
Acer campestre	Field maple
Alnus glutinosa	Alder
Betula pendula/pubescens	Silver/downy burch
Carpinus betulus	Hornbeam
Corylus avellana	Hazel
Fraxinus excelsior	Ash
Pomoideae	Pomaceous fruits: *Sorbus, Malus, Pyrus, Crateagus*
Quercus sp.	Oak
Salix/Populus sp.	Willow/aspen or poplar
Taxus baccata	Yew

(*Quercus* sp.). A single finely finished peg associated with a beam (context 19147) was found to be of the coniferous species yew (*Taxus baccata*), the only representation of this species in the waterlogged wood analysis.

The causeway
A variety of wood types were used to construct the causeway/trestle support 12224 and its associated spread of debris 12270, with hazel roundwood and mature hazel (*Corylus avellana*), oak, ash (*Fraxinus excelsior*) and alder (*Alnus glutinosa*) identified.

Revetments
A simple assemblage was observed for revetments 19429 and 19430, which were constructed from mature oak, oak roundwood cut at nine to ten years old and two hazel roundwood pieces. The uprights/stakes in contexts 12684 and 12689, also thought to be part of a revetment, were formed from large roundwood of field maple (*Acer campestre*) and hazel respectively. The stake from 12338, which formed part of the NE–SW revetment, was identified as hazel.

The wood from revetment structure 12281 (section 11853), to the west of causeway 12224, was identified as roundwood of oak, hazel, birch and pomaceaous fruit wood (Pomoideae). Where discernible the roundwood had been cut at 10 years old.

Two pieces of worked horizontal timbers and a small stake, believed to pre-date the main revetment construction, were found to be degraded, but the stake from context 12632 was identifiable as hazel, the timber from 12629 as willow/aspen (*Salix/Populus* sp.), while that from 12628 compares well with hazel or alder.

Wattle

The wattle structure(s) from 12320–1 and 19049 (section 11844) were constructed using large numbers of hazel roundwood pieces cut at up to 12 years old, with occasional pieces of birch and willow/aspen roundwood. However, the wattle recovered from context 12563 was of 2–5 year old field maple roundwood. The wattle from contexts 19083–6 was solely of hazel roundwood, normally cut at 5 years. The sails and rods forming wattle structure 12549 were dominantly of hazel, but one roundwood piece with an oblique point was identified as Pomoideae. The hurdle from context 12210, which may have acted as a filter in front of the mill chutes, was constructed from willow/aspen and hazel roundwood.

Possible fish trap and miscellaneous other timbers and stakes

The wattle associated with the possible fish trap 19441 proved to be of hazel and alder twigwood, both types capable of providing supple thin whips for weaving.

A number of other miscellaneous timbers and stakes associated with the mill were recovered and submitted for identification. As shown in Table 51, a variety of woody taxa were utilised for these pieces, which included a timber of field maple, uprights of birch and hazel, and c 8–10 year old roundwood stakes of ash (*Fraxinus excelsior*), hazel, alder, Pomoideae and field maple. A well-finished wooden bowl (SF 12771; see Goodburn, Chap 4, Fig. 8, 2) was identified as *Carpinus betulus* (hornbeam), an attractive and workable timber still commonly used today for creating wooden bowls.

Discussion

The taxa identified in this analysis were, in the main, commonly found in the wood charcoal analysis for Saxon contexts at Springhead and Northfleet (see Barnett above). However, the nature of this exploitation and sourcing of the wood for the mill and revetment construction contrasts significantly. The wood charcoal from domestic and agricultural contexts showed utilisation of a wide range of taxa of open woodland and hedgerows for fuel, with assemblages generally mixed and reflecting local availability, with no good evidence of management of woody taxa at this time. In the case of the mill however, although some flexibility clearly occurred in resourcing, generally a very narrow range of wood types were utilised for construction. Mature oak

timbers were chosen for large timbers, notably for the main mill and chute construction. This was a pragmatic choice since oak, as well as being capable of providing large pieces, is hard and durable, even under wet conditions.

Substantial numbers of rod-like young roundwood pieces were also sourced to form stakes, wattle panels, pegs and uprights. Hazel was clearly favoured, the nature and volume of the pieces indicating management of hazel stands by coppice rotation, with a crop taken at 5–12 years. Other types were also utilised however, some of which may also have been coppiced, including field maple, birch, ash, alder and willow. The one anomalous piece was the well-finished peg of yew (context 19147). This is the only piece found in both the wood and charcoal analysis for this period, with the only other occurrence being a fragment of charcoal from a Roman context at Springhead. This peg has been described as being used in a beam and was likely chosen as a durable (*cf* Edlin 1949) and more decorative piece for the main mill building as opposed to the types chosen for use in the wet areas of the mill mechanism.

As noted in the discussion of the Saxon wood charcoal (see Barnett, above), there is scant data from elsewhere on Saxon selection of wood for construction and fuel to compare to the assemblage analysed here. The probably domestic fuel assemblages at the Anderson's Road and St Mary's Stadium sites in Southampton (Chisham 2006; Gale 2005) included the types represented at Northfleet, but with a greater range of taxa utilised. The maintenance of coppiced stands of trees at this time is, however, indicated by the Domesday Book with areas distinguished as *silua minuta* (coppice-wood) (Rackham 1990). The selection and use of wood specifically for mill construction is discussed by Watts and Goodburn (Vol 1, Chap 6).

Marine Shell from Springhead
by Sarah F Wyles

Although the vast majority of the marine shell assemblage was recovered from Roman contexts, the analysis of a small number of shells of Saxon date from Springhead enables some comparisons. A group of 176 shell fragments from two contexts from late Saxon crop dryer 300260 were selected for detailed analysis. The same methods used for analysing the Roman marine shell were employed on this group of shells and the results are summarised in *Tables 53* and *54*.

Results

The assemblage examined represented a MNI of 107, all of which were oysters (*Ostrea edulis*) (*Table 53*). Of these, 29% of the 85 left valves were deemed measurable, while only 26% of the 91 right valves could be measured. These percentages are significantly lower than the general percentages seen in the Roman assemblage.

Only 2% of the measurable shells showed knife marks and notches. Some of the shells (8%) had indications of staining and around 36% of the analysed assemblage was recorded as being worn and 16% as being flaky. This is similar to the results seen from the shells from Roman Springhead but less than those from Northfleet villa.

The shells were analysed for evidence of whether they were fished from natural beds using techniques such as dredging or farmed from deliberately laid oyster beds. Although no shells with oyster fragments, spats or complete shells attached were recorded, 20% of the shells were considered misshapen. The majority of the left valves have a maximum diameter of between 62 mm and 90 mm, while the majority of the right valves are between 55 mm and 87 mm. The shells generally have a greater width than length. The mean size of left valve width is 76 mm, whereas the mean size of right valve widths is 71 mm. It seems unlikely that this assemblage is a result of some selection procedure as the appearance of some of the shells was rather poor. In addition to the misshapenness, 6% of the assemblage appeared to be rather thin and about 14% rather thick.

Some indication of infestation was observed on about 10% of the assemblage. The infestation was usually only slight and the assemblage generally comprised healthy shells; no 'rotten backs' were recorded. All of the infested shells showed traces of the burrows left by the polychaetic worm *Polydora ciliata*. There were no signs of chambering, which can be caused by changes in salinity levels. The shells were slightly elongated, as shown by the correlation co-efficient, and, therefore, are likely to have been recovered from a hard substrate.

Student T-tests were carried out on the maximum diameter of the measurable left valve. There was a population match between this group and four of the groups from the sites at Roman Springhead.

Discussion

The group of shells analysed comes from a single late Saxon feature and is, therefore, unlikely to be representative of the Saxon settlement(s) as a whole. Nevertheless, it is probably the case that marine shellfish augmented rather than formed a significant part of the Saxon diet. A mixture of worn, flaky, stained and broken shells indicates a pattern of slow or intermittent disposal of this group of shells. There is no evidence to suggest whether the shells were disposed of from an area used for food preparation or one used for consumption.

The irregularity of the shells and the lack of other small marine shells, together with paucity of small oysters, may be indicative of a managed oyster bed being fished with a dredge net of a fixed size; there is no evidence of any selection procedure.

The preferences of the polychaetic worm, *Polydora ciliata*, together with the lack of chambering, suggests that these oysters were recovered from beds in shallow rather than deep waters and possibly open coastal rather than estuarine environments. The shape of the shells indicates that they are likely to have been recovered from a hard substrate source. Studies on the oysters from mid-Saxon deposits at the Royal Opera House and comparisons with other London sites, as well as Saxon sites elsewhere, has shown that the London assemblages are closely associated with oysters originating in East Anglia, with no similarity to oysters from the south coast (Winder with Gerber-Parfitt 2003). The population test on the Springhead group seems to indicate a continuation of the exploitation of those natural beds used in the Roman period, situated in North Kent, the Thames Estuary and Essex, with apparently little or no change in the management and exploitation of the beds between the Roman and Saxon periods.

Bibliography

Note: the use of 'a', 'b' etc suffixes to denote publications by the same person in the same year has been standardised across the four volumes so that some entry suffixes here may not run in true consecutive order.

ADS, 2006 CTRL Digital Archive, Archaeology Data Service, http://ads.ahds.ac.uk/catalogue/projArch/ctrl

Allan, J P, 1984 *Medieval and Post-medieval Finds from Exeter, 1971–1980.* Exeter Archaeol Rep 3, Exeter

Anderson, T and Andrews, J, 1997 The human skeletons, in *The Anglo-Saxon Cemetery on Mill Hill, Deal, Kent* (ed K Parfitt and B Brugmann), 214–36. Soc Medieval Archaeol Monogr Ser 14, London

Archibald, M, 1991 Coinage and currency, in *The Making of England. Anglo-Saxon Art and Culture AD 600–900* (ed L Webster and J Backhouse), 35–7. Brit Mus Press, London

Avery, B W, 1990 *Soils of the British Isles.* CAB International, Wallingford

Baker, J and Brothwell, D, 1980 *Animal Diseases in Archaeology.* Academic Press, London

Barclay, C, 1995 The Ryther treasure trove, *Brit Numis J* 65, 132–50

Barclay, A, Lambrick, G, Moore, J and Robinson, M, 2003 *Lines in the Landscape. Cursus Monuments in the Upper Thames Valley: excavations at the Drayton and Lechlade Cursuses.* Thames Valley Landscapes Monogr. 15, Oxford

Barton, K J, 1962 Settlements of the Iron Age and pagan Saxon period at Linford, Essex. *Trans Essex Archaeol Soc* 1 (3 Ser), 57–104

Battarbee, R W, 1986 Diatom analysis, in *Handbook of Holocene Palaeoecology and Palaeo-hydrology* (ed B E Berglund), 527–70. Wiley, Chichester

Bayley, J and Butcher, S, 2004 *Roman Brooches in Britain: a technological and typological study based on the Richborough Collection.* Rep Res Comm Soc Antiq London 68, London

Betts, I M and Smith, T P, 2006 Building material from Parsonage Farm, Westwell, Kent (ARC PFM98), in Booth (ed) 2006

Blackmore, L, 2008 The pottery, in *Early and Middle Saxon Rural Settlement in the London Region* (ed R Cowie and L Blackmore), 168–93 Mus London Archaeol Service Monogr 41

Blackmore, L, 1993 La céramique du Vème aux Xème siècle á Londres et dans la région Londonienne, in *Travaux du Groupe de Recerches et d'Etudes sur la céramique dans le Nord Pas-de-Calais*, Actes du Colloque d'Outreau 1992 (ed D Piton), 129–50

Blair, P W, 1977 *Introduction to Anglo-Saxon England*, 2 edn. University Press, Cambridge

Böhme, H W, 1974 *Germanische Grabfunde des 4. bis 5. Jahrhunderts zwischen unterer Elbe und Loire.* Münchner Beiträge zur Vor- und Frühgeschichte 19, Munich

Booth, P, 2006 Ceramics from Section 1 of the Channel Tunnel Rail Link, Kent, in ADS 2006

Boyle, A., 1995, Personal equipment, in *Two Oxfordshire Anglo-Saxon Cemeteries: Berinsfield and Didcot* (ed A Boyle, A Dodd, D Miles and A Mudd), 222–4. Thames Valley Landscape Monogr 8, Oxford

Brugmann, B, 2004 *Glass Beads from Early Anglo-Saxon Graves.* Oxbow, Oxford

Bullock, P, Fedoroff, N, Jongerius, A, Stoops, G and Tursina, T, 1985 *Handbook for Soil Thin Section Description.* Waine Res Publicat, Wolverhampton

Butterfield, B G and Meylan, B A, 1980 *Three-dimensional Structure of Wood: an ultrastructural approach.* Chapman and Hall, London

Cameron, E 2000 *Sheaths and Scabbards in England AD 400–1000.* Brit Archaeol Rep 301, Oxford

Campbell, B M S, 1983 Agricultural progress in medieval England: some evidence from eastern Norfolk. *Econ Hist Rev* ns 36(1), 26–46

Campbell, B M S, 2000 *English Seigniorial Agriculture.* Cambridge University Press, Cambridge

Cappers, R T J, Bekker, R M and Jans, J E A, 2006 *Digital Seed Atlas of the Netherlands.* Barkhuis Publishing/Groningen Univ Library, Groningen

Carruthers, W, 2004 The plant remains, in *Tatberht's Lundenwic: archaeological excavations in Middle*

Saxon London (ed J Leary), 112–14. PCA Monogr 2, London

Chadwick Hawkes, S. and Grainger, G, 2006 The Anglo-Saxon Cemetery at Finglesham, Kent. Oxford Univ School Archaeol Monogr 64, Oxford

Chantraine, H, 1961 s v uncia, in Paulys Realencyclopädie der classischen Altertumswissenschaft (ed A F Pauly) vol. 9 A/1, Col. 604–65. Stuttgart

Chisham, C, 2006 The charcoal, in A mid-Saxon site at Anderson's Road, Southampton (C Ellis, and P A Andrews), Proc Hampshire Fld Club Archaeol Soc 61, 114–16

Clapham, A R, Tutin, T G and Moore, D M, 1987 Flora of the British Isles, 3 edn. University Press, Cambridge

Clapham, A R, Tutin T G and Warburg, E F, 1965 Flora of the British Isles. Cambridge University Press, Cambridge

Coleman, D C and Fry, B (eds), 1991 Carbon Isotope Techniques. Academic Press, San Diego

Courty, M A, 2001 Microfacies analysis assisting archaeological stratigraphy, in Earth Sciences and Archaeology (ed P Goldberg, V T Holliday and C R Ferring), 205–39. Kluwer, New York

Courty, M A, Goldberg, P and Macphail, R I, 1989 Soils and Micromorphology in Archaeology. University Press, Cambridge

Cupere de, B., Lentacker, A., Van Neer, W, Waelkens, M. and Verslype, L, 2000 Osteological evidence for the draught exploitation of cattle: first applications of a new methodology, Int J Osteoarchaeol 10, 254–67

Dark, P, 2000 The Environment of Britain in the First Millennium AD. Duckworth, London

Davies, A, 2003 The plant remains, in Middle Saxon London: excavations at the Royal Opera House 1989–99 (G Malcolm, D Bowsher and R Cowie), 289–302 Museum of London Archaeological Service Monograph 15, London

Davis, A, 2006a The charred plant remains from Cuxton, Kent, in Giorgi and Stafford (eds) 2006

Davis, A and Moulins, D de, 1988 The plant remains, 139–147 in Two middle Saxon occupation sites at Jubilee Hall and 21–22 Maiden Lane (R Cowie, R, Whytehead and R Blackmore), Trans London Middlesex Archaeol Soc 39, 47–163

Denys, L, 1992 A Check List of the Diatoms in the Holocene Deposits of the Western Belgian Coastal Plain with a Survey of their Apparent Ecological Requirements: I. Introduction, ecological code and complete list. Service Geologique de Belgique Professional Pap 246, 41

Dinç, U, Miedema, R, Bal, L and Pons, L J, 1976 Morphological and physio-chemical aspects of three soils developed in peat in the Netherlands and their classification. Netherlands J Agric Sci 24, 247–65

Dixon, J M, 2002 Biological flora of the British Isles: Briza media L. J Ecology 90, 737–52

Dobney, K and Ervynck, A, 2000 Interpreting developmental stress in archaeological pigs: the chronology of linear enamel hypoplasia. J Archaeol Sci 27, 597–607

Driesch, A, von den, 1976 A Guide to the Measurement of Animal Bones from Archaeological Sites. Bull 1, Cambridge, Massachusetts

Drinkall, G and Foreman, M, 1998 The Anglo-Saxon Cemetery at Castledyke South, Barton-on-Humber. Sheffield Excav Rep 6, Sheffield

Dunning, G C and Goodman, W L, 1959 The Anglo-Saxon plane from Sarre, Archaeol Cantiana 73, 196–201

Duchaufour, P, 1982 Pedology. Allen & Unwin, London

Eagles, B and Ager, B, 2004 A mid 5th to mid 6th-century bridle-fitting of Mediterranean origin from Breamore, Hampshire, England, with a discussion of its local context', in Bruc Ealles Wel 1 (ed M Lodewijckx), 87–96. University Press, Leuven

Earwood, E, 1993 Domestic Wooden Artefacts in Britain and Ireland from Neolithic to Viking Times. University of Exeter Press, Exeter

Ebel-Zepezauer, W, 2000 Studien zur Archäologie der Westgoten com 5.–7. Jh n Chr, Iberia Archaeologica 2. Philipp von Zabern, Mainz

Edlin, H L, 1949 Woodland Crafts in Britain: an account of the traditional uses of trees and timbers in the British countryside. Batsford, London

Evison, V I, 1987 Dover: the Buckland Anglo-Saxon Cemetery. Hist Build Monum Comm England Archaeol Rep 3, London

Flower, R J, 1993 Diatom preservation: experiments and observations on dissolution and breakage in modern and fossil material. Hydrobiologia 269/70, 473–84

Gale, R, 2005 Charcoal, in The Origins of Mid-Saxon Southampton: excavations at the Friends Provident St Mary's Stadium, 1998–2000 (V Birbeck), 154–6. Wessex Archaeol, Salisbury

Gallois, R W, 1965 *The Wealden District*. HMSO, London

Giorgi, J and Stafford, E (eds), 2006 Palaeo-environmental evidence from Section 1 of the Channel Tunnel Rail Link, Kent, in ADS 2006

Goldberg, P and Macphail, R I, 2006 *Practical and Theoretical Geoarchaeology*. Blackwell, Oxford

Goodall, A R, 1984 Non-ferrous metal objects, in *Excavations in Thetford 1948–59 and 1973–80* (A Rogerson and C Dallas), 68–76. E Anglian Archaeol 22, E Dereham

Goodman, W L, 1964 *The History of Woodworking Tools*. G Bell, London

Green, F J, 1981 Iron Age, Roman and Saxon crops: the archaeological evidence from Wessex, in *The Environment of Man, the Iron Age to Anglo Saxon Period* (ed M Jones and G Dimbleby), 129–154. Brit Archaeol Rep 87, Oxford

Green, F J, 1994 Cereals and plant food: a reassessment of the Saxon economic evidence from Wessex, in *Environment and Economy in Anglo-Saxon England* (ed J Rackham), 83–8. Counc Brit Archaeol Res Rep 89, York

Greig, J, 1991, The British Isles, in *Plants and Ancient Man: studies in the palaeoethnobotany* (ed W van Zeist and W A Casparie, 229–334. Balkema, Rotterdam

Grierson, P and Blackburn, M, 1986 *Medieval European Coinage 1: the early Middle Ages (5th–10th centuries)*. University Press, Cambridge

Grime, J P, Hodgson, J G and Hunt, R, 1988 *Comparative Plant Ecology: a functional approach to common British species*. Unwin Hyman, London

Grünewald, M, 1990 *Der römische Nordfriedhof in Worms, Funde von der Mainzer Strasse*. Bücher Bessler, Worms

Guido, M 1999 *The Glass Beads of Anglo-Saxon England c AD 400–700*, Rep Res Comm Soc Antiqs London 58, Oxford

Habermehl, K H, 1975 *Die Altersbestimmung bei Haus- und Labortieren*, 2 edn. Verlag Paul Parey, Berlin

Hamerow, H, 1993 *Excavations at Mucking volume 2: The Anglo-Saxon settlement*. Engl Herit Archaeol Rep 21, London

Hansen, M, 1986 *The Hydrophilidae (Coleoptera) of Fennoscandia and Denmark Fauna*. Fauna Entomologyca Scandinavica 18, Leiden

Hendey, N I, 1964 *An Introductory Account of the Smaller Algae of British Coastal Waters. Part V: Bacillariophyceae (Diatoms)*. Min Agric Fish Food Ser 4, London

Hillman, G, 1981 Reconstructing crop husbandry practices from the charred remains of crops, in *Farming Practice in British Prehistory* (ed R J Mercer), 123–62. University Press, Edinburgh

Hillman, G, 1984b Interpretation of archaeological plant remains: the application of ethnographic models from Turkey, in *Plants and Ancient Man: studies in the palaeoethnobotany* (ed W van Zeist and W A Casparie, 1–42. Balkema, Rotterdam

Hillson, S W, 1979 Diet and dental disease. *World Archaeol* 2(2), 147–62

Hinton, D A, 1996 *Southampton Finds Vol. 2: the gold, silver and other non-ferrous alloy objects from Hamwic, and the non-ferrous metalworking evidence*. Southampton Archaeol Monogr 6, Southampton

Hinton, D A and Parsons, A L, 1996 Pins, in Hinton 1996, 14–37

Hirst, S and Clark, D, 2009 *Excavations at Mucking Vol 3. The Anglo-Saxon Cemeteries*. Museum of London, London

Horton, B P, Edwards, R J and Lloyd, J M, 1999 A foraminiferal-based transfer function: implications for sea-level studies. *J Foram Res* 29 117–29

Horwood, A R H, 1919 *British Wild Flowers in their Natural Haunts*. Gresham, London

Hustedt, F, 1953 Die Systematik der Diatomeen in ihren Beziehungen zur Geologie und Ökologie nebst einer Revision des Halobien-Systems. *Sv Bot Tidskr* 47, 509–19

Hustedt, F, 1957 Die Diatomeenflora des Fluss-Systems der Weser im Gebiet der Hansestadt Bremen. A*b naturw Ver Bremen* 34, 181–440

Jarvis, M G, Allen, R H, Fordham, S J, Hazleden, J, Moffat, A J and Sturdy, R G, 1984 *Soils and Their Use in South-East England*. Soil Surv England Wales, Harpenden

Jessop, L, 1986 *Coleoptera: Scarabaeidae*. Handbk ident British Insects 5/11, London

Jones, M K, 1981 The development of crop husbandry, in *The Environment of Man: the Iron Age to the Anglo-Saxon period* (ed M Jones and G Dimbleby), 95–127. Brit Archaeol Rep 87, Oxford

Juggins, S, 2003 C2 *User Guide: software for ecological and palaeoecological data analysis and visualisation*. University of Newcastle, Newcastle upon Tyne

Kay, Q O N, 1971 Biological flora of the British Isles: *Anthemis cotula* L. *J Ecology* 59(2), 623–36

Kay, Q O N, 1994 Biological flora of the British Isles: *Tripleurospermum inodorum* (L.) Schultz Bip. *J Ecology* 82, 681–97

Kazanski, M, 1998 Les fibules germaniques orientales et danubiennes en Gaule (périodes C2–D2), in *100 Jahre Fibelformen nach Oscar Almgren. Internationale Arbeitstagung 25.–28. Mai 1997, Kleinmachnow, Brandenburg* (ed J Kunow), 375–86. Forschungen zur Archäologie im Land Brandenburg 5, Wünsdorf

Kenward, H K, 1978 *The Analysis of Archaeological Insect Assemblages: a new approach.* Archaeol York 19/1, London

Kenward, H K and Hall A R, 1995 *Biological Evidence from Anglo-Scandinavian Deposits at 16–22 Coppergate.* Archaeol York 14/7, York

Kenward, H K, Hall, A R and Jones, A K G, 1980 A tested set of techniques for the extraction of plant and animal macrofossils from waterlogged archaeological deposits. *Sci and Archaeol* 22, 3–15

Kleemann, J., 1991, *Grabfunde des 8. und 9. Jahrhunderts im nördlichen Randgebiet des Karolingerreiches*, doctoral diss, Universität Bonn (published as: *Sachsen und Friesen im 8. und 9. Jahrhundert – Eine archäologische-historische Analyse der Grabfunde*, Veröffentlichungen der urgeschichtlichen Sammlungen des Landesmuseums zu Hannover 50. Oldenburg 2002)

Koch, A, 1998, Fremde Fibeln im Frankenreich: ein Beitrag zur Frage nichtfränkischer germanischer Ethnien in Nordgallien, *Acta Praehistorica et Archaeologica* 30, 69–89

Koch, U, 1984 *Der runde Berg bei Urach 5. Die Metallfunde der frühgeschichtlichen Perioden aus den Plangrabungen 1967–1981.* Kommission für Alamannische Altertumskunde Schriften 10, Heidelberg

Koch, K, 1992 *Die Käfer Mitteleuropas/Ökologie* Band 3, Krefeld

Koch, U, Welck, K v and Wieczorek, A, 1996 *Die Bevölkerung Nordgalliens: Einheimische und Fremde, in Die Franken – Wegbereiter Europas. Vor 1500 Jahren: König Chlodwig und seine Erben* (eds A Wieczorek, P Périn, K v Welck and W Menghin), 840–52. Exhibition Catalogue Reiss-Museum Mannheim, Mannheim/Mainz

Krammer, K and Lange-Bertalot, H, 1986–1991 *Bacillariophyceae.* Gustav Fisher Verlag, Stuttgart

Laidlaw, M and Mepham, L, 1999 Pottery, in *Prehistoric, Roman and Early Saxon Settlement at Prospect Park, London Borough of Hillingdon* (D E Farwell, P Andrews and R Brook), 29–43. Wessex Archaeol, Salisbury

Landuydt, C J 1990 Micromorphology of iron minerals from bog ores of the Belgian Campine Area, in *Soil Micromorphology: a basic and applied science* (ed L A Douglas), 289–301. Elsevier, Amsterdam

Leeds, E T, 1945 The distribution of the Angles and Saxons archaeologically considered. *Archaeologia* 91, 1–106

Lewis, J S, Wiltshire, P and Macphail, R I, 1992 A Late Devensian/Early Flandrian site at Three Ways Wharf, Uxbridge: environmental implications, in *Alluvial Archaeology in Britain* (ed S Needham and M G Macklin), 235–48. Oxbow Monogr 27, Oxford

Lindroth, C H, 1974 *Coleoptera: Carabidae.* Handbk Ident British Insects 4/2, London

Long, D A, 2006 More early planes: an account of thirteen woodworking planes dating from the late second century AD to the eleventh century AD, *Instrumentum* 24, 15–18

Long, D A, Steedman, K and Vere-Stevens, L, 2002 The Goodmanham plane: a unique Roman plane, of the fourth century AD, discovered in Yorkshire in 2000, *Tools and Trade* 13, 9–20

Lucht, W H, 1987 *Die Käfer Mitteleuropas (Katalog).* Goecke and Evers, Krefeld

MacGregor, A, 1985 *Bone, Antler, Ivory and horn: the technology of skeletal materials since the Roman period.* Croom Helm, London

Macphail, R I, 1999 Sediment micromorphology, in *Boxgrove. A Middle Pleistocene Hominid Site at Eartham Quarry, Boxgrove, West Sussex* (M B Roberts, and S A Parfitt), 118–48. Engl Herit Archaeol Rep 17, London

Macphail, R I and Cruise, G M, 2001 The soil micromorphologist as team player: a multianalytical approach to the study of European microstratigraphy, in *Earth Science and Archaeology* (ed P Goldberg, V Holliday and R Ferring), 241–67. Klewer, New York

Macpherson-Grant, N and Mainman, A J, 1995 *Early to late Saxon, in Excavations in the Marlowe Car Park and Surrounding Areas* (K Blockley, M Blockley, P Blockley, S Frere and S Stow), 818–97. Archaeol Canterbury 5, Canterbury

Magnell, O, 2006 Tracking wild boar and hunters: osteology of wild boar in Mesolithic South Scandinavia. *Acta Archaeologica Lundensia* 8, 1–19

Marzinski, S, 2003 *Early Anglo-Saxon Belt Buckles (late 5th to Early 8th Centuries AD): their classification and context.* Brit Archaeol Rep 357, Oxford

McKinley, J I, 2006a Prehistoric, Roman and Anglo-Saxon human remains from Saltwood Tunnel, Kent CTRL specialist report series, in McKinley (ed) 2006b

McKinley, J I (ed), 2006b Human remains from Section 1 of the Channel Tunnel Rail Link, Kent, in ADS 2006

Metcalf, DM, 1993 *Thrymsas and Sceattas in the Ashmolean Museum, Oxford.* Roy Numis Soc/ Ashmolean Mus, London

Miedema, R, Jongmans, A G and Slager, S, 1974 Micromorphological observations on pyrite and its oxidation products in four Holocene alluvial soils in the Netherlands, in *Soil Microscopy* (ed G K Rutherford), 772–94. Limestone, Kingston, Ontario

Moffett, L, 1988 *The Archaeobotanical Evidence for Saxon and Medieval Agriculture in Central England, c 500 AD to 1500 AD.* Unpubl MPhil thesis, University of Birmingham

Morris, C A, 2000 *Wood and Woodworking in Snglo-Scandinavian and Medieval York*, Archaeology of York 17(13), York

Morrison, K F and Grunthal, H, 1967 *Carolingian Coinage.* American Numis Soc Notes and Monogr 158, New York

Moulins, D de, 1989 Plant remains: the Peabody site, 134–9 in Excavations at the Peabody Site, Chandos Place, and the National Gallery (R L Whytehead and R Cowie), *Trans London Middlesex Archaeol Soc* 40, 35–176

MPRG, 1998 *A Guide to the Classification of Medieval Ceramic Forms.* Med Pot Res Grp Occas. Paper 1, Southampton

Murphy, P J, 1985 The cereals and crop weeds, in West 1985, 100–8

Murphy, C P, 1986, *Thin Section Preparation of Soils and Sediments.* A B Academic, Berkhamsted

Murphy, P, 1994 The Anglo-Saxon landscape and rural economy: some results from sites in East Anglia and Essex, in *Environment and Economy in Anglo-Saxon England: a review of recent work on the environmental archaeology of rural and urban Anglo-Saxon settlements in England* (ed J Rackham), 23–39. Engl Herit, London

Murray, J W, 2006 *Ecology and Applications of Benthic Foraminifera.* University Press, Cambridge

Myres, J N L, 1977 *A Corpus of Anglo-Saxon Pottery of the Pagan Period.* University Press, Cambridge

North, J J, 1989 *Sylloge of Coins of the British Isles. 39: the J J North Collection of Edwardian Silver Coins 1279–1351.* University Press, Oxford

North, J J, 2004 *English Hammered Coinage, vols 1–2.* Spink and Son, London

Parfitt, K and Brugmann, B, 1997 *The Anglo-Saxon Cemetery at Mill Hill, Deal, Kent.* Society for Medieval Archaeology Monograph 14, Leeds

Payne, S and Bull, G, 1988 Components of variation in measurements of pig bones and teeth and the use of measurements to distinguish wild boar from domestic pig remains. *Archaeozoologia* 2, 27–66

Pelling, R and Robinson, M, 2000 Saxon emmer wheat from the upper and middle Thames valley, England. *Environ Archaeol* 5, 117–19

Philp, B, 1973 *Excavations in West Kent, 1960–70.* Kent Archaeol Rescue Unit, Dover

Pilet, C, 1980 *La necropole de Frénouville; étude d'une population de la fin du Ille à la fin du VIIe siècle.* Brit Archaeol Rep, S83, Oxford

Pollard, R J, 1988 *The Roman Pottery of Kent.* Kent Archaeol Soc, Maidstone

Powers, N, 2006 Human bone from an Anglo-Saxon cemetery at Cuxton, Kent, in ADS 2006

Pringle, S, 2005 *Assessment of Ceramic Building Material from Ebbsfleet Roman Villa, Kent* (ARCEBB01), unpubl assess rep

Rackham, O, 1986 *The History of the Countryside.* Dent, London

Rackham, O, 1990 *Trees and Woodland in the British Landscape.* Phoenix, London

Rackham, J, 1995 Appendix: skeletal evidence of medieval horses from London sites, in *The Medieval Horse and its Equipment* (ed J Clarke), 169–71. Boydell & Brewer/Mus London, London

Raymond, F, 2003 Pottery, in *Bronze Age, Roman and Saxon Sites on Shrubsoles Hill, Sheppey and at Wises Lane, Borden, Kent* (C Coles, S Hammond, J Pine, S Preston, and A Taylor), 22–41. Thames Valley Archaeol Services Monogr 4, Reading

Rees, S E, 1979 *Agricultural Implements in Prehistoric and Roman Britain.* Brit Archaeol Rep 69, Oxford

Reineck, H E and Singh, I B, 1986 *Depositional Sedimentary Environments.* Springer, Berlin

Rigold, S E, 1975 The Sutton Hoo coins in the light of the contemporary background of coinage in England, in *The Sutton Hoo Ship-Burial, vol. 1* (R Bruce-Mitford), 653–77. Brit Mus Publ, London

Ripoll Lopez, G, 1998 *Toréutica de la Bética (Siglos VI y VII D C)*. Reial Acadèmia de Bones Lletres, Barcelona

Roberts, C and Cox, M, 2003 *Health and Disease in Britain from Prehistory to the Present Day*. Sutton, Stroud

Robinson, M and Hubbard, R N L, 1977 The transport of pollen in the bracts of hulled cereals, *J Archaeol Sci* 4, 197–9

Rodwell, J S (ed), 1991a *British Plant Communities, vol 1: woodlands and scrub*. University Press, Cambridge

Rodwell, J S (ed), 1991b *British Plant Communities, vol 2: mires and heaths*. University Press, Cambridge

Rodwell, J S (ed), 1992 *British Plant Communities, vol 3: grasslands and montane communities*. University Press, Cambridge

Rodwell, J S (ed), 1995 *British Plant Communities, vol 4: aquatic communities, swamps and tall-herb fens*. University Press, Cambridge

Rodwell, J S (ed), 2000 *British Plant Communities, vol 5: maritime communities and vegetation of open habitats*. University Press, Cambridge

Rogers, J and Waldron, T, 1995 *A Field Guide to Joint Disease in Archaeology*. Wiley, Chichester

Ross, S, 1989, Pins, in Excavations at the Peabody Site, Chandos Place, and the National Gallery (R L Whytehead and R Cowie with L Blackmoore). *Trans London Middlesex Archaeol. Soc.* 40, 35–176

Roth, H, 1986 *Kunst und Handwerk im frühen Mittelalter. Archäologische Zeugnisse von Childerich I. bis zu Karl dem Großen*. Konrad Theiss Verlag, Stuttgart

Roth, H and Wamers, E (eds), 1984 *Hessen im frühen Mittelalter. Archäologie und Kunst*. Sigmaringen, Thorbecke

Ryves, D B, Juggins, S, Fritz, S C and Battarbee, R W, 2001 Experimental diatom dissolution and the quantification of microfossil preservation in sediments. *Palaeogeog, Palaeoclimat, Palaeoecol* 172, 99–113

Scaife, R G, 2000b Palynology and palaeoenvironment, in *The Passage of the Thames: Holocene environment and settlement at Runnymede* (S P Needham), 168–87, Runnymede Bridge Res Excav 1, London

Schmid, P, 1994 Oldorf – eine frühmittelalterliche friesische Wurtsiedlung. *Germania* 72, 231–67

Schön, M D, 2001 Grabfunde der Römischen Kaiserzeit und Völkerwanderungszeit bei Sievern, Ldkr. Cuxhaven. *Probleme der Küstenforschung im südlichen Nordseegebiet* 27, 75–248

Schulze-Dörrlamm, M, 1986 Romanisch oder Germanisch? Untersuchungen zu den Armbrust- und Bügelknopffibeln des 5. und 6. Jhs. n. Chr. aus den Gebieten westlich des Rheins und südlich der Donau. *Jahrbuch des Römisch-Germanischen Zentralmuseums* 33(2), 593–720

Schweingruber, F H, 1990 *Microscopic Wood Anatomy*, 3 edn. Swiss Federal Institute for Forest, Snow and Landscape Research, Birmensdorf

Sellens, A, 1978 *Woodworking Planes: a descriptive register*. privately printed.

Stace, C, 1997 *New Flora of the British Isles*, 2nd edn. University Press, Cambridge

Stevens, C J, 2006b The charred plant remains from North of Saltwood Tunnel, Saltwood, Kent, in Giorgi and Stafford (eds) 2006

Stevens, C J, 2006d The charred plant remains from Little Stock Farm, Mersham, Kent, in Giorgi and Stafford (eds) 2006

Stoodley, N, 1999 *The Spindle and the Spear. A Critical Enquiry into the Construction and Meaning of Gender in the Early Anglo-Saxon Burial Rite*. Brit Archaeol Rep 288, Oxford

Stoops, G, 2003 *Guidelines for Analysis and Description of Soil and Regolith Thin Sections*. Soil Sci Soc America, Madison

Sumbler, M G, 1996 *British Regional Geology: London and the Thames Valley*. HMSO, London

Tester, P J, 1956 An Anglo-Saxon occupation site at Dartford. *Archaeol Cantiana* 70, 256–9

Timby, J, 1988 The pottery, in *The Coins and Pottery from Hamwic, Southampton* (ed P Andrews), 73–125. Southampton Finds Vol 1, Southampton

Turner, J 1981, The vegetation, in *The Environment of Man: the Iron Age to the Anglo-Saxon period* (ed M Jones and G Dimbleby), 67–73. Brit Archaeol Rep 87, Oxford

Tusser, T, 1965 *Five Hundreth Pointes of Good Husbandrie* (1580 edn, eds W Payne, and J Heritage). English Dialect Soc, Kraus Reprint, Vaduz

Tyler, S, 1995 The early Saxon pottery, in *North Shoebury: settlement and economy in south-east Essex 1500 BC–AD 1500* (J J Wymer and N R Brown), 99–102. E Anglian Archaeol 75, Chelmsford

Tyler, S, 1998 Saxon pottery from Slough House Farm, in *Archaeology and Landscape in the Lower Blackwater Valley* (S Wallis and M Waughman), 157–8. E Anglian Archaeol 82, Chelmsford

Ulrich, R B, 2007 *Roman Woodworking*. Yale University Press, New Haven 2007

Urbon, B, 1991 Spanschäftung für Lanzen und Pfeile, *Fundberichte aus Baden-Württemberg* 16, 127–31

Vierck, H E F, 1972 Date and origin of a small long brooch, in *Excavations at Shakenoak Farm, near Wilcote, Oxfordshire* (eds A C C Brodribb, A R Hands and D R Walker), 78–83. Privately printed

Vierck, H E F, 1977 Zur relativen und absoluten Chronologie der anglischen Grabfunde in England, in *Archäologische Beiträge zur Chronologie der Völkerwanderungszeit* (eds G Kossack and J Reichstein), 42–52. Antiquitas Reihe 3, Vol 20, Bonn

Vos, P C and Wolf, H de, 1993 Diatoms as a tool for reconstructing sedimentary environments in coastal wetlands; methodological aspects. *Hydrobiologia* 269/70, 285–96

WA, 2006 *Archaeological Investigations at Springhead Quarter, Northfleet, Kent, Archaeological Assessment Report and Updated Project Design.* Unpubl Client Rep 58847.01

Walton Rogers, P, 2007 *Cloth and Clothing in Early Anglo-Saxon England, AD 450–700.* Counc Brit Res Rep 145, York

Walton-Rogers, P, 2006 Early Anglo-Saxon costume and textiles from Saltwood Tunnel, in ADS 2006

Wamers, E, 1986 *Schmuck des frühen Mittelalters im Frankfurter Museum für Vor- und Frühgeschichte.* Archäologische Reihe 7, Frankfurt am Main

Wamers, E, 1994 *Die frühmittelalterlichen Lesefunde aus der Löhrstraße (Baustelle Hilton 2) in Mainz.* Mainzer Archäologische Schriften 1, Mainz

Waton, P, 1982 Man's impact on the chalklands: some new pollen evidence, in *Archaeological Aspects of Woodland Ecology* (eds M Bell and S Limbrey), 75–92. Brit Archaeol Rep S146, Oxford

Watson, J and Edwards, G, 1990 Conservation of materials from Anglo-Saxon cemeteries, in *Anglo-Saxon Cemeteries: a reappraisal* (ed E Southworth), 97–106. Alan Sutton, Stroud

Welch, M, 1983 *Early Anglo-Saxon Sussex*, Brit Archaeol Rep 112, Oxford

Werff, A van der and Huls, H, 1957–1974 *Diatomeenflora van Nederland*

Werner, J, 1955 Byzantinische Gütelschnallen des 6. und 7. Jahrhunderts aus der Sammlung Diergardt, *Kölner Jahrbuch für Vor- und Frühgeschischte* 1, 36–48

West, S, 1985 *West Stow, the Anglo-Saxon Village.* E Anglian Archaeol 24, Bury St Edmunds

Wheeler, R E M, 1935 *London and the Saxons.* London Mus Catalogue 6, London

Whelan, J M, 1993 *The Wooden Plane: its history, form and function.* Astragal Press, New Jersey

Whittaker, J E, 2001 *Preliminary Environmental Assessment of Samples from the Site of an Anglo-Saxon Mill, Northfleet, Kent (ARC EBB01) – Ostracods and Foraminifera.* Unpubl Rep, Natur Hist Mus, London

Whittaker, J E, 2007 CTRL *Section 2 Post-excavation Archaeological Works – Prehistoric Ebbsfleet (Palaeolithic). STDR4 00, Borehole 7.2: Full Microfossil Analysis Report.* Unpubl Rep Natur Hist Mus, London

Williams, D and Vince, A, 1997 The characterization and interpretation of early to middle Saxon granitic-tempered pottery in England. *Medieval Archaeol* 41, 214–20

Wiltshire P E J, Edwards K J and Bond, S, 1994 Microbially-derived metallic sulphide spherules, pollen, and the waterlogging of archaeological sites. *Proc Amer Assoc Sediment Palynol* 29, 207–21

Winder, J M with Gerber-Parfitt, S, 2003 *The oyster shells, in Middle Saxon London: excavation at the Royal Opera House 1989–94* (G Malcolm, D Bowsher with R Cowie), 325–32. Mus London Archaeol Service Monogr 15, London

Wood, R, 2005 *The Wooden Bowl.* Stobert Davies, Ammanford

Wren, C R, 1993 *The Voided Long-cross Coinage, 1247–1279.* Plantagenet, Herne Bay

Yalden, D, 1999 *The History of British Mammals.* Poyser, London

Index

by Susan M. Vaughan